Hinduism
What It Really Is
Sanatana Dharma

Vastu Sastra, Vedic Astrology and Gemology

Jada Bharata Dasa, John Howley

Spiritual Guides
Travel Guide Series

Hinduism, What It Really Is, Sanatana Dharma, With Vastu Sastra, Vedic Astrology and Gemology

Writer: Jada Bharata Dasa, John Howley
Editor: Kathryn Bellach
Proofreaders: Gadagraj Dasa, Pundarika Vidyanidhi
Cover Design: Kurma Rupa

Published by John Howley and Spiritual Guide.

If you interested in purchasing a copy or copies of this book you can contact:

Jada Bharata, Krishna Balarama Mandir, Bhaktivedanta Swami Marg
Vrindavana, Mathura District, UP India (Residence MVT 6-C 201)
Phone 0565-446-008; Fax 91-565-446-008; email jadabharat@hotmail.com

Krishna Culture
PO Box 926337, Houston TX
Phone (800) 829-2579; Fax (713) 290-8720; Email: krsnacultr@aol.com
Website www.krishnaculture.com

Bhaktivedanta Library Services, Petite Somme 2 Durbuy 6940
Belgium Phone 32 86 323-280; fax 32 86 322-029;
Email: bls.orders@pamho.net; Website www.blservices.com

Spiritual Guides Website: www.spiritualguides.net

The publisher and writers of Hinduism have done their best to make sure that the facts in this book are accurate and up to date, however the publisher, Spiritual Guide, and the writers can accept no responsibility for any loss, injury, or inconvenience sustained by anyone reading this book.

ISBN 0-9653858-3-3

The first edition published in January, 2001 by John Howley and Spiritual Guides.
© Copyright by John Howley. Text, photographs as indicated, and maps.

All rights reserved. No part of this book may be reproduced, stored in a retrieval system, photocopied or transmitted, except brief extracts for the purpose of review, without the written permission of the copyright owner and publisher.

Printed in India by Rekha Printers Pvt. Ltd., New Delhi 110 020.

Jada Bharata (John Howley)

Jada Bharata Dasa, the author, was born in the USA. He studied to be an accountant at both Drexel and Rutgers Universities. He became a member of ISKCON, to study the Vedic (Indian) scriptures and to learn about the culture of India. He studied the Vedic scriptures for over twenty years reading the Srimad Bhagavatam nine times and many of the other Vedic scriptures numerous times.

He first went to India in 1981 for three weeks as part of a package tour. Since then he has been to India twelve more times, spending over eight years in India. He now resides full time in India in Vrindavan, 150km southeast of Delhi, and spends four months a year traveling around India.

Spiritual Guides Publishers

Started in 1993, Spiritual Guides was established to publish travel books on India and Nepal, and books on spiritual and alternative subject matters. Spiritual Guides specialises just on these subjects in order to do the best job possible.

Questions, Corrections or Comments

I really appreciate any letters that are sent in. If you have any question or comments please feel free to contact me. My email address is jbharata@hotmail.com. If you contact me by email you can expect a quick response.

Acknowledgments

I would like to thank my editors, Kathryn Bellach and Charles Paulin, who went to great extents to improve my English and point out to me inconsistencies. I was especially amazed at Kathryn's expertise on all the subject matters in this book. I would also like to thank Pundarika Vidyanidhi who checked the astrology section for factual content. Gadagraj Dasa, who has studied astrology and gemology for years, helped me greatly by making some critical corrections and observations. Kurma Rupa did an excellent job of designing the cover, which I am sure anyone would agree.

I would also like to thank my spiritual teachers, Satsvarupa Dasa Goswami and His Divine Grace A.C. Bhaktivedanta Swami Prabhupada, who helped reveal to me the greatest asset of India—its spiritual benefits. Without their instructions and mercy a book like this would not have been possible for me to have written.

I would also like to greatly thank the authors of the books listed in the bibliography. As this book is only meant to be an introduction, it is suggested that any of the books in the bibliography can be used to get a better understanding on these interesting subject matters. They are all recommended reading.

Please visit our web Site at:
www.spiritualguides.net

The site includes:

The entire Spiritual India book done by Spiritual Guides, which includes a detailed account of the holy places, temples, forts, beaches, palaces, treks, wildlife parks and much more.

- Information on Vrindavana, Mayapur and Jagannath Puri
- Astrology Section
- Vastu Sastra
- Fengshui
- Vedic Gemology
- Tarot Card Reading
- Good Shopping Sources in India
- Vegetarian Restaurants in the US and other Countries
- Vegetarian recipes and ingredients

Updates of the India, Vrindavan books will be put on the site regularly. Such as:

New Restaurants and Hotel (also restaurants that have closed).
Updated phone numbers.
Updated taxi prices from airports and train stations.
Present taxi prices between Delhi and Vrindavan.
Updated train and plane schedules and prices in India.

The site will include articles and comments from travelers in India.

Also Included: Important India, Nepal, spiritual, vegetarian, natural health shops, and travel web links.

Table of Contents

Introduction — 1

Deities — 3

Krishna — 3
Krishna's Pastimes — 3
Radharani — 5
Vishnu — 5
Incarnations of Vishnu — 8
Matsya — 9
Kurma — 12
Varaha — 12
Narasimha — 13
Vamana — 16
Parasuram — 16
Lord Rama — 17
Balarama — 18
Lord Buddha — 18
Kalki — 19
Other Vishnu Incarnations — 19
Siva — 19
Parvati — 21
Nataraja Siva — 21
Brahma — 22
Lakshmi — 23
Sri Nathaji (Sri Gopala) — 23
Jagannatha, Balarama and Subhadra — 24
Durga — 25
Kali — 26
Ganesh — 26
Hanuman — 27
Garuda — 27
Karttikeya — 27
Nandi — 28
Ganga — 28
Narada Muni — 28
Garuda — 29
Ananta Shesha (Shesha-naga) — 29
Universal Administrators — 29
Indra — 29
Surya — 30
Kuvera (Kubera) — 30
Soma — 31
Agni — 32
Kamadeva — 32
Varuna — 32
Vayu — 33
Vishwakarma — 33
Yamaraja — 33
Weekly or Planet Gods — 34
Ravi-var (Surya or Sunday) — 34
Som-var (Moon or Monday) — 34
Mangal-var (Mars or Tuesday) — 34
Budh-var (Mercury or Wednesday) — 35
Brihaspati-var (Jupiter or Thursday) — 35
Shukra-var (Venus or Friday) — 35
Shani-var (Saturn or Saturday) — 35
Rahu — 36

General Information — 37

Hinduism — 37
The Word Hindu — 38
Basic Philosophy — 38
AUM/ OM — 39
Hindu Trinity — 39
Worship — 40
The Vedas — 40
Puranas — 41
Bhagavad Gita — 42
Mahabharata — 42
Ramayana — 44
Srimad-Bhagavatam — 45
Guru — 45
Four Main Schools of Thought and Markings of Different Sects — 46
Vaishnava Philosophy — 47
Vaishnava Sampradayas — 47
Karma — 48
Reincarnation — 48
Samsara — 49
Kundalini Yoga — 49
Bhakti — 50
Mantra — 50
Ahimsa — 50
Ashram — 51
Ashtanga Yoga — 51

Atman	52
Caturmasya	52
Sudarsana Cakra	53
Swastika	53
Tantra	53
Shalagram-shilas	54
Siva Lingas	54
Siva Jyotirlingas	55
Holy Places	55
Vrindavana and Braja Mandala	56
Ayurvedic Medicine	56
Cows	57
Daksha and Lord Siva Story	57
Dance	58
Bharata Natyam Dance	58
Kathakali Dance	59
Other Dance Styles	60
Ganges and Yamuna Rivers	60
Ganges Story	61
Jyotisha (Astrology)	62
Kumbha-mela	62
Kumbha-mela Story	63
Marriages	64
Ekadasi	64
Yugas	65
Foods	66
Funeral Rites	67
Music	67
Musical instruments	68
Namaste and Greeting	68
Personalities	69
Caitanya Mahaprabhu	69
Madhvacarya	69
Ramanujacarya	69
Sankaracarya	70
Sri Andal	71
Bhaktivedanta Swami Prabhupada	71
Sadhu	72
Samskara Purificatory Process	72
Mandala	73
Manus	73
Moksha	73
Nirvana	74
Mudra	74
Padma (Lotus Flower)	74
Rudraksha Beads	74
Sacred Trees and Plants	75
Sacred Mountains	75
Temples	76
Important Temples and Deities	76
Temple Design	77
Dravidian Temple Design	78
Dravidian Temple Enclosures	79
Vertical Construction of Temples	80
Andhra Pradesh Temples	80
Kerala Temple Design	81
Orissan-style Temples	81
North India Temples	82
Temple Priests	82
Temple Worship	83
Main Deity's Consort	84
Varnasrama Dharma)	84
108 Divya Desams & the Alwars	85
Tirtha Yatra	86
Yantras	86
Writing and Worshipping Yantras	87
Yoga	88
Vedic Sciences	88
Islam	88
Buddhism	90
Sikhism	92
Jainism	93
Zoroastrianism	94
On Chanting Hare Krishna	95
Bhagavad Gita Verses	97

Vedic Astrology 101

Prashna	102
The Zodiac	103
Tropical vs. Sidereal	103
Planets	105
Ketu and Rahu	106
Planets and the Days That They Rule	106
Attribute of Planets	107
Sun	107
Moon	107
Mars	108
Mercury	108
Jupiter	109
Venus	110
Saturn	110
Rahu	111
Ketu	112
Karakas	112
Signs	113
Appearance of Signs	113

Qualities of the Signs	113	Sun Mahadasha	136
Parts of the Body	114	Moon Maha dasha	136
Aries	115	Mars Maha dasha	136
Taurus	115	Rahu Maha Dasha	137
Gemini	115	Jupiter Maha Dasha	137
Cancer	116	Saturn Maha Dasha	137
Leo	116	Mercury Maha Dasha	138
Virgo	117	Ketu Maha Dasha	138
Libra	117	Venus Maha Dasha	138
Scorpio	118	Harmonic and Navamsa Chart	139
Sagittarius	118	Transits or Movement of Planets	139
Capricorn	119	Times Planets Spend in each Sign	140
Aquarius	119	Retrograde Motion	141
Pisces	120	Judgment of a Horoscope	141
Twelve Houses	121	Things Taken Into Consideration	141
Significance of the Twelve Houses	121	Marriage Selection	142
Constellations	122	Judgment by	143
Lunar and Solar Year and Month	124	Remedial Measures	143
Hindu Tithis (Days)	125	Potential Problems Time of Birth	143
Influence of the Planets	125	Different Styles of Charts in India	144

Vedic Gemology 146

Natural Tendencies of Planets	126
Positive Effect	126
Negative Effect	126
Relationships between Planets	126
Table of Friend and Enemy Planets	127
Relationship of Planets and Signs	128
Ownership	128
Exaltation	128
Debilitation	128
Moolatrikonas	128
Different Angles	129
Conjunction	129
Combust	130
Planetary War	130
Drishti or Aspect	130
Ascendant or Lagna	131
Janma Rashi (Moon Sign)	132
Hemming	132
Predictions	132
Yogas	133
Specific Situations	133
Time of Special Influence	133
Age of Planets	134
Major Periods (Mahadasha)	134
Sub-Periods (Antardasha)	134
How to Calculate the Periods	135
Length of Mahadashas	135

Astrological Remedial Measures	147
Gems for Health	147
Wearing Gems	148
Power of Colors	148
Relation of the Planets	149
Setting in a Ring	149
Fingers	150
When and Where to Wear	151
Installation of Gems	151
Gemstone Chart	152
Testing for Positive Effect	152
Diamond (Hiraka)	152
Astrological Effects of Diamond	154
Ruby	158
Astrological Effects of Ruby	158
Sapphire	161
Blue Sapphire (Neelam)	162
Effects of a Blue Sapphire	163
Yellow Sapphire	164
Effects of a Yellow Sapphire	165
Padparadscha	167
Emerald (Panna)	167
Astrological Effects of Emerald	168
Pearl	170
Astrological Effects of Pearls	172

Coral	175
Astrological Effects of Coral	175
Zircon	177
Hessonite	178
Effects of Hessonite Garnet	178
Jade	179
Cat's Eye	180
Astrological Effect of Cat's Eye	181
Garnet	183
Turquoise	183
Quartz	184
Rock Crystal	184
Topaz	185
Citrine	186
Opal	186
Moonstone	186
Peridot	187
Amethyst	187
Bloodstone	188
Agate	188
Lapis Lazuli	188
Tourmaline	189
Aquamarine	189
Spinel	190
Purchasing Gemstones Overseas	190
Prices of Gems	191
Carat—Weight and Size	192
Color	192
Clarity	193
Cut and Polishing	193
Hardness	194
Stability	194
Toughness	194
Luster	195
Brilliance	195
Refractive Index	195
Difference In Light	195
Specific Gravity	196
Cleavage	196
Fire	196
Synthetic or Treated Gems	196
Gem Substitutes	197
Birthstones Sidereal System	198
Birthstones	198
Constellations and Gems	199
Navaratna Ring or Pendant	200
Prescribing a Gem	200
To prescribe a gem	201

Vastu Sastra — 202

The Land	202
Roads in Relation to Land	205
Negative Location of Land	207
Building Material	207
Shape of the Land	207
Well or Water Source	208
Compound Wall and Gate	209
Outside of Main Building	210
Parking	210
Roof	211
Inside the Building	211
Entrance Gate and Main Door	212
Overhead Water Tank	214
The House	214
Worship (Temple) Room	214
Kitchen	215
Living (Sitting) Room	216
Bedrooms	216
Safe Room	217
Dining Room	217
Bathrooms	217
Study Room	218
Storage Room	218
Stairways	218
Basement	219
Position of Rooms	220
Upper Floor	221
Trees and Plants	221
House Warming	222
Purchasing the Adjacent Plot	223

Festival — 225

Months	225
Magha (Jan-Feb)	225
Phalguna (Feb-March)	226
Chaitra (March-April)	227
Vaishaka (April-May)	227
Jyaistha (May-June)	227
Asadha (June-July)	227
Sravana (July-Aug)	229
Bhadra (Aug-Sept)	229
Asvina (Sept-Oct)	230
Kartika (Oct-Nov)	230
Aghan (Nov-Dec)	232
Pausa (Dec-Jan)	232

Glossary — 233

Introduction

After spending several years traveling around India doing research on another book I wrote, *Holy Places and Temples of India*, I had the good fortune to meet many people. After our encounters I realized that many people were looking for an easy to understand book on Hinduism. They wanted to understand more about the different gods that they are seeing in temples. They also wanted to understand the religious beliefs of the people, and they wanted more information about temples.

One person told me that he had searched in many book shops throughout India trying to find a book that would help him in understanding Hinduism, but after much endeavor, he could not find one that gave him the answers that he wanted, in an easy to understand book. As I have spent the last three and a half years in India doing research on this subject, I decided to write a book on this subject, with the aim of helping the reader to understand the seemingly intricate aspects of Hinduism.

While trying to understand Hinduism one may at times become bewildered. Depending on whom one talks to, people's understanding of Hinduism may vary greatly. I have tried to present the subjects in this book in an objective manner, mainly dealing with points that are accepted by most people.

A point of disagreement may be the origin of the Vedas and when they were written. Often the academic view point is that the Vedas were written at a particular point of time and that the stories in the Vedas do not present real historical facts, but are just myths or stories to present certain moralistic points. In contrast a believer presents the Vedas as coming directly from God through his representatives and the stories are actual historical fact that happened, many times, so much in the distant past, that it is inconceivable to many modern historians and scientists. Since there are no historical facts which can give the exact date of when the Vedas were written. neither viewpoint can be proved and therefore both must be accepted on faith.

Hinduism is in one sense considered a religion. Hinduism is also called *Sanatana-dharma*. The English word for religion is a little different from *Sanatana-dharma*. Religion conveys the idea of faith, and faith may change. One may have faith in a particular process, and he may change this faith and adopt another, but *Sanatana-dharma* refers to that activity which cannot be changed. *Sanatana-dharma* is not sectarian, but it is actually the duty of all living entities in the world.

There are basically three schools of thought in Hinduism. There are the Vaishnavas, the Shaivites (followers of Siva and Shakti), and the believers of the impersonal school of thought. According to Vaishnavas there is only one God, but he may be known by different names. In the Christian religion he is known as Jehovah, in the Muslim religion he is known as Allah, and in Hinduism he is known as Krishna or Vishnu. Some people in the Hindu religion believe that Siva is Supreme. Others believe that everything is one, and that when you reach the stage of self-realization you become one with God, or in other words, you become God.

God can expand himself into unlimited forms. Avataras or incarnations are directly God. There are also servants of God who are called demigods because they have been given great power to help manage the universe, but they are just servants of God who are much more powerful than humans. They are not God. The demigods also worship the Supreme Lord themselves. People will worship the demigods to get certain material results. This is because the demigods are in charge of different material facilities. After long worship the worshipers will receive a benediction, but the benediction bestowed by the demigods is just temporary.

Many people say that the gods of Hinduism were developed over a long period of time and were changed by people who migrated to India. Other people say that these gods are eternal and have been mentioned in the Vedas from time eternal. They were not invented or developed over time. Otherwise what would be the value of this being a religion.

A question that may be asked is, why are the deities worshiped? The correct name of the deities in the temples is *arca-vigraha*, which means "the worshipful form of the Lord." The deity in the temple, made of stone, metal, or wood, is a form of a god which is authorized in the Vedic scriptures to accept worship. In Hinduism the deity forms of the different gods are considered nondifferent from the actual gods.

Also included in this book are chapters on Vedic astrology, gemology and Vastu Sastra. These sections are not expected to be detailed instructions on the subject matter, but are written in easy to understand English and hopefully will give the readers a basic understanding of these difficult subject matters. The section on astrology should help the reader better understand what a Vedic astrologer is talking about when he is explaining a chart.

DEITIES

Krishna

Krishna is considered to be the Supreme Personality of Godhead by Vaishnavas. He is the son of Vasudeva and Devaki. His complexion is blackish, the color of a new rain cloud. He stands in a threefold bending form, and plays on a flute. When worshiped in a temple, he will often be seen with his consort, Radha. In paintings, he may be seen dancing with the cowherd girls (*gopis*), playing with the cowherd boys, or as the chariot driver of Arjuna on the battlefield of Kurukshetra. He is also seen with cows because he was born as a cowherd boy. He is often seen in Deity form as a small baby crawling, with a sweet in one hand.

He appeared in Mathura in Uttar Pradesh about 5,000 years ago. He performed many of his pastimes in Vrindavan. Both of these places still exist and are located about 150km from Delhi, between Agra and Delhi.

While he was present he killed the evil king Kamsa and many other demons to protect his devotees. He is the speaker of the *Bhagavad Gita*, which is like the "Bible" of Indian philosophy. Krishna was married to 16,108 wives in Dwarka. His main consort in Dwarka is Rukmini, an incarnation of Lakshmi, the goddess of fortune.

Krishna appears on earth once in a day of Lord Brahma or once every 4,320,000,000 years, during the twenty-eighth millennium of the seventh Manu, at the end of Dvapara-yuga. According to *Srimad Bhagavatam* Krishna is the source of all *avataras* (incarnations), and therefore all of the *avataras* are present in Krishna. When Krishna incarnates, all the features of the other incarnations are already present within Him. Krishna is unborn and eternal as confirmed in the *Bhagavad-gita* and other Vedic literatures.

Krishna's face is decorated with ornaments, such as earrings shaped like sharks. Krishna has a very beautiful face, His checks are brilliant and Krishna's smile is attractive to everyone.

Krishna's Pastimes

Krishna was born of Devaki, the wife of Vasudeva, while they were imprisoned in Mathura. They were imprisoned because their eighth son, Krishna, was destined to kill the evil King Kamsa. When Krishna was born, the doors of the prison mystically opened and the guards fell asleep. Vasudeva walked out of the prison and took Krishna across the Yamuna River to Gokula to be cared for by his foster parents, Nanda and Yasoda. When Vasudeva arrived in Gokula, he found Yasoda asleep after having just delivered a baby girl. He exchanged babies and returned to the prison. When Kamsa found out that Devaki's eighth child had been born, he rushed to the prison. He seized the baby, but the baby slipped from his hands and flew into the air, as a goddess. She said, "Fool, you cannot kill me. The baby that is destined to kill you has already been born elsewhere."

Krishna spent his childhood with Nanda and Yasoda in Vrindavan. Kamsa sent many demon followers to Vrindavan to kill him. First he sent Putana, a child-killing witch, who assumed the form of a beautiful woman. She offered to nurse baby Krishna after covering her breast with poison, but Krishna sucked both her breast and her life-airs, killing her.

He then killed Trinavarta, the wind demon, who grabbed Krishna and flew away with him. Krishna made himself so heavy that the demon fell to the ground and died. The Aghasura demon, in the form of a gigantic snake, swallowed Krishna and his cowherd boy friends. Krishna then expanded himself and killed Aghasura. Aristasura, the bull demon and Keshi, the horse demon, both fought with Krishna and were killed.

He also punished Kaliya, a many-hooded serpent. This snake had poisoned the Yamuna River. Krishna danced on his head and eventually the Kaliya snake surrendered to him, realizing that he was the Supreme Personality of Godhead.

He also carried out many pastimes with the cowherd boys, cows, and *gopis* (cowherd girls). There are many paintings of Krishna dancing with the cowherd girls. This dance is called the Rasa Dance. Krishna expanded himself into many forms and it appeared to each girl that he was dancing only with her.

One day Krishna told his father, Nanda Maharaja, to stop worshiping Indra, the god of rain, and instead to worship Govardhan Hill, a sacred hill in Vrindavan. Nanda Maharaja did this and Indra became so angry that he sent torrential rains. Krishna lifted Govardhan Hill and held it over the residents of Vrindavan like an umbrella, thus protecting them. This pastime has been depicted in many paintings and sculptures.

Krishna then went to Mathura to kill Kamsa. He stayed in Mathura until he was 28. At the age of 28 he moved to Dwarka. In Dwarka he married 16,108 wives. His chief wife was Rukmini. He became Arjuna's charioteer during the battle of Kurukshetra, and this is when he spoke the famous *Bhagavad-gita*.

Radharani

She is also known as Radha and Radhika. She is the most important of the *gopis* (cowherd girl) of Vrindavana. She is the main consort of Krishna and is often seen standing with Him on the altar in temples. Radharani is Krishna's consort during His pastimes in Vrindavana. She is always shown as a beautiful woman. She is a very important deity for devotees of Krishna, because it is believed that one has to get her mercy to be able to approach Krishna properly.

Vishnu

Vishnu is the maintainer of the material creation. Another name for Vishnu is Narayana. He is one of the Hindu trinity, along with Lord Siva and Lord Brahma, and superintends the mode of goodness. He is full in all six opulences—wealth, influence, beauty, fame, strength, and renunciation. He is renounced because he is not attached to anything in the material world. Lord Vishnu is considered to be the Supreme Personality of Godhead by Vaishnavas.

As Garbhodakashayi Vishnu, Brahma appears from his navel and creates the universe. His consort is Lakshmi (also called Shridevi). Shridevi usually holds a lotus flower with the petals open. His other consort is Bhudevi, who carries a blue lotus flower (sometimes the petals are closed). If both consorts are with Lord Vishnu, Lakshmi is on his right and Bhudevi on his left.

He usually has four hands, which hold a conch shell (*sankha*), a disc (*chakra*), a club (*gada*), and a lotus flower (*padma*). He has a blue complexion and wears yellow garments. He wears a jewel on his chest called *kaustubha*.

The club and the wheel are the Lord's symbols of punishment for the demons and miscreants. The lotus flower and conchshell are used to bless the devotees. When his incarnation is present on this planet, Lord Vishnu kills the demons and protects his devotees simultaneously.

Vishnu's carrier is known as Garuda, who is half-bird (eagle) and half-man. Garuda is seen in many Vishnu temples kneeling reverently in front of the temple.

Lord Vishnu is often seen reclining on a bed made up of the coils of the serpent Ananta Shesha (Shesha-naga) with Lakshmi and Bhudevi at his feet. There are unlimited incarnations of Lord Vishnu, but there are ten major incarnations.

Baladev Subhadra Jagannath

Sri Nathji

Lord Rama

Ganesh

Hanuman

Brahma

Laksmi

Lord Vishnu

Saraswati

Lord Siva

Durga

A Deity of Lakshmi-Narayana may be seen with Lord Narayana (Vishnu) sitting down, with Lakshmi sitting on his lap. Narayana may have a disc and lotus in his hands.

Lord Vishnu expands into three forms to create and maintain the universe. They are 1) Maha-Vishnu who is seen lying on Ananta Shesha in the Causal Ocean. In this form He creates the material universe by his breathing. 2) Garbhodakashayi Vishnu, who enters the universe and maintains it. 3) Kshirodakashayi Vishnu, who enters the heart of every living entity as the Supersoul and is found in every atom.

Lord Vishnu has a cheerful, lotus-like face and his body is the color of a blue lotus. On His breast He bears the mark of Srivatsa, which is a curl of white hair. The brilliant Kaustubha gem, decorated with jewels and pearls, is suspended from His neck. He wears a garland of beautiful flowers around His neck. The smiling face of Lord Vishnu is pleasing to the entire world.

Incarnations of Vishnu

An incarnation of Lord Vishnu is called an *avatara*. Vishnu descends on earth whenever there is a decline in religious practice and a predominant rise of irreligion. In the Vedas it is said that the Lord, although one without a second, manifests himself in innumerable forms. Each and every incarnation has a particular mission, and all these forms and their missions are described in the revealed scriptures. Still, the essence of the mission is always the same—to lead people to God consciousness and obedience to religious principles. Sometimes Vishnu descends personally, and sometimes he sends his bona fide representative in the form of his son or servant, or he comes himself in a disguised form.

The Lord descends from his abode to this world, and therefore he is called *avatara*, which means "one who descends." Sometime people may think an *avatara* is an incarnation who assumes a material form of flesh and bones, but *avatara* actually refers to one who descends from a higher region. The Lord's abode is situated far above this material world, and he descends from that higher position; thus he is called *avatara*.

Vishnu has ten major incarnations who are collectively known as the Dasavatara. They are Matsya, the fish; Kurma the tortoise; Varaha, the boar (who killed Hiranyaksa and saved the earth); Narasimha, the half-man, half-lion (Narasimha killed the demon Hiranyakasipu and saved his pure devotee Prahlada); Vamana, the dwarf Brahmin (who begged three paces of land from Bali Maharaja, the king of the demons, and in so doing reclaimed the universe for the demigods); Parasuram, the ax-bearing warrior (who although born a Brahmin, killed twenty-one generations of *ksatriyas* (warrior caste) because of their failure to follow religious principles); Rama, the ideal king (who saved his wife from Ravana, king of Lanka. The *Ramayana* narrates his activities); Balarama, Krishna's brother; Lord Buddha; and Kalki, the killer of the demoniac population at the end of Kali-yuga.

Besides the major incarnations there are innumerable others. The Lord manifests in many species of life to maintain the faithful and to annihilate the unfaithful.

Sometimes Lord Vishnu appears in person as Lord Krishna or Lord Rama. Sometimes He appears as a *shaktavesha-avatara* such as Lord Buddha. (*Shaktavesha-avataras* are incarnations of Vishnu's power invested in a living entity.) Living entities are also part and parcel of Lord Vishnu, but they are not as powerful; therefore when a living entity descends as an incarnation of Vishnu, he is especially empowered by the Lord.

Matsya

The first incarnation of Lord Vishnu is Matsya, the fish incarnation. Matsya's lower body resembles a fish and his upper body a man. He has four hands, in which he holds a club, lotus, disc, and club. Sometimes his hands are depicted with the palm held outward, indicating blessings for his devotees. In pictures he is often depicted as a fish.

At night when Brahma sleeps, the three worlds are flooded with the waters of the Causal Ocean and all beings inhabiting them are annihilated. At the end of the past millennium (the end of Brahma's day) Brahma felt tired and desired to lie down. The Vedas were emanating from his mouth and a great demon named Hayagriva stole them. Understanding this, Lord Vishnu assumed the form of a fish to save the Vedas and kill the demon.

When the entire world was covered with water, the Lord again took the form of a fish and saved King Satyavrata, who lived on a boat attached to the fish's horn. Along with saving the king, he also saved the sages, herbs, seeds, and representatives of the other living entities.

Once King Satyavrata was practicing austerity on the bank of the Kritamala River, drinking only water. Cupping his palms to scoop up some water from the river to offer as an oblation, he inadvertently scooped up a small fish. The fish appealed to the king for protection, asking him to provide the fish with a safe place. The king then put the fish in a water jug. The fish immediately expanded his body and became too big for the jug. Satyavrata then placed the fish in a large well, but that was soon not large enough. The King then placed the fish in a lake, but the fish again ex-

Lord Krishna

Indra

Nataraja Siva

Lord Vishnu

Lord Narasimha

Lord Varaha

Buddha

panded and the lake became too small. Finally, the king placed the fish in the sea, but that also became too small. The king then realized that the fish was an incarnation of Lord Vishnu.

The fish then told the King that there would be an inundation throughout the universe within a week and that he would protect the king. As the fish had told him, the Ocean rose and the king saw a boat coming toward him. He got into the boat along with the saintly people, herbs, seeds, and representatives of other living entities. He then offered prayers to Matsya. Matsya taught King Satyavrata and the saintly persons Vedic knowledge.

Kurma

The second incarnation, Kurma is Lord Vishnu in the form of a tortoise. Kurma means "tortoise." He is sometimes seen in the form of a half-man, half-tortoise. He is often depicted with four arms. In his upper two hands he holds a disc and a conchshell. In his lower two hands he holds a club and a lotus. Sometimes these two hands are depicted in protection and boon-giving postures (*mudras*).

Kurma's shell served as the pivot for Mandarachala Mountain, when the demigods and the demons used the mountain as a churning rod while churning the milk ocean (see Kumbha-mela story). The demons and demigods were producing nectar from the sea by using Mandara Mountain as the churning rod (the same nectar that is said to drop during the Kumbha-mela, giving eternal life). Because the churning rod needed support, Lord Vishnu accepted the form of a tortoise and allowed the demigods and the demons to rest the mountain on his back..

There is only one Kurma temple in India, at Srikurman (Kurma-ksetra) in Andhra Pradesh. Srikurman is located 100 km northeast of Visakhapatnam and 200 km southwest of Puri, on the shore of the Bay of Bengal, 15 km east of the town of Srikakulam. The present temple is at least 700 years old. The original temple was supposedly built in 200 AD. The Deity in this temple consists of two stones, about two feet long, coming out from the ground, which represent the head and body of Sri Kurma.

Varaha

Lord Varaha, the third incarnation, appeared as a giant boar to save the earth and to kill the demon Hiranyaksa, who had been terrifying the universe. Varaha is often depicted as half-man, half-boar, and is engaged in picking up the earth. He is also sometimes depicted entirely as a boar. He may be seen holding a conchshell, disc, lotus, and club. Sometimes he is lifting the earth planet and other times, fighting with Hiranyaksa. He may also be seen holding a club, and one hand may be in the protective or boon-giving postures.

Varaha dove to the bottom of the ocean to save the earth after Hiranyaksa put it there. Hiranyaksa was Hiranyakasipu's brother, the demon who was killed by Lord Narasimha. Hiranyaksa was so proud, that he wanted to fight with Lord Vishnu in the form of a boar. Lord Varaha then got into a vicious club fight with Hiranyaksa. Hiranyaksa struck Varaha with his hard fist, but Varaha slapped Hiranyaksa indifferently at the root of his ear and killed him instantly.

In the material world a boar or pig is considered most abominable, but Adi-sukara (the original boar), the Supreme Personality of Godhead, was not treated as an ordinary boar. Even Lord Brahma and the other demigods worshiped the Lord's form as a boar.

Narasimha

In his fourth incarnation, Lord Vishnu appears in the form of half-man, half-lion, to kill the king of the demons, Hiranyakasipu, the older brother of Hiranyaksa. He is usually depicted with four hands. The upper hands hold a disc and lotus; the bottom hands are either seen tearing out Hiranyakasipu's innards or in the boon-giving and protective postures.

Hiranyakasipu was powerful. After performing extreme austerities, he received a benediction from Lord Brahma. He asked to be immortal, but Brahma told him he could not grant such a wish because he himself was mortal. Hiranyakasipu then received the blessing that he could not be killed by man, beast, demigod, or any kind of weapon or hands. He would also not die in the air, in water, or on the ground, nor be killed either inside or outside, neither during the day nor at night.

The Lord assumed the incarnation of a half-man, half-lion and killed Hiranyakasipu. He killed him on his lap, so that he was killed neither on land nor in water. He was killed in the doorway of the assembly hall, which was neither inside nor outside. He was torn apart by Narasimha's nails, which was neither a weapon nor hands. He was killed at dusk, which was neither day nor night.

Prahlada Maharaja was the son of Hiranyakasipu, and because the boy was a great devotee of Lord Vishnu, his father tortured him. To save his devotee Prahlada Maharaja, Lord Narasimha appeared to kill Hiranyakasipu.

Parasurama

Balarama

Matsya

Kurma

15

Kalki

Nandi

Vamanadeva

Vamana

Lord Vishnu appeared as Vamana, a dwarf-Brahmin, and attended Bali Maharaja's sacrifice. Bali Maharaja was the grandson of Prahlada Maharaja, and due to being born in a demon family, was king of the demons. Bali had managed to overcome Indra, the king of heaven, and Indra approached Lord Vishnu for help.

Vamana begged three steps of land from Maharaja Bali. As it is the duty of a king to grant charity to Brahmins, Maharaja Bali replied, "Why take so little? I can give you much more than that."

Lord Vamana replied "O my dear King, even the entirety of whatever there may be within the three worlds to satisfy one's senses cannot satisfy a person whose senses are uncontrolled. One should be satisfied with whatever he achieves by his previous destiny, for discontent can never bring happiness. A person who is not self-controlled will not be happy even with possessing the three worlds."

Vamana then expanded his body to take up the earth and all the heavens in his first two steps. There was nothing left for Bali Maharaja to give for the third step, so he offered his head. After taking everything from him, Lord Vamana made Bali king of the underworld.

Vamana holds a water-pot in one hand and an umbrella in the other. He wears either a loincloth or a deerskin. He wears a ring of *kusa* grass on his third finger and sometimes holds a book.

He is also called Trivikrama. *Tri* means "three," and *vikrama* means "victory." Vamana attained victory over Bali Maharaja by taking three steps. Lord Vishnu, as Vamana, may be seen stretching his leg to take a big step.

Parasuram

Parasuram, the sixth incarnation, was born as a Brahmin, but later acted as a *ksatriya*. He is seen in a human form holding a battle ax in one hand. Sometimes he is seen with four hands carrying a sword, ax, bow, and arrows. There are just a few temples dedicated to Parasuram in India. *Parasu* means "ax," and thus his name means "Rama with an ax." He was the son of the sage Jamadagni and Renuka. Siva showed Parasuram how to fight and also provided him with his ax. Parasuram taught Arjuna how to fight.

One time, the powerful *ksatriya* king, Kartaviryarjuna, who had one thousand arms, stole Jamadagni's *kamadhenu* (wish-fulfilling) cow. Parasuram then killed the king to regain the cow. After killing the king, Jamadagni, told him that killing a king is sinful, and that as a Brahmin he should have tolerated the offense. Jamadagni advised Parasuram to atone for his sin by traveling to various holy places.

While Parasuram was traveling, the king's sons avenged their father by killing Jamadagni. Parasuram then killed twenty-one generations of the *ksatriya* race in order to purify the *ksatriya* race.

Lord Rama

Lord Rama is the hero in the famous story, the *Ramayana*. He is also known as Raghunath and Ramacandra. Rama is the husband of Sita. He appeared in Ayodhya as the son of King Dasaratha.

Lord Rama is almost always worshiped with his consort Sita, his brother Laksman, and his monkey servant Hanuman. He is depicted with two arms, and in one hand he holds a bow. His wife Sita stands on his left, and she is often depicted holding a blue lotus. On his right side stands Laksman, who usually holds a bow and arrows. Hanuman usually kneels in front of Lord Rama.

His father, Maharaja Dasaratha, had three wives. From these three wives Maharaja Dasaratha had four sons. One of his wives, Kaikeyi, served Dasaratha nicely and received two boon from him. She said she would ask for the benedictions at another time. At the time of Ramacandra's coronation, Kaikeyi asked her husband to enthrone her son Bharata and to send Ramacandra to the forest for fourteen years. Maharaja Dasaratha then ordered Ramacandra to go to the forest.

Rama went to the forest with Laksman and Sita. When Marica assumed the form of a golden deer, Lord Ramacandra wanted to capture the deer to please Sita. While he was chasing the deer, the ten-headed demon, Ravana, kidnapped Sita and carried her to Lanka. As Rama and Laksman searched the forest for Sita, they met the dying Jatayu, who had been fatally wounded while trying to rescue Sita. Rama then killed the monkey Vali and made friends with Sugriva, the monkey king.

The monkeys were sent out to find Sita. Hanuman, Rama's eternal servant, found Sita in Ravana's capital on the island of Lanka. Hanuman jumped across the sea. When Lord Rama came with the monkey army, they built a bridge by floating boulders on the water. This happened at Rameswaram.

With Laksman's help, along with the help of the monkey army, Rama was able to kill Ravana and his army. Rama then made Ravana's brother, Vibhisana, king of Lanka. Rama then returned to his own kingdom in Ayodhya to become king.

Balarama

The eighth incarnation of Lord Vishnu, Balarama, is Krishna's older brother. He is white and has two hands. He usually carries a plow or a club (and sometimes both). He is often seen in pictures with Krishna and with the cowherd boys. He usually wears a blue *dhoti*. He is also known as Baladeva, Balabhadra and Halayudha or Haladhara. He married Revati, the daughter of King Raivata. They had two sons named Nisatha and Ulmuka.

Balarama is the son of Vasudeva. He first appeared in the womb of Vasudeva's wife Devaki, but was mystically transferred to Rohini's womb. (Rohini is another of Vasudeva's wives). This was done to prevent Kamsa from killing him at his birth. Kamsa was destined to be killed by Devaki's eighth son, and to not take any chances he was killing all the sons born to Devaki at birth.

Balarama trained both Bhima and Duryodhana in club-fighting. Eventually, his students faced one another in the final combat of the Kurukshetra war. Because of this, Balarama chose to remain neutral during the conflict.

Balarama killed the ass-demon named Dhenakasura. One time Duryodhana locked up Krishna's son Samba in Hastinapura. Balarama went there and demanded his release. When Duryodhana refused he took his plow and started to drag the city into the Yamuna. To save the city Duryodhana released Samba.

Lord Buddha

Buddha is considered to be the ninth incarnation of Lord Vishnu. He is often seen sitting on a lotus, wearing yellow cloth. His hands are in the protective and boon giving positions. Siddhartha Gautama, who was later called Buddha, appeared around 563 BC (the Mahabodhi Society accepts 624 BC). He was born in a warrior caste. He got married when he was 16, and he had one son. He left home when he was twenty-nine in search of the answer to life. After about six years he went to Bodh Gaya and sat under the Bodhi tree. While meditating he was tempted by the demon Mara, who offered him all the desires of the world. Not taking any of these temptations, he received enlightenment. You can see these scenes depicted in many of the Buddhist carvings around India.

He appeared in Lumbini, which is now in Nepal, preached his own conception of nonviolence, and condemned the animal sacrifices sanctioned in the Vedas. During the time when Lord Buddha appeared, animal killing was being done unrestrictedly on the plea of Vedic sacrifice. Lord Buddha preached nonviolence. He preached that he did not believe in the tenets of the Vedas and stressed the adverse psychological effects of animal killing. Lord Buddha appeared to stop this and to establish the Vedic principle of nonviolence.

Technically Lord Buddha's philosophy is called atheistic because there is no acceptance of the Supreme Lord and he denied the authority of the Vedas. But that is an act of camouflage by the Lord, because he is an incarnation of the Lord. He rejected the Vedas outwardly because people were supporting their cow and animal killing from the pages of the Vedas. Lord Buddha preached the preliminary principles of the Vedas in a manner suitable for the time.

Kalki

At the end of Kali-yuga (the present age), Kalki, the tenth incarnation, appears. He rides a white horse and carries a flaming sword raised above his head. With this sword, he kills the demoniac and atheistic population of the world. He appears at the time of Pralaya (the great deluge). By the end of Kali-yuga morality and law and order has for the most part disappeared. Vedic sacrifices have been forgotten and foreign barbarians will occupy the land. At this time Lord Vishnu in the form of Kalki comes to restore law and order.

Other Vishnu Incarnations

Besides Lord Vishnu's ten main incarnations, there are many others. There are also *shaktavesha avataras* (empowered incarnations). Twelve other main incarnations: (1) the four Kumaras, (2) the sage Narada, (3) Nara and Narayana Rishis, (4) sage Kapila (who taught Sankhya philosophy), (5) Dattatreya, (6) Yajna, (7) Rishabhadeva, (8) King Prithu, (9) Dhanvantari (doctor), (10) Veda-Vyasa (author of *Mahabharata* and *Srimad-Bhagavatam*, who was empowered to present the Vedic scriptures), (11) Mohini Murti (who bewildered the demons and gave nectar to the demigods), (12) Hayagriva (who had a horse head and who killed the demons, Madhu and Kaitabha, then recovered the Vedas, which they had stolen).

Siva

Siva is one of the Hindu trinity along with Lord Vishnu and Lord Brahma. He is the destroyer. At the end of Kali-yuga (the present age), he will perform the dance of destruction and the entire universe will be destroyed. Lord Siva is in charge of *tamo-guna*, or the mode of ignorance. He may be depicted holding a trident, as do many of his followers. He may also hold a mace or battle-ax, an antelope, or an hour-glass drum known as a *damaru*. He may have two or four arms.

He has three eyes. The third one, situated between the eyebrows, is normally closed, except at the time of destruction. He has a crescent moon in his matted hair, and his body is smeared with ashes. He has three horizontal lines on his head, and he wears a cobra around his neck. He has fair skin. He wears a tiger skin, and he sometimes wears a garland of skulls. While he is meditating he sits on a tiger skin. He never accepts luxurious dress, garlands, ornaments, or ointments.

Lord Siva has a blue throat, because he once drank the poison produced from the churning of the milk ocean. He held the poison in his throat to save humanity from being destroyed.

Siva is worshiped in the form of the Siva-linga, or phallus, in most temples. His carrier is Nandi, the bull. Most Siva temples have a trident on top of the temple tower.

Siva is also known as Gangadhara, or one who bears the weight of the Ganges River as it falls to earth from the heavens. When the Ganges descended to earth, it fell on his head and through his *jata* (matted hair), forming many small streams. Eventually these streams combine and form the Ganges at Haridwar.

He resides at Mount Kailash, which is a mountain located in the Himalayas in Tibet. He sits facing south.

Siva is known as Nataraja, the cosmic dancer. He is also known by other names, such as Rudra, Mahadeva, Sankara, Pashupati (the lord of the animals), and Bhairava, his terrible form. He is also known as Ashutosha, or one who is easily pleased, and Bhutanatha or lord of the *bhutas*, or ghosts and spirits. He is called Mahadeva, or the greatest of the demigods, because no one is equal to him in the material world. Hari Hara is a form that is half-Vishnu and half-Siva.

His consort is Parvati, also known as Kali or Durga. Lord Siva is the husband of Durga, goddess of the material energy. Because Lord Siva is her husband, he is known as the controller of the material energy.

Lord Siva's duty is dangerous because he has to employ the energy of goddess Durga. In pictures Goddess Kali (Durga) is sometimes seen standing on Lord Siva's prostrate body, because Lord Siva has to fall flat in order to stop Kali from killing the demons. Since Lord Siva controls the material energy, worshipers of Lord Siva attain opulent positions within the material world. Durga is described as keeping all living entities in the darkness of ignorance.

He is also known as the husband of Sati (also called Gauri), who entered the fire at the sacrifice performed by her father, Daksha. She was then reborn as Uma, and again married Siva.

The story of the third eye is that one time Uma, Siva's consort, playfully held her hands over Siva's eyes. At once darkness spread over the entire universe and not even the sun or moon could be seen. At once Lord Siva produced the third eye so that light could return to the universe.

Siva can see the past, present and the future. One of his eyes is like the sun, another like the moon, and his third eye, which is between his eyebrows, is like fire. He can generate fire from his middle eye, and he is able to vanquish any powerful living entity, yet he does not live pompously in a nice house nor does he possess any material properties, even though he is the master of the material world. He is unstained by material contamination. Lord Siva is not connected with anyone, nor is anyone his enemy. Since he is one of the three controllers of the universal affairs, he is equal to everyone.

Parvati

Parvati is Lord Siva's wife and the mother of his sons, Karttikeya and Ganesh. Parvati lives with Siva on Mount Kailash. Her carrier is a lion. She is seen as a beautiful woman with two arms. She is called the daughter of the Himalaya mountains. She also takes on other forms such as Durga and Kali.

She is worshiped as the consort of Lord Siva in Siva temples, and is not worshiped alone in her own temple. She may hold a mirror or spear in her hands. If she has four hands she may hold a spear and a chisel in two of her hands and the other two hands may be in the protective and boon-giving modes. In pictures she may be seen in meditation, trying to attract Lord Siva.

Nataraja Siva

In this form Lord Siva is depicted in his famous Ananda Tandava dancing pose, with one leg in the air and he has four arms. *Nata* means "dance" and *raja* means "king." Thus he is known as "king of the dance." Lord Siva is depicted dancing on a dwarf named Apasmara, who is said to represent ignorance or false ego, which makes souls forget their true identity. Nataraja destroys false ego. He is encircled by a ring of flames and is holding a drum. One of his hands is in the Abhaya Mudra posture ("Fear not, I will protect you").

One time, Siva went to a forest to subdue ten thousand holy men. The holy men became angry and sent a tiger to kill him, but Siva subdued the tiger and used its skin as a cape. The sages then sent a poisonous snake, which he restrained and used as a garland. They then sent a black dwarf armed with a club. Lord Siva danced on the dwarf's back with his leg in the air. This dance was so splendid that the holy men had to accept Lord Siva as their master.

Another story about Nataraja is that Kali (Parvati) was once the patron goddess of the Tillai Forest (what is now the city of Chidambaram in Tamil Nadu). Lord Siva came to this forest to dance for two of his devotees Patanjali and Vyaghrapada. They worshiped the *svayambhu-linga*, a self manifested Siva-linga. Kali did not like him being there, so she challenged him to a dancing contest and the loser would have to leave the forest. Lord Vishnu was the judge. Their dancing went on for some time and during this time they were equal in their dancing, but then Siva did a dance where he lifted his leg over his head. This dance is called the Ananda Tandava. At this point Kali knew she could not win and so she left.

The Sabhanayaka Nataraja Temple in Chidambaram is the original temple dedicated to the Nataraja form (Celestial Dancer) of Lord Siva. The Nataraja deity there has been the model for innumerable bronze statues of Siva performing this dance.

Brahma

Brahma is the god of creation. He is one of the three main Hindu gods, which include Lord Vishnu and Lord Siva. He sits on a lotus which has sprouted from Lord Vishnu's naval. He has four heads, usually bearded, four arms, and matted hair. He holds a spoon, a pot of holy water, a scepter, beads (rosary), and a part of the *Vedas* (a book). He may also hold a bow, lotus, or scepter. Sometimes two of his hands are in a protective and boon-giving mode.

His four faces represent the four Vedas and his four hands the four directions. He is the father of Lord Siva. He may wear a tiger skin or the skin of a black antelope. He rides on a swan or sits in the lotus position on a chariot pulled by seven swans. If he is colored, he is pink or red.

His consort is Saraswati, but in Pushkar Gayatri is also worshiped as his consort. His consort Saraswati is supposed to have cursed him at Pushkar. (This story can be read in the section about Pushkar.)

He was born from the lotus flower that emanated from Lord Vishnu's navel. One day of Brahma is a thousand cycles of the four *yugas* (known as a *kalpa*), which equals 4.32 billion years. His night is the same. He lives for 100 years.

There are only a few Brahma temples in India. The one at Pushkar in Rajasthan is the main temple.

Lakshmi

Lakshmi is Lord Vishnu's consort, and the goddess of wealth and good fortune. She may sit at Lord Vishnu's feet or be depicted standing or sitting next to him. She is also seen reclining on Lord Vishnu's chest. She usually has two arms when she is worshiped with Lord Vishnu, and four arms when she is worshiped alone. She appeared when the demigods and demons churned the milk ocean.

She sits or stands on a lotus, and often holds a lotus flower. When she has four arms, she holds lotuses in her two upper hands. Gold coins may be seen dropping from her lower two hands, or her lower hands may be in a boon-giving posture. She is normally a bright golden color.

Lakshmi is often seen in paintings half submerged in water with two elephants on either side of her. She has two elephants who spray bathing water on her. Rukmini, the wife of Lord Krishna and Sita, the wife of Lord Rama, are incarnations of Lakshmi. She sometimes rides on the back of Garuda, along with Lord Vishnu.

There are no temples dedicated exclusively to Lakshmi, but she is usually worshiped as a side deity in Vishnu temples. She is also seen in deity form on the main altar of Vishnu temples, usually at the Lord's feet. She is worshiped in most people's homes—many Hindus have a picture of Lakshmi on their home altars—to attain wealth.

People do not generally know that Lakshmi is fickle, and that unless she is worshiped with her consort, Lord Vishnu, her mercy will only be temporary. The Dipawali festival of light (October/November) is associated with Lakshmi. Houses are brightly lit by lamps because it is believed that wealth (Lakshmi) will not enter a house which is dark. Most houses are decorated with oil lamps and electric lights on this day.

Sri Nathaji (Sri Gopala)

Sri Nathaji is a beautiful black marble Deity of Lord Krishna, standing with His left hand upraised lifting Govardhana Hill. His right hand, closed in a fist, rests on His hip. The original Deity of Sri Nathaji is located in

Nathdwar, 48 km northeast of Udaipur, in Rajasthan. The temple of Sri Nathaji is said to be the second richest in India, after the Balaji Temple in Tirupati. Every day Sri Nathaji is offered large quantities of opulent foodstuffs. He is a very popular Deity in Rajasthan and Gujarat. His picture can be seen throughout these two states.

The servitors of Sri Nathaji say that the Deity is the original form of Sri Krishna. Since this form of Lord Krishna includes all others, His devotees see Him both as Sri Radhanath (the Lord of Radha) and as child Krishna.

The Deity appears in large black stone, from which His form emerges in bas-relief. The stone around the Deity bears several marks: two cows, a snake, a lion, two peacocks, a parrot by the Lord's head, two sages seated on His right side and a third on His left, and then below the sages is another snake. Around the Lord's neck is a flower garland, resembling a black snake.

This Deity is said to have been originally installed by Vajranabha, the great-grandson of Lord Krishna, 5,000 years ago. Over 500 years ago the Deity was found by Madhavendra Puri in some bushes next to Govardhana Hill in Vrindavana. Madhavendra Puri then established the worship of Sri Gopala in a temple on Govardhana Hill. Madhavendra Puri handed the service of the Deity to the son of Vallabhacarya named Vitthala. Sri Nathaji was brought to Nathdwar by Rana Raj Singh of Mewar in the 17th century. The Deity was brought to Rajasthan to protect Him from the destructive reign of the Muslim ruler Aurangzeb, who terrorized the Vrindavana area in 1665.

Jagannatha, Balarama and Subhadra

These are the main Deities in the Jagannatha Temple, which is located in Puri, Orissa. Jagannatha is another name for Lord Krishna, which means Lord of the Universe. Balarama is his brother and Subhadra is his sister. Lord Jagannatha is black in color, Balarama is white in color, and Subhadra is yellow in color. The pole next to the Deities represents the Sudarsana-chakra of Lord Krishna. These Deities can be seen all over Orissa, but are also seen in many other Krishna temples throughout India.

There is an interesting story that describes how these Deities got their present form. Once there was a king named Indradyumna. Lord Jagannatha came to him in a dream and told him I shall come floating from the sea in my wooden form as Daru-brahman at the place called Bakimuhan. The king went to this place and saw a huge piece of wood which had the marks of a conch, club, disc and lotus on it.

King Indradyumna had the best sculptors come to carve the Deity of Lord Jagannatha from Daru-brahman. As soon as they started, their chisels broke to pieces. The Supreme Lord Himself came in disguise as an old artist. He said that if he was able to work behind closed doors for 21 days then the Deities could be carved. The old sculptor then took Daru-brahman into the temple and the doors were closed. After 14 days passed, the king could not hear the sounds of the artist's tools and he became full of anxiety. The king then personally opened the door of the temple by force.

The king did not see the sculptor, but instead he saw the three forms of Lord Jagannatha, Subhadra and Balarama. Their fingers and toes were unfinished. Thinking himself a great offender the king decided to give up his life. He then laid on a bed of *kusa* grass and began to fast. Lord Jagannatha appeared to him in a dream. He told the king that He is eternally situated here in Jagannatha Puri in the form of Lord Jagannatha as Daru-brahman. I have no material hands and feet, but with my transcendental senses I accept all the items offered by my devotees. The fact that you broke your promise is part of the pastime for me to manifest this form of Jagannatha. Those devotees whose eyes are smeared with the salve of love will always see me as Krishna, holding a flute.

Durga

Durga is also known as Kali, Parvati, and Uma. Durga is sometimes seen as a beautiful woman. She has a yellow complexion. Durga means "impenetrable like a mountain fort." As Durga, she is in her punishing or threatening mode. This is the darker form of Siva's consort. Lord Siva is in charge of destruction, which he carries out with the help of his material energy, Durga. Her carrier may be a tiger or a lion. She may be seen seated in a yogic posture on a lotus throne. She is also seen carrying weapons to destroy the demons.

Durga is often worshiped in her own temples. She is known as the *Shakti* energy of the Lord and is powerful. She is often worshiped to attain material boons. There are nine forms of Durga.

She may have four or eight arms, and holds knives and severed heads. With her other hands, she makes a gesture of "Fear not," and grants boons. She may also hold a cup, a wheel, a conch shell, a bell, an arrow, a trident, a snake, a sword, a club, and a water pot.

She is also called Mahishasura-mardini, because she killed the buffalo demon. It is said that Durga took birth to kill Mahishasura, because he had received a boon from Brahma that neither man, woman, nor animal could kill him.

In the form of Chamundi she has a terrifying aspect and wears a garland of skulls. Snakes and scorpions adorn her body. Chamundi was created to kill the demons Chanda and Munda.

Kali

Kali is a fierce form of Lord Siva's consort. She may ride a tiger, breathe fire, and wear a garland of human skulls and snakes. Kali means "black," and thus her skin is black. In this form, she is also known as Bhadrakali or Mahakali. She has blazing eyes and is often depicted with her long tongue protruding. She wears snakes around her neck and carries weapons in each of her ten hands (sometimes she is depicted with only eight hands). If she has eight hands, she carries a bow, an arrow, a disc, a sword, a shield, a noose, a spear, and a conch. If she has ten hands, she also carries a skull and a moon disc.

Ganesh

Ganesh is the god of prosperity and wisdom. He is also the god of science and skills. Ganesh has an elephant head and is the eldest of Lord Siva and Parvati's two sons. He is worshiped to remove obstacles one may face in an endeavor, and his worship is popular in India. He has two wives, Siddhi (achievement) and Riddhi (success).

He wears a snake-belt or a serpent across his chest, and he is usually depicted as red or yellow, with four to ten arms. He holds an ax, a goad, a rope, a dish of sweetballs, and other items. His fourth hand is offering a boon. His carrier is a rat, which can travel through the smallest hole or chew its way though obstructions.

He is worshiped in many temples dedicated solely to him. He is also found at the entrance of many temples to others because by worshiping him, one's obstacles in worshiping the main deity in that temple can be removed. He is seen on the altar in many businesses and is worshiped in most Indian people's homes.

When Lord Siva returned once from a long trip, he found Ganesh guarding Parvati's door. Siva wanted to enter, but Ganesh refused him entrance. Not recognizing Ganesh as his son—Ganesh had grown up while he was away—he cut off his head. Parvati insisted that Siva bring her son back to life, so Siva replaced his son's head with the head of the first living being he saw, an elephant.

When Vyasadeva recited the *Mahabharata*, Ganesh recorded it. He told

Vyasadeva that he would only write if Vyasa dictated continuously and did not hesitate. He is also called Ganapati, or Lord of the *ganas* (head of the army of dwarf-demons). In South India, he is known as Vinayaka.

He is called Ekadanta because he has one broken tusk. It is said that this tusk broke when the elephant had his head cut off. It is also said that his tusk was knocked out by Parasurama. The story is that Parasurama arrived one day to see Siva, and Ganesh would not let him pass. When Parasurama tried to get by Ganesh they started fighting and Parasurama broke his tusk. Parvati was about to curse Parasurama, but Brahma stopped her and promised that even though he had only one tusk, that Ganesh would still be worshipped by all men and even the demigods would worship him.

Hanuman

He is a monkey and Lord Rama's eternal servant in the *Ramayana*. He represents the perfect servant of God. He was sent by Rama along with many other monkey warriors to find Sita. He jumped from the mainland of India to Lanka in one leap and there he found Sita. At this time Hanuman was captured and had his tail set on fire. He escaped and set Lanka on fire with his flaming tail. He helped Rama defeat Ravana and save Sita. He is the son of Vayu, the wind-god. He was able to enlarge his body. He has a red face and yellow fur.

While the battle with Ravana was going on he flew to the Himalayas to collect medicinal herbs to help the wounded Laksman, the brother of Lord Rama. After the battle he was granted his wish to be the eternal servitor of Lord Rama.

He has many temples of his own and is also worshiped along with Sita and Rama. Every Rama temple has a Hanuman deity. Hanuman is a very popular deity. He is often painted bright orange. He is mostly seen with two arms with a monkey body. He also has other forms with five or ten heads.

Karttikeya

Karttikeya is the god of war. He led the demigods in the war against the demon Taraka. He is Siva's youngest son, and the brother of Ganesh. He is known as Subrahmanya, Kumar, Murugan, Skanda and Sena-pati (army commander). He is usually depicted with six heads and twelve arms, but may sometimes be seen with one head and two arms. He rides a peacock named Paravani and is yellow-colored. He has two wives named

Devasena and Valli. He is worshiped by women in order to receive a male child.

In South India he is usually worshiped as Subrahmanya, the pious and sacred one. In South India there are six major temples in which Subrahmanya is worshiped. He is also worshiped as a side deity in many Siva temples.

In his hands he carries a conchshell, sword, bow, arrows, spear, noose, shield, banner and a disc. He may have one hand in a protective pose and the other in a charitable position. In temples in South India he may be seen with 12 arms. During Kartika (October/November) a clay deity of Karttikeya is worshiped and then submerged in a river.

Ananta Shesha (Shesha-naga)

He is king of the *nagas* or serpents. He is also called Ananta or the "Eternal One." He rules the underworld region called Patala. He has thousands of hoods. Lord Vishnu is often seen reclining with his head on the chest of Shesha. Shesha lives in the Causual Ocean serving Lord Vishnu with his hundreds of headss spread over the head of Lord Vishnu. He wears royal purple cloth and a pearl necklace.

He lives in Mani Mandapa (the jeweled palace). He is also known as Sankarshan and Anantadeva. He is considered non-different from Lord Vishnu.

Ananta Shesha's main mission is to dissolve this material creation. At the time of devastation, Anantadeva becomes slightly angry. Then from between his two eyebrows appears three-eyed Rudra, who is carrying a trident. This Rudra is the embodiment of the eleven Rudras, or incarnations of Lord Siva. The eleven Rudra expansions of Lord Siva together devastate the entire universe.

Ganga

The Goddess Ganga has a fair complexion and she wears a white crown. Ganga is another name for the Ganges, the most sacred river in India. If she has two hands she holds a water lily in her right hand and a stringed instrument in her left. If she has four hands she holds a water lily, a water pot, beads, and one hand is in the protective position. Many holy cities are located along the Ganges. Hindus aspire to die on the bank of the Ganges, as they believe they will reach heaven if they do so. After cremation the ashes of a person are often thrown into the Ganges.

Narada Muni

He is a famous sage who appeared from the forehead of Lord Brahma. He is mentioned in many of the Puranas. He visited Krishna and instructed Veda Vyasa to write the *Srimad Bhagavatam* to instruct people on the highest purpose of life. He also inspired Valmiki to write the *Ramayana*. He is said to have invented the *Veena* (a string instrument) and he taught music to the Gandharvas, who are musicians and singers in heaven. In a deity form, he is usually seen standing, holding a *Veena*.

Garuda

He is the half-man, half-bird (half-eagle) carrier of Lord Vishnu. Many times he is seen kneeling outside a Vishnu temple. He is the king of the birds. Often both Vishnu and Lakshmi are seen seated together on his back being carried by him.

He is the son of Kasyapa and Vinata. He is the enemy of snakes. He has wings with which he hits and kills demons. He is also called Taraswin or the swift one.

Nandi

Nandi is Lord Siva's bull carrier. He is found in almost all Siva temples and usually faces the Siva-linga. He is usually sitting, but may be presented standing. In paintings he is white with brown eyes, a black tail, and horns with red points. He has a thick neck and his horns are as hard as diamonds. He is usually facing the Siva-linga and can be very large. Sometimes he is close to the Siva-linga. He may also be by the entrance of a Siva temple.

Universal Administrators

Indra

Indra is the king of the heavenly planets. He is the lord of the sky, rain, lightning, and thunder. Indra rides a white elephant known as Airavata, the king of the elephants. He may also ride on a golden chariot drawn by horses. He may be depicted either with two arms or four, and he holds a thunderbolt (*vajra*) in one hand. He may also carry a bow and arrows, conchshell, a net, or a hook. Indra is the god of the eastern direction. He may have a golden or reddish complexion. He can send rainstorms wherever and whenever he wishes. He is also known as Sahasraksha, "thousand-eyed." He may be shown with eyes all over his body. He lives in the city called Indrapura, or heaven.

Indra figures in many of the Vedic stories, often in descriptions of battles between the demons and demigods, and at times when he is in difficulty, he is seen approaching Lord Vishnu for help. In temples he is not directly worshiped, but he is often seen in carvings on Vishnu temples, often sitting on an elephant.

His wife is Indrani (also known as Aindra or Paulomi). She is the goddess of the sky. She has beautiful golden skin. She is the ideal Indian woman, devoted to her husband and beautiful.

Surya

Surya is the sun-god. He rides across the sky on a chariot drawn by seven red horses. His charioteer is Aruna, the dawn god, who holds a whip. Aruna is the older brother of Garuda, Lord Vishnu's carrier. Surya may have two or four arms and may hold a lotus, a wheel, or a conchshell. The fourth hand may be offering protection. If he has two hands, both hands may be holding lotus flowers.

Ushas, the goddess of dawn is related to him. Surya's son is Vaivasvata and his son is Iksvaku. The Ashvins, his twin sons, ride before him in their own golden chariots. He lives in his own capital called Vivasvati.

Because he is the sun-god and controls light and heat, he has much influence over agricultural production. Therefore, many people worship him. He is glorified in the famous Gayatri *mantra,* which is chanted by Brahmins.

Surya is mentioned throughout the Vedic literatures. He is considered one of the most important deities. Figures of Surya can be seen in temples dedicated to other gods all over India. He does not usually have his own temple, except in a few cases. The most important such temple is the Sun temple at Konark, Orissa.

Kuvera (Kubera)

Kuvera is the god of wealth and the treasurer of the demigods. He watches over the world's wealth, including gold, silver, jewels, pearls, etc. He carries a money bag and a bowl. He is the protector of the northern direction. He has a white, dwarfish body, and rides on the Pushpaka chariot, which was given to him by Brahma. He has eight teeth and three legs. He may have two or four hands. If he has two hands, he usually holds a money bag and a bowl. He may also hold a vase, a club, a bowl, and a piece of fruit.

He is the lord of the Yakshas, who are minor forest gods. Yakshas usually have handsome human forms, but they may also appear ugly. Yakshas are usually good, but are occasionally wicked. They are mystical and can assume the form of trees or take other shapes.

He is the son of Visravasa and Idavida. His capital is called Prabha or Alaka. It is a lovely place on Mount Mandara in the Himalayas. His wife's name is Yakshi or Kauveri and she is the daughter of Mura. They had three sons and one daughter. He is called Dhana-pati (Lord of Wealth) and Nata-raja (king of men), because whomever has wealth also rules men.

He is not such an important god and is not usually worshiped in temples. He is often seen carved on temple walls and is mentioned in many Vedic stories.

He inherited the kingdom of Lanka from his father, Visravasa. His half-brother, Ravana, performed great austerities and got a boon to be invincible. Ravana defeated his brother and took his chariot Pushpaka and the island of Lanka. At this time Viswakarma, the architect of the demigods, built Kuvera a palace on Mount Kailash. He also has a beautiful garden called Caitrarath on Mount Mandara. His kingdoms are found in the Himalayas. One reason is because the mountains contain great mineral wealth.

Soma

Soma is the moon-god, and is also known as Chandra. It is said that he is the son of Atri Rishi and Anasuya. His son is Budha, the planet Mercury. The Lunar dynasty descends from him. He is the deity for Monday. It is considered auspicious to be born on a full moon. He has two hands, one holding a mace and the other in a protective mode. His complexion is copper-colored. He rides on a three-wheels chariot flying a red flag, which is pulled by three or ten horses.

He is married to Rohini, daughter of Daksha, and Daksha's other twenty-seven daughters. Because he showed his preference for Rohini, the other daughters complained to their father. Daksha cursed Soma and he became inflicted with leprosy. The daughters feeling this was too severe a punishment asked their father to lift the curse. This could not be done, but he agreed to mitigate it. Because of this, the moon gradually becomes grey-colored and disappears. Later, it again recovers and becomes full.

Agni

Agni is the god of fire and is red-colored. He is depicted either with one or two heads, red eyes, three legs, and two to seven arms. It is said that he has seven arms to reach the seven worlds and that his three legs represent the three important fires of a person's life: sacrificial, marriage, and funeral. His wife's name is Svaha.

He carries a fan, a spear, a cup and a spoon, and other items used for fire sacrifices. Whenever a fire is lit Agni is born, especially a sacrificial fire. His wife's name is Svaha.

At the end of a person's life, Agni accepts the body through the funeral fire. Fire is said to make everything pure, which is why the body is burned at the time of death. Agni purifies it.

He rides on a ram and has a potbelly. Flames issue from his mouth to consume the butter which is offered by priests in the sacrificial fire. Agni is the friend of every household, as fire is needed for cooking.

Many Vedic verses address him. Priests performing sacrifices pour clarified butter on fire and chant "Svaha," which is the name of Agni's consort. Many important events of a person's life are overseen by Agni.

Kamadeva

Kamadeva is the god of love, Cupid. He is handsome and fair. He carries a sugarcane bow strung with humming bees. He shoots arrows from his bow which have five flower-tipped shafts of desire. His carrier is a parrot or a peacock. His wife, Rati (passion), and his friend, Vasanta (spring), help him select what arrow will be used on his current victim. He roams the earth, especially during springtime, and fires his arrow often at sages, young girls, and married women.

Siva burned him to ashes because he disturbed his mediation. It is said that Kamadeva's arrow had hit his mark and Siva, therefore, married Parvati. During this time Kamadeva was dead and love disappeared from the earth. Eventually Kamadeva was born as the son of Krishna named Pradyumna.

He is said to be the son of Lakshmi and Vishnu and he is also said to be the son of Sraddha, the god of faith.

Varuna

He is the god of the oceans. He has a fair complexion and may have two or four hands. In one of his right hands he holds a noose called Nagapasa. He punishes wrongdoers and liars and he ties guilty people in his noose. Varuna rides on a crocodile-like monster called Makara, which has the head and legs of an antelope. His wife is Varuni. He sits on a diamond throne and is surrounded by the various gods of the rivers and lakes. He is the son of Aditi. His kingdom is called Sukha (happiness) or Pushpa-giri (flower mountain). He controls the Western direction.

Vayu

Vayu is the wind-god and the god of breath. He is the father of both Bhima from the *Mahabharata* and Hanuman from the *Ramayana*. He is considered the God of Life, since breath is the first thing every child needs. He may have two or four hands and may hold a wheel or a goad. He is not mentioned very much in the Vedas. He rules the northwest direction.

He rides on a chariot pulled by a pair of purple or red horses or deer. Sometimes his chariot can be pulled by forty-nine or a thousand horses. He may also be seen riding a deer carrying a white flag.

Vishwakarma

He is the architect of the demigods or heavenly planets. He is the presiding deity of the craftsman. He usually has four hands holding a book, a noose, a water-pot and a club in his right hand. He may hold craftsmen tools in his left hand or they may be seen placed near his seat. His daughter Sanjana married Surya, the Sun god.

He created the residences, chariots and weapons of the demigods. He built the city of Dwarka for Lord Krishna and Lanka for Ravana. He presented the Satapatya Veda, which explains the science of architecture.

Yamaraja

Yamaraja is the lord of death and judges men when they die. He has a green complexion and wears red cloth. He may have two or four arms. He carries a club in one hand and a noose in the other with which he catches his victims. He rides on a black buffalo. He is the god of the south.

When people die they are brought before Yamaraja and Chitragupta (his Record Keeper). Chitragupta has recorded all the activities of a person's life. Persons who have done pious activities go to heaven and ones who have done sinful activities go to hell. Yamaraja appears to a pious person looking like Vishnu, with a lotus-like smiling face. To the sinners he looks terrible with extremely long hair and eyes like deep wells. It is said that after death the soul takes four hours and forty minutes to reach Yamaraja.

Therefore the body of a dead person is not supposed to be cremated before this time has passed.

People are afraid of Yamaraja because he awards punishment to the miscreants, but those who worship Vishnu (Krishna) have nothing to fear from him. To the devotees he is a cordial friend, but to the nondevotees he is fear personified. He is the twin brother of Yami, who became the river Yamuna.

He is said to be the first mortal to die and having found the path to the other world, guides others after they die. He has two voracious dogs who each have four eyes. They guard the path to his abode.

Brahma had Viswakarma, the architect of the demigods, create the abode of Yamaraja because he realized that a place was needed to judge the wicked. This place is said to have a perfect climate, and there is no afflictions from the body, mind or enemies.

Weekly or Planet Gods

Ravi-var (Surya or Sunday)

This day is influenced by the Sun. Ravi is another name of Surya, the sun-god. He has a red complexion, and thus it is auspicious to wear red on this day. He may have two or four hands, which carry two lotus flowers or a conchshell and a disc. He rides on a chariot with one wheel pulled by seven horses. Sunday is a good day to start a new endeavor. Usually Ravi is a malefic planet in astrology.

Som-var (Moon or Monday)

Monday is under the influence of the moon planet (Soma). It is good to fast and wear white on Mondays. Soma has a white complexion and carries a mace. He rides on a chariot with three wheels pulled by three horses. Someone who is born under the influence of Soma will be respectable, rich, powerful, have many friends, and be honored. The Moon is usually an auspicious planet.

Mangal-var (Mars or Tuesday)

Mangala (Mars) has a red complexion. He has four arms and carries a club and a trident. He usually rides a ram, but also rides in a chariot. A person under the affect of this planet has a tendency to suffer, be accident-prone, to be robbed, attacked, put in prison, or have his good name ruined. This planet is usually detrimental and is often worshiped so that one can become free of its detrimental effects. One can wear red to help ward off the effects of this planet. If a king starts a war on this day, he will be victorious. One should not start an auspicious activity on this day. A copper triangle is his symbol.

Budh-var (Mercury or Wednesday)

This is the day of Mercury (Budha) who has a light green complexion. He also wears green clothes and a green garland. He has four arms and carries a club, a sword and a shield. It is considered especially auspicious to feed Brahmins on this day. Soma, the moon god, is his father and Tara is his mother.

Budha's influence is normally neither favorable nor unfavorable. Budha exerts its influence in reference to the other planets.

Gurupati-var (Jupiter or Thursday)

Brihaspati is the priest of the demigods, and he is also called Guruvara. He has four arms and holds beads (a rosary), a club, and a ball. He has a golden complexion. The color of Thursday is yellow. He usually sits on a lotus or rides on a chariot pulled by eight horses. Someone under the influence of Brihaspati will have a lot of wealth. Brihaspati rules the planet Jupiter

Shukra-var (Venus or Friday)

Shukra is the planet Venus. Shukra means "bright." Shukra is the teacher of the demons and knows how to bring the dead back to life. He has a white complexion. He is seen with four hands, two hands are holding a club and beads (a rosary) and the other two hands may be in the protective or boon giving positions. A silver square is his symbol. He is usually seen sitting on a lotus, but sometimes may be seen riding on a chariot with many flags and pulled by eight horses. Shukra is usually a very auspicious planet. A person under the influence of Shukra will be honored across the land and will attain a high office.

Shani-var (Saturn or Saturday)

Shani is the planet Saturn. This planet is potentially the most detrimental. If this planet is wrongly placed in a person's chart, it can cause great misfortune, such as poverty and loss of loved ones. Shani is black-colored and is seen with four hands, which may hold a trident, a bow and arrow, or a rosary. One of his hands may be in the gift-bestowing position.

He rides either a vulture or in an iron chariot.

There are several Shani shrines found in temples of other gods throughout India. By worshiping Shani one can rid oneself of the misfortunes that this planet causes. To gain the ultimate benefit, this planet should be worshiped on Saturdays.

Due to his wife's curse, Shani can cause destruction by just looking at someone. Therefore he is seen looking down, so as not to destroy anything.

Rahu

The ascending node in astrology, Rahu's influence on a person's chart usually means trouble. Rahu is the planet that causes eclipses and is the ruler of meteors. He is originally a Daitya (demon) and is shown as a monster demon. He has a dragon head and a tail like a comet. He at times devours the Sun and the Moon, causing eclipse. He is originally a Daitya (demon) and is shown as a monster demon. He rides on a chariot pulled by eight black horses.

When Mohini Murti was distributing *soma* nectar to the demigods, Rahu assumed the form of a demigod and drank nectar. The Sun and Moon realized what was going on and told Mohini Murti (actually Lord Vishnu), who immediately cut off Rahu's head. He had drunk the nectar, but it had only reached his neck, so his body died but his head remained alive and rose into the air. To avenge himself, Rahu attacks the Moon every month and occasionally eclipses the Sun.

GENERAL INFORMATION

Hinduism

Hinduism is the major religion in India. About eighty percent of the population is Hindu (over 700 million people). Hinduism is the most popular religion in Asia. Large numbers of people also practice it in Nepal, Fiji, and the island of Bali in Indonesia.

Hinduism is also called *sanatana-dharma*. The English word "religion" does not quite encompass the meaning of *sanatana-dharma*. "Religion" conveys the idea of a particular faith, but faith may change. One may have faith in a particular process or path, and he may then change and adopt another. *Sanatana-dharma* refers to that activity which cannot be changed. *Sanatana-dharma* is therefore not something sectarian. Rather, it refers to the duty all living entities in this world possess—to understand our spiritual essence and to understand our relationship with God. *Sanatana-dharma* is also different from what many people in the West have come to understand as *dharma*. *Dharma* is commonly understood as performing the duty of serving family and country. *Sanatana*, however, means "eternal, that which has neither beginning nor end." *Sanatana-dharma* is the eternal occupation of the living entity. That eternal *dharma* is to serve God.

There are basically three schools of thought in Hinduism, the Vaishnavas, the Shaivites (followers of Siva and Shakti), and the impersonalists. According to Vaishnavas, there is only one God, but he may be known by different names. In the Christian religion he is known as Jehovah, the Muslims call him Allah, and the Vaishnavas call him Krishna or Vishnu. Shaivites believe that Siva is supreme. Impersonalists believe that everything is one, and that when they attain self-realization they will become one with God and become formless.

God can expand himself into unlimited forms. *Avataras*, or incarnations, are God directly. There are also servants of God called demigods—living beings who have been given the power to administer the universe. These demigods are sometimes worshiped as supreme, although they are actually only powerful living beings and not the Supreme Divinity in themselves. According to the Hindu pantheon, there are 33 million demigods, all of whom worship the Supreme Lord. Hindus worship demigods to obtain material benefits because the demigods administer various material facilities. After long worship, the worshipers usually receive their benediction, but the benediction is generally temporary.

Many people say that the gods of Hinduism were developed over a long period of time and were changed by people who migrated to India. Other people say that these gods are eternal and have been mentioned in the Vedas from time eternal. According to the Vedic scriptures the second conclusion is correct.

The Word Hindu

The word "Hindu" was first used by the Persians to refer to the people who lived on the southern side of the Sindus River (now known as the Indus River). The Sindus River divides what was at one time the Middle East (Persia and Afghanistan) and India (then known as Bharata). Because of problems in pronouncing the initial "s", the river was called "Hindu," so the people who lived on the other side of the Sindus River in India, were called Hindus. The name "Hindu" came to refer to both the people and their religion.

Nowadays, the word "Hindu" is used to describe worshipers of the Hindu gods—those who worship Vishnu, Krishna, Siva, Durga, or anyone else. Their scriptures *(sastra)* are the Vedas.

The words "Hindu" and "Hinduism" are not mentioned in the Vedas and are not Sanskrit words. These words have never been used in any scripture or by any *acharya* or spiritual teacher. To indicate Vedic society, the scriptures use the word *"aryan"* or *"sanatana-dharma."*

Basic Philosophy

There are two types of living entities, the *isvara* (the Supreme), which means the controller and the *jiva* (individual soul), the controlled living entities. The *jiva* is controlled all the time. The living entity is part and parcel of the Supreme, but he eternally remains an individual living entity birth after birth. According to the Vaishnavas school of thought the living entity, however great he may be in the material estimation, can never equal the Supreme Lord. According to the impersonal school of thought, at one point the individual soul becomes one with God.

A common understanding in Hinduism is that we are not our bodies, but we are eternal spirit souls. At the present time we are under the influence of the material nature, but our duty is to get freed from this influence.

The nature of the material world is that problems automatically appear, even without us wanting them. They are like a forest fire that somehow blazes without being set by anyone. No one wants fire, and yet it takes place, and we become perplexed. The Vedas advise that in order to solve the perplexities of life and to understand the science of the solution, one must approach a spiritual master who is in the disciplic succession.

AUM/ OM

OM, or *pranava*, is the seed of transcendental realization, and it is composed of the three transcendental letters a-u-m. By chanting OM in conjunction with the breathing process—a transcendental but mechanical way of entering trance—as devised by experienced mystics, one is able to bring the mind, which is usually materially absorbed, under control. OM is the seed of all transcendental sound, and only transcendental sound can bring about the desired change of the mind and the senses. OM is the direct, literal representation of the Supreme Absolute Truth. By chanting OM and controlling the breathing system, one is able to reach the ultimate state of the *pranayama* system of yoga and be fixed in *samadhi* (trance).

The sound of OM is eternal and goes beyond the conceptions of time. It is pronounced with a nasalized ending, a sound between an N and an M. OM is used to begin sacrifices, mediation, prayers, and before the performance of yoga. To obtain the true benefit of this powerful mantra, one must chant it with full concentration. OM is the symbolic sound representation of the Supreme Personality of Godhead. There is no difference between the Supreme Personality of Godhead and OM.

These three symbolic representations are used by Brahmins while chanting Vedic hymns and during sacrifices performed for the satisfaction of the Supreme. In the Vedic hymns, the word OM is always present.

Hindu Trinity

There are three main Hindu gods: Brahma, the creator, Vishnu, the maintainer, and Siva, the destroyer. There are also three modes of nature: passion, goodness, and ignorance. Passion is for creation, goodness for maintenance, and ignorance for destruction. Brahma is in charge of the mode of passion, Vishnu the mode of goodness, and Siva the mode of ignorance.

Worship

Most Hindus perform daily worship in their homes on a small altar. Often they set aside an entire room as a shrine and worship only in that room. They will place pictures of their family gods on the altar and offer their worship to the pictures. Often there are many pictures which may include Vishnu, Krishna, Siva, Ganesh, Lakshmi, Durga, Rama, and Hanuman. They may also have a deity form of one of the gods or a Sivalinga on the altar. Worship is usually performed early in the morning and again in the evening. Most Hindus rise from bed before dawn to begin their worship.

A person engaged in home worship will perform *aratik*, which usually consists of offering incense, a lamp, and flowers. Other items may also be offered. Food is also offered to the different gods.

It is considered important for all Hindus to make regular visits to temples. A person may visit a temple every day or even several times a day. They may also visit several different temples in a day. Other people, especially those who live a good distance from a temple, may visit the temple only on festival days. Important festivals must be observed.

Mantra meditation or chanting the holy names of God is also considered worship. Devotees sing songs *(bhajans)* to glorify God.

The Vedas

The *Vedas* are written in Sanskrit, which is one of the oldest (if not the oldest) languages in the world. *Veda* means "knowledge."

According to the *Bhavisya Purana*, the *Vedas* include the original four *Vedas*—*Rig*, *Atharva*, *Yajur*, and *Sama*—the *Upanisads*, the *Mahabharata* (which includes the *Bhagavad-gita*), the *Pancaratna*, the *Ramayana*, and the *Puranas*. Many scholars say that only the original four *Vedas* (*Rig*, *Atharva*, *Yajur*, and *Sama*) can be considered real Vedic literature. This is neither accepted by the *Vedas* themselves nor by the important Vedic teachers such as Sankara, Ramanuja, or Madhvacarya. The *Chandogya Upanisad* states that the *Puranas* and *Itihasas* (histories) are the fifth *Veda*.

The main criterion for a literature to be accepted as Vedic is that it must have the same purport and conclusion as the original Vedic scriptures. Any work that expands on the Vedic conclusion without changing its meaning can be accepted as Vedic.

The Vedic scriptures are vast. The *Mahabharata* has 110,000 couplets, the *Rig Veda* 1,017 hymns, and the eighteen main *Puranas* hundreds of thousands of verses.

The *Rig Veda* has hymns glorifying gods such as Indra (King of Heaven), Surya (Sun) and Agni (fire). It also describes different sacrifices that can be performed. The *Yajur Veda* explains the rules of some religious rituals. It describes how to do a Vedic sacrifice and how to make an altar. The *Sama Veda* (1549 hymns) deals with chanting. *Sama* means "melody." It discusses such gods as Indra, Agni and Soma (the Moon god). The *Atharva Veda* (6000 verses) contains many *mantras* that are used in *sacrifices* and is said to have been written by the Sage Atharva.

There are more than 108 *Upanishads*. The *Upanisads* are mainly dialogues between sages or between gods and sages to establish philosophical conclusions. They often contain stories. The thirteen most important ones are: *Katha, Isa, Chandogya, Prasna., Kena, Mundaka, Aitareya, Taittirya, Brihad Aranyaka, Kaushitaki, Maitri, Mandukya* and *Svetasvatara*. Some of the *Upanishads* are named after the sages that are mentioned in them.

Vedic literature provides knowledge of self-realization and liberation (*moksha*) from material bondage and suffering. It teaches that the material body is temporary and that one should not resign himself to this temporary and miserable world but try to find permanent happiness. This is done by serving the Supreme Personality of Godhead, who is known in the *Vedas* as Krishna or Vishnu.

The *Vedas* are considered eternal. They do not come from any materially conditioned person but from the Supreme. They cannot be understood by logic or experimentation, as they are inconceivable. They must be understood by hearing from an authoritative source. The knowledge of the *Vedas* is considered complete and infallible.

One of the main *Vedas* is the *Manusmriti* (the codes of Manu). This is one of the *Dharma Sutras* or *Vedas* that give men moral rules of conduct and duties to perform. It describes what is sinful, what punishment should be given, performance of sacrifice, the duties of women, funeral ceremonies, purification rituals and many other subjects. It basically deals with the laws of man.

Puranas

Purana means "old." The *Puranas* are stories which expound the *Vedic* conclusions. Often the pastimes of God and his devotees are described. There are many *Puranas*, but there are 18 major *Puranas*. Six *Puranas* deal with Lord Vishnu, six address Lord Siva and six deal with Lord Brahma. They are usually in question and answer form. There are also *Upa* (additional) *Puranas*. The Puranas are named after different gods.

The *Puranas* establish the meaning of the *Vedas*, as they are the natural commentaries on the *Vedas*. The highest *Purana* is the *Srimad Bhagavatam* (*Bhagavat Purana*).

Bhagavad Gita

The *Bhagavad-gita* presents the discussion between Krishna and Arjuna just prior to the famous Battle of Kurukshetra. *Bhagavad-gita* means "Song of God." Early in the work, Arjuna accepts Krishna as his spiritual master after seeing his friends and relatives on the opposing side and losing his desire to fight. Sri Krishna begins his instructions to Arjuna, which present the conclusions of Vedic knowledge.

The *Bhagavad-gita* is considered by many to be the most important chapter of the *Mahabharata*, and it is the essence of its instructions. It consists of eighteen chapters and seven hundred verses. The battle of Kurukshetra, which lasted for eighteen days, was fought between the Pandavas and the Kauravas and their respective armies totaled approximately five million men. Many scholars accept this battle as allegorical, but followers of Vedic culture believe the battle actually took place about five thousand years ago.

The *Gita* is like the "Bible" of India. It is the most popular book read by Hindus, and is studied by scholars around the world. Its first instruction is that we are not the body but eternal spirit soul temporarily encaged within the body. It concludes that the perfection of life is total surrender to God and to act according to His desire. Krishna says, "Always think of me, become my devotee, worship me and offer your homage unto me. Thus you will come to me without fail. I promise you this because you are my very dear friend."

Bhagavad-gita is highly recommended reading for one who wants to understand the essence of the Vedic teachings.

Mahabharata

The Mahabharata is the most famous story in India. It was composed in Sanskrit by Veda Vyasadeva, and is said to have 110,000 verses. Bharata is the original name for India. *Mahabharata* therefore means the history of "Greater India."

The *Mahabharata* is about the five sons of Maharaja Pandu—Yudhisthira, Bhima, Arjuna, Nakula, and Sahadeva, and the events leading up to and following the Battle of Kurukshetra.

Two brothers, Pandu and Dhritarastra, were heirs to the throne of

India. Dhritarastra, the older brother, was blind and thus disqualified. Pandu became king. When Pandu died, however, Dhritarastra's eldest son, Duryodhana, claimed the throne over Pandu's eldest son, Yudhisthira. Duryodhana was, after all, only disqualified due to his father's blindness.

The five Pandavas, or sons of Pandu, were eventually forced into exile by Duryodhana's intrigues. During this time, the five brothers married Draupadi, and had many adventures together, which led to their names becoming attached to many temples and places around India.

After a period of time, the Pandavas returned to the court and requested that their kingdom be returned. When Duryodhana refused, the Pandavas proposed that the kingdom be divided equally between the cousins. The court ministers convinced Duryodhana to agree. The Kauravas (sons of Dhritarastra) got Hastinapur for their capital and the Pandavas got Indraprastha (now greater Delhi).

Eventually, Duryodhana devised a dice game in which the Pandavas were cheated of their entire kingdom, including their wife Draupadi. The Kauravas attempted to strip Draupadi in public, but Krishna protected her. The Pandavas then had to go into exile for twelve years in the forest and then live for one year incognito. During the thirteenth year, the Pandavas lived in the service of the King of Virata.

When their exile was over, the Pandavas returned and demanded that their kingdom be restored. Again Duryodhana refused. The Pandavas, hoping to avoid war, requested five villages to rule. Again Duryodhana refused. Ultimately, his refusal led to the battle at Kurukshetra (north of Delhi). It was just prior to this battle that the *Bhagavad-gita* was spoken.

While preparing for war, Arjuna and Duryodhana were given the choice of having either Krishna or Krishna's army on their side. The only stipulation was that Krishna himself would not fight. Duryodhana chose Krishna's army, and Arjuna happily chose Krishna. Krishna thus became Arjuna's charioteer. On the morning of the first day of battle, Krishna recited to Arjuna the *Bhagavad-gita*.

The Kauravas side was at first commanded by Grandfather Bhisma, but he was eventually wounded during the battle. The battle lasted for eighteen days, and millions of soldiers were killed. Most of the Kauravas were killed in this battle. On the last day of battle, Bhima and Duryodhana fought a duel with clubs. After a vicious fight in which Bhima smashed Duryodhana's thighs and won, the Pandavas won back their kingdom.

Yudhisthira was then crowned Emperor. Not long after the battle of Kurukshetra, the Pandavas renounced the kingdom and installed their grandson Pariksit on the throne. They then headed to the Himalayas to start their journey toward Heaven. Eventually, Yudhisthira was the only one to reach his goal, but upon reaching the heavenly kingdom, Yudhisthira insisted that his four brothers and Draupadi be admitted along with him.

Ramayana

This is the story of Lord Rama, the seventh incarnation of Lord Vishnu. There was once a king named Dasaratha who had three wives, Kausalya, Sumitra, and Kaikeyi. Regrettably, he had no sons from any of his wives. Thus he performed a sacrifice by which to obtain a son, and from the sacrifice came nectar for his wives to drink. Kausalya, the senior wife, was given half the nectar, and the other two were given the other half to share. Sumitra divided her share into two portions. After they drank the nectar, Kausalya gave birth to a son named Rama, Sumitra had the twins Laksman and Satrughna, and Kaikeyi gave birth to Bharata.

Rama later married Sita, the daughter of King Janaka. King Janaka organized a *svayamvara*, a competition to see who was qualified to marry his daughter. The winner had to string Lord Siva's bow and hit a target. Only Rama was able to string the bow, what to speak of hit the target. As Rama was Lord Vishnu and Sita was Lakshmi, this marriage was predestined.

King Dasaratha decided to retire as King of Ayodhya and to crown Rama, his eldest son, king. On the eve of the coronation, Kaikeyi, Dasarath's youngest wife, was convinced by her maid Mandara that Dasarath was trying to cheat Bharata out of the kingdom. Accordingly, she asked her husband to crown Bharata and to exile Rama to the forest for fourteen years. Dasaratha was unwillingly obliged to comply, as he had previously promised Kaikeyi that he would fulfill any desire as a gift for her having saved his life in the past.

In this way, Rama, along with his devoted wife, Sita, and his brother Laksman, went to the forest, and not long after Dasarath expired. When Bharata, who was away at the time, returned to Ayodhya, he did not wish to rule due to his affection for Rama. He followed Rama to the forest and begged him to return. Rama refused, however, in order to maintain his father's promise. Bharata agreed to rule on Rama's behalf, set Rama's sandals on the throne, and lived a life of asceticism outside the city gates until Rama's return.

While in the forest, Ravana, king of Lanka, kidnapped Sita and brought her to his kingdom. Rama and Laksman then went out to search for Sita.

During this time they met Sugriva, the monkey king, and Hanuman, his minister. The devoted Hanuman eventually found Sita in Lanka. Rama and Laksman, along with the monkey army, attacked Lanka. After much fighting, the ten-headed Ravana was killed and Sita was recovered. Rama then returned to Ayodhya and assumed the throne.

Srimad-Bhagavatam

The *Srimad-Bhagavatam* is also known as the *Bhagavat Purana*. It is dedicated to Lord Vishnu and describes the history of various incarnations of Lord Vishnu and his devotees. It is made up of twelve books, 332 chapters, and 18,000 verses. According to Vaishnavas, the *Srimad-Bhagavatam* is the most important *Purana* because it directly discusses the glories of Lord Krishna. Veda Vyasadeva wrote it on the instruction of his *guru*, Narada Muni. It is a discourse in which Maharaja Pariksit, the last member of the Pandava dynasty, questions Sukadeva Goswami (the son of Veda Vyasadeva) about the purpose of life.

The *Srimad-Bhagavatam* describes stories about the ten incarnations of Lord Vishnu. The tenth book deals in detail with the pastimes of Lord Krishna himself. The last book discusses Kali-yuga, the present age of quarrel, and the future.

Guru

Literally, *guru* means "heavy," and the *guru should* be heavy with knowledge. The guru is the spiritual guide of his students. He initiates his students when he knows they are sincere, and gives them a *mantra* to chant. To achieve a *mantra*'s full effect, it should be received from a spiritual teacher. The true *guru* is considered the representative of God. He is always a pure servant of God; being a human being he can never become God.

The *guru* must come in a bona fide disciplic succession and have complete knowledge of the Absolute Truth. The faithful disciple becomes the next *guru*. His or her relationship, therefore, is not only with the *guru* but also with the *guru's* spiritual succession or unbroken chain of masters. This chain of disciplic succession is called *sampradaya* or *parampara*.

A true *guru* teaches by example. He must have renounced the four sinful activities: intoxication, gambling, illicit sex (sex outside of marriage), and meat-eating. He has to have complete control of his senses and of his speech.

Disciples must surrender themselves completely and become humble servants of the *guru*. They must make following the *guru's* instructions their life's mission. The most important attributes of a disciple are faith, service, and submissive inquiry. The disciple should not serve a spiritual master blindly, but must also inquire from him about the ultimate solution to life's problems and about the Absolute Truth. The disciple should also be careful to ensure that the *guru* practices what he preaches.

The secrets to the goal of life given by the bona fide *guru* are open to everyone regardless of caste, creed, or nationality, but they remain secrets unless the disciples has the sincerity and the honest desire to know the goal of life. To understand the goal of life, a disciple must follow regulations of purification assigned by the *guru*.

There are two types of *gurus*, *diksha-guru* (initiating spiritual master) and *shiksha-guru* (instructing spiritual master). One keeps his *diksha-guru* for life. A *shiksha-guru* is one who provides instructions on the path. For a *shiksha-guru* to be effective, he much speak exactly the same instructions as the *diksha-guru* has spoken and not contradict him.

Four Main Schools of Thought and Markings of Different Sects

1. **Vaishnavas**, who worship Lord Vishnu and Krishna.
2. **Shaivites**, who worship Lord Siva.
3. **Shaktas**, who worship the goddess Durga or Kali.
4. **Smartas**, who worship five major deities: Vishnu, Siva, Shakti, Ganesh, and Surya, the sun-god.

Worshipers of Siva may also worship Ganesh and Karttikeya (Skanda), Siva's sons. Shaktas may worship the many forms of Durga, such as Parvati or Kali. Durga is the most commonly worshiped form and has many temples of her own throughout India.

The different sects wear different markings on their foreheads, chests, and arms to identify to which sect they belong (the markings are applied also to sanctify the body). You can tell the difference between the sects by the forehead marks. Vertical marks mean devotees of Vishnu; horizontal marks indicate devotees of Siva. Siva's devotees usually wear *rudraksha* beads around their necks, while devotees of Vishnu or Krishna wear *tulasi* beads.

Worshipers of Siva have two or more horizontal lines, with or without a dot above or below them. Also a crescent moon or a trident, Siva's own markings, indicate a Shaivite. There may also be an oval or half-oval, said to symbolize Siva's third eye.

Vaishnavas are divided into worshipers of Lord Krishna and his consort Radha, worshipers of Lord Vishnu and his consort Lakshmi, and worshipers of Lord Rama and his consort Sita. Lord Krishna is often worshiped by himself or with Rukmini, his chief wife. Often Krishna and Vishnu are worshiped in temples alone, without their consorts. Often each type of worshiper has their own sectarian markings.

Deities of Ganesh or Karttikeya wear the marks of Siva on them. Krishna, Rama, Hanuman, and Indra have the marks of Vishnu on them. Brahma has the markings of both Vishnu and Siva on him.

These markings are made of *tilaka* (sacred clay), ashes from a sacred fire, cow dung, sandalwood, turmeric, or lime. They may be yellow, red, black, or ashen white.

Vaishnava Philosophy

Vaishnava philosophy accepts that there is only one God. He takes many names and forms in different religions. Christians call him Jehovah, Muslims, Allah, and Hindus, Vishnu or Krishna. According to Vaishnavas, Krishna is the Supreme Personality of Godhead, and all other gods and living entities are his servants. This is the essential difference between material life and spiritual life. Spiritual life means that God is the object of our service, and material life means our service is devoid of relationship with God.

A common misconception is that Krishna is an incarnation of Vishnu. Actually, Krishna is supreme. Even though Vishnu and Krishna are basically nondifferent, still, one expanded from the other. According to scripture, Vishnu is an expansion of Krishna. The analogy is that when one candle lights another, they both have the same potency, but one is always the original flame. Vishnu is the administrative form of Lord Krishna, while Krishna is always engaged in enjoying with his devotees.

Another common misconception is that God is ultimately formless. If one accepts that God is all-powerful, then why is he not powerful enough to be a person? Rather, it is seen that behind all energy a person is working. A common idea is that Lord Siva is supreme, but according to Vaishnava philosophy even Lord Siva, who is very powerful, is Vishnu's servant. Also there is the misconception that there are many gods in Hinduism, but according to Vaishnava philosophy there is only one God, which is commonly accepted by most religions.

Vaishnava Sampradayas

There are four Vaishnava *sampradayas* (lines of disciplic succession): namely, the Brahma-sampradaya, the Sri-sampradaya, the Kumara-sampradaya, and the Rudra-sampradaya. These *sampradayas* are also known respectively as the Madhva-sampradaya, the Ramanuja-sampradaya, the Nimbarka-sampradaya, and the Vishnuswami-sampradaya after the four major *acaryas* in each *sampradaya*.

Karma

Karma refers to the scientific law of cause and effect. Whatever we do will come back to us at a later date, if not in this lifetime, in a future birth. From time immemorial, the individual soul has been acting in the material world and enjoying or suffering the reactions. His actions bring about his transmigration from one material body to another. Both pious and impious actions bind a person to this wheel of transmigration, because both piety and impiety create a reaction. Everyone creates their own *karma* out of their particular desires to enjoy this world in different ways. Neither God nor anyone else can be held responsible for our *karma*; we create our own destiny.

In one sense, all *karma* is bondage. Even pious activities bind a person to the material world. The goal of life is to be free from *karma*, and to therefore become free from the wheel of repeated birth and death. A person cannot become free from *karma* simply by renouncing activity. He or she must engage in transcendental activities—that is, by serving the Supreme Personality of Godhead, who will then intervene and free us from previous *karmic* reactions.

Vikarmas activities are actions that are irreligious and should not be performed. These activities give you bad reactions. A person acting in God consciousness is performing transcendental activities and these activities are considered *akarma* or activities that have no reaction. To engage in the service of God makes one immune to all sorts of reactionary elements of work.

Reincarnation

Reincarnation refers to the science of repeated birth and death. The logic is that the soul is eternal and the body is temporary. When a person dies, only the body dies. The soul receives another body according to his or her *karma*. As a result of *karma*, a person may take birth in a wealthy family or in a family of insects. The *Padma Purana* states that there are 8,400,000 species of life. The Vedic conclusion does not agree with Darwin's theory of evolution. According to the *Vedas*, all species were created simultaneously and did not evolve over a period of time. Rather, the soul evolves through each of them until it reaches the human form of life, when there is a chance to cultivate self-realization and become liberated.

Samsara

Samsara means "repeated birth or death, or transmigration." As a result of *karma* a person takes birth after birth, sometimes as a rich person and sometimes as a poor person. According to the *Padma Purana* there are 8,400,000 species of life and the fallen soul has to take birth in everyone of them. After evolving through these millions of birth, a soul (*jiva*) takes birth as a human. At that time they have the chance to take to self-realization. If they do not, they are again subjected to *samsara*.

Kundalini Yoga

In a mystical sense *chakras* are in the center of the body. There are six *chakras* that are at different levels of the body up along the spine. In this process one meditates on the different *chakras* in the body in proper order. One then moves one's vital energy from the base of the spine to the top of the head. To have the desired effect one should engage in this process under the guidance of a competent guru. The *chakras* cannot be seen by the naked eye.

Each *chakra* has the form of a lotus, with the petals representing different mystical qualities. Different deities are represented by each *chakra*. It is said that the goddess Devi (Kundalini, the serpent power) surrounds the *muladhara chakra*. When it is awakened by different *Tantric* yoga processes, it rises to the *sahara-padma chakra*.

There are six major *chakras* in the body. They are **Muladhara** (base of the spine), **Svadhisthana** (private area), **Manipuraka** (stomach area), **Anahata** (lower chest), **Visuddha** (base of the neck) and the **Ajna** (in the middle of the head, just above the eyes). The Ajna *chakra* is often referred to as the third eye. Located above the top of the head is the **Sahasra chakra**, which is often considered the seventh *chakra*.

To reach the ultimate stage, a *yogi* blocks the evacuating hole with the heel of the foot. He then progressively moves the life air on and on to the six different *chakras*. One reaches the Svadhisthana *chakra*, which is the powerhouse of the life air and then one proceeds up until he reaches the Ajna *chakra*. One then pushes the life air up between the eyebrows, and then, blocking the seven outlets of the life air, should then reach the cerebral hole and give up his material connections, having gone to the Supreme.

The life air passes through seven openings, namely two eyes, two nostrils, two ears and a mouth. Generally it passes through the mouth at the time of an ordinary man's death. But the yogi who controls the life airs in this way, generally releases the life air by puncturing the cerebral hole in the head.

Bhakti

Bhakti refers to the expression of love, service, and devotion to a personal God. The *Bhagavad-gita* presents *bhakti-yoga* as the highest goal, and Arjuna is asked to serve the Supreme Personality of Godhead, Sri Krishna, without a motive other than love and without material consideration. *Bhakti-yoga* is opposed to the concept of becoming one with the Supreme. It is believed that service to God is eternal and that the individual soul is never equal to or becomes God. Chaitanya Mahaprabhu, Ramanujacarya, and Madhvacarya all taught the *bhakti* path as the most efficient means to reach God realization.

Mantra

A *mantra* is a Vedic hymn that causes the mind to meditate on a particular deity. A *mantra* is meant to be received by a bone fide *guru* if it is to have complete effect. The *mantra* can consist of only one word, such as OM (aum), or it can consist of multiple syllables or words. A *mantra* is usually repeated many times. Often one keeps track of the repetitions on beads. This practice is called *japa*. *Japa* is performed when a person constantly repeats a *mantra* so that only he or she can hear it. *Sadhus* may chant over a 100,000 names of God in a day. Great care must be taken to chant the *mantra* correctly and with attention if the practitioner wishes to receive the ultimate benefit the *mantra* offers.

Gaudiya Vaishnavas consider that by chanting the Lord's holy names, specifically the *maha-mantra, Hare Krishna Hare Krishna, Krishna Krishna Hare Hare/ Hare Rama Hare Rama, Rama Rama Hare Hare,* one will attain transcendental devotion to God. It is considered that Krishna and his name are nondifferent.

Shaivites chant the *mantra Om Namah Shivaya*. Another famous *mantra* is *Sree Ram Jaya Ram, Jaya Jaya Ram/ Sree Ram Jaya Ram, Jaya Jaya Ram*.

The most famous *mantras* are the *gayatri-mantra* and OM (aum). To get the proper effect from chanting the *gayatri-mantra* one must receive it from a *guru*. The *gayatri-mantra* is "*OM bhur bhuvah svah, tat savitur varenyam, bhargo devasya dhimahi, dhiyo yo nah prachodayat.*" The *gayatri-mantra* is usually given to a teenage Brahmin when they receive their sacred thread and become "twice-born." There are many other *mantras* in Hinduism.

Ahimsa

Ahimsa means nonviolence, not wishing to harm, or actually harming any being at any time. This means plants, insects, animals or humans. This means that no living entity should be injured or killed unless it is absolutely necessary. It also means that no mental misery should be inflicted on anyone. For this reason many Hindus are vegetarians so as not to injure animals, which are considered a higher form of life than plants. It is stated that every living entity has to live by killing another entity; that is the law of nature. *Jivo jivasya jivanam*: one living entity is the life for another living entity. But for a human being, that violence should be committed only as much as necessary.

Ahimsa means that one should act in such a way that will not put others into misery or cause them confusion. The human body is meant for spiritual realization, so anything not done to further that end commits violence on the human body. Mahatma Gandhi preached these teachings not only verbally, but also by his personal example in the way he lived.

Ashram

Living quarters at a temple or holy place. It also refers to a remote hermitage of a saintly person or sage. Sages would often do their personal meditation in their ashrams and they would also teach their students there. It is usually a very basic place, but sometimes they can be very large, consisting of a temple, guesthouses, teaching facilities, etc. An ashram is usually a very peaceful and tranquil place, making it a perfect place to meditate on God.

Another meaning has to do with the four spiritual orders of life according to the Vedic social system. This includes *brahmacarya* (student life), *grihastha* (married life), *vanaprastha* (retired life), and *sannyasa* (renounced order).

Ashtanga Yoga

There are eight disciplines: Yama, Niyama, Asana, Pranayama, Pratyahara, Dharana, Dhyana and Samadhi. These processes are recommended for controlling the senses and for spiritual advancement. This process was mainly propounded by the Sage Patanjali in the Yoga Sutra. The Patanjali system of yoga instructs one on how to control the functions of the body's air in a technical manner so that ultimately all the functions of the air within become favorable for purifying the soul of material attachment. According to this yoga system, *pratyag-atma* is the ultimate goal.

Yama means giving up vices. This means to make one's life pure.
Niyama means doing pure activities. This is purity of the body. **Asana**

means doing yoga postures. This is the Hatha-yoga exercises that are commonly seen in the West.

Pranayama involves controlling the airs within the body so as to reverse the directions of their passage. The *apana* air goes downward, and the *prana* air goes upward. The *pranayama-yogi* practices breathing the opposite way until the currents are neutralized into *puraka*, equilibrium. Offering the exhaled breath into the inhaled breath is called *recaka*. When both air currents are completely stopped, one is said to be in *kumbhaka-yoga*. By practice of *kumbhaka-yoga*, one can increase the duration of life for perfection in spiritual realization. By practicing *pranayama* one can increase the duration of life and therefore give oneself more time to attain perfection in this life, rather than waiting for the next.

Pratyahara means to withdraw one's senses from the sense objects like a tortoise withdraws his body into his shell. **Dharana** mean to fix one's mind on an object. **Dhyana** means meditation.

Samadhi (trance) means that one realizes the Supersoul through transcendental mind and intelligence, without the misgivings of identifying the self with the Superself. It means that the mind is fixed for understanding the self. At this stage there is no longer any connection with mundane pleasure, for one is then transcendental to all sorts of happiness derived from the senses. *Samadhi* is never possible for persons interested in material sense enjoyment. Unless the yogi reaches this stage he is unsuccessful.

Atman

This is another name for the soul. It is spiritual, eternal, free from deterioration and is never born or dies. It is the size of one ten-thousandth the tip of a hair, so it is so small that it is beyond conception and cannot be seen. When the body dies, the soul remains alive, passing into another body at death. The *karma* of the soul passes into the new body at death along with the soul.

Caturmasya

Caturmasya is a four-month period when austerities are performed during the rainy season. Traditionally *sannyasi* and *sadhus* do not travel during this period, but remain in a holy place. The fourth month of Caturmasya, Kartika (Oct/Nov) is dedicated to Lord Krishna in his Damodara form. Damodara is a name of Krishna that refers to when he was tied with a rope around his stomach. Caturmasya goes from the first day (full Moon day) of Shravana (middle of July) to the last day of Kartika (middle of November).

Sudarsana Cakra

The *cakra* (disc) of Lord Vishnu is called Sudarsana, which means "auspicious vision." The Sudarsana cakra is always concerned with annihilating the demons. The illuminating principles in this world such as the sun, the moon, and fire emanate from the effulgence of Sudarsana. Similarly, illumination by knowledge also comes from Sudarsana, because with the illumination of Sudarsana one can distinguish one thing from another, the superior from the inferior.

When Lord Vishnu throws this disc it never misses its mark. It is very sharp and can slice off the top of a mountain. It can burn down an entire city and can kill thousands of men in battle in a single throw. It cuts and burns at the same time. It is the most powerful weapon.

Swastika

The Swastika symbol is widely used in Hinduism and is an auspicious sign. It means "auspicious" or "well-being." It is put on doorways to keep away black spirits. The Swastika is the sign of the sun god, Surya. The right-handed Swastika goes in a clockwise direction and the left-handed Swastika goes in a counter clockwise direction. The left-handed Swastika is often considered inauspicious. Usually Swastikas are white on a black background.

Tantra

Tantra is a practice to attain transcendental ecstasy by performing certain rites, which may be mystical. *Tantra* means "to expand." Most of the rites that are performed are focused toward Devi, the wife of Siva in her Shakti (energy) manifestation. Five *makaras* (magically changed things) are needed for a *tantra* ritual: *mamsa*—flesh, *matsya*—fish, *madya*—wine, *maithuna*—sexual union, and *mudra*—mystic gestures. Some worshipers of Shakti worship her as Uma and Gauri. Others, who are usually much more radical, worship her as Kali or Durga and group sexual rites may be performed. These erotic *Tantric* rituals are against the normal principles of Hinduism.

By pronouncing the correct *mantras* in the correct way and by using *yantras*, the Tantric *yogi* may be able to force the gods to give them mystical powers, which may lead them to divine ecstasy. *Om mani padme hum* which means "bliss, which is the jewel within the lotus," is a famous six syllable *Tantric* chant. Some *tantra* teaches that you get liberation by enjoyment.

Many *tantra* literatures are kept secret, so many of the rituals are unknown. Often these rituals have nothing to do with the *Vedas*.

Shalagram-shilas

Shalagram-shilas are self-manifested Deities of Lord Vishnu or Krishna appearing as small stones. Shalagram-shilas are usually collected from the Gandhaki River in Nepal, near Muktinatha. They are often black or a dark color, and are round or oval. Brahmins usually worship Shalagram-shilas in their homes. These stones are sold on the streets in Kathmandu and look like fossils.

Shalagram-shilas are always considered nondifferent from Krishna Himself. The *Padma Purana* says: "Lord Vishnu may be worshiped in the form of a Deity made of eight kinds of material: stone, wood, metal, paint, written word, earth, jewels, and words within the mind. But you should know that the worship of *shalagram-shila* is worship of Sri Krishna Himself, since the Lord exists eternally in the *shalagram-shila*."

In the *Bhavisya Purana*, Lord Krishna says to His devotee, Tulasi: "In the form of small stones, I live always on the banks of the Gandhaki River. The millions of worms who live in that place adorn those stones with the sign of my *cakra*, by carving them with their small teeth."

According to their markings, or *chakras*, one can identify the *shalagrams* as one of the many incarnations of the Lord, such as Narasimha, Matsya, Kurma, Varaha, etc. Brahmins often have a Shalagram-shila in their house and perform daily worship by bathing and offering *aratik* to it.

Siva Lingas

Siva is worshiped as a Siva-linga in temples. A Siva-linga is usually made of stone and has three parts. The base is square with an oval or octagonal platform, topped by a cylindrical, round stone. It is common to have a temple of Siva without a form of Siva, but to simply worship a *linga*.

The linga may either be carved or natural. The natural *lingas* are usually collected from a riverbed, often the Krishna River in South India. A Siva-linga is bathed, offered flower garlands, covered with milk, and offered food as part of the worship. A Siva-linga may be *chala* (movable) or *achala* (immovable). A *chala linga* may be in a house, carried, or sometimes worn around the neck. The *achala lingas* are installed in temples.

Lord Siva is worshiped as five element *lingas* at five different major temples in South India:

1. Sky or space (ether), Akash-linga, in Chidambaram, Tamil Nadu.
2. Water, Appu-linga, at the Jambukeswaram temple near Tiruchirappalli (Trichy), Tamil Nadu.

3. Fire, Agni-linga, at the Arunachaleswar Temple, in Tiruvannamalai, Tamil Nadu.
4. Earth, Prithvi-linga, in Kanchipuram, Tamil Nadu, or some say Gokarna, Karnataka.
5. Air, Vayu-linga, in Sri Kalahasti, Andhra Pradesh.

Siva Jyotirlingas

There are twelve Siva Jyotirlingas, which are symbols of creation and power. They are said to be self-manifested. Temples where they are installed are considered important.

1. Sri Somnath in Somnath, Gujarat
2. Sri Mallikarjuna in Srisailam Hill, Andhra Pradesh
3. Sri Mahakaleswara in Ujjain, Madhya Pradesh
4. Sri Omkareswar, bank of the Narmada River, Madhya Pradesh
5. Sri Vaidyanatha in Chitabhumi (Deoghar), near Patna, Bihar
6. Sri Nageswara near Dwarka, Gujarat
7. Sri Viswanatha in Varanasi, Uttar Pradesh
8. Sri Bhima Sankara in Mahabaleswara, Maharashtra
9. Sri Rameswara in Rameswaram, Tamil Nadu
10. Sri Trimbakeswara near Nasik, Maharashtra
11. Sri Kedarnath in the Himalayas, Uttar Pradesh
12. Sri Ghrisneswara in Sivalaya near the Ellora Caves, Maharashtra

Holy Places

There are thousands of holy places throughout India. Some have more spiritual significance than others, and the benefits and spiritual advancement a person can receive when making a pilgrimage is relative to the place. Faithful Hindus visit holy places to perfect spiritual realization.

There are four *dhamas* or kingdoms of God: Badrinath, Rameswaram, Puri, and Dwarka. Each represents a planet in the spiritual sky. The spiritual sky consists of the *brahmajyoti* (the effulgence around God's body, the light into which yogis seeking liberation desire to merge) and the Vaikunthas (spiritual planets).

There are seven sacred cities known as the Saptapuris (Mokshapuris): Ayodhya, Mathura, Mayapuri (Haridwar), Kashi (Varanasi), Kanchi (Kanchipuram), Avantipuri (Ujjain), and Dwarka. The seven most sacred rivers are the Ganges, Yamuna, Godavari, Saraswati, Narmada, Sindhu, and Kaveri. There are four Kumbha-melas, located at Allahabad, Haridwar,

Ujjain, and Nasik.

There are eight self-manifested holy places (Svayam Vyakta Ksetras) out of a list of 108 major Vishnu temples (108 Vaishnava Divya Desams): Sri Rangam, Tirumala, Sri Mushnam, and Thotadri in South India; Shalagram, Pushkar, Naimisaranya, and Badrinath in North India.

The most important holy places for Gaudiya Vaishnavas are Vrindavan, Mathura, Puri, and Mayapur. Other important holy places are Dwarka, Ayodhya, Kurukshetra, Naimisaranya, Nasik, Ujjain, Rameswaram, Gaya, Gangotri, Yamunotri, Kedarnath, Badrinath, Varanasi, and Prayag. Vrindavan and Mathura are important because Lord Krishna appeared and performed his childhood pastimes there. Dwarka is important because Lord Krishna lived there later and performed many pastimes there.

The Himalayas are considered a holy mountain range. The Himalaya Range is about 2,500 km long and 350 km wide, and there are hundreds of peaks over 6000m (20,000 ft) high.

Vrindavana and Braja Mandala

Braja Mandala covers an area of 1453 square miles surrounding Vrindavana and Mathura. Braja is where Sri Krishna performed His pastimes 5,000 years ago. There are twelve principle forests in Braja and all of them are considered places of pilgrimage. Other major places in the Braja area are Nandagram, Varsana, Gokula, Govardhana Hill, and Radha Kund. It is believed that all the results of traveling on all the pilgrimages within the three worlds can be achieved simply by touching the holy land of Mathura.

Vrindavana and Mathura are the most important Vaishnava holy places in all of India because Mathura is the birthplace of Lord Krishna and Vrindavana is where He carried out His childhood pastimes.

It is said in the *Padma Purana* that "Simply by residing for one day in Mathura one will attain Hari-bhakti, devotion to Hari (Vishnu)." In the *Adi-varaha Purana* it is stated: "Any person who dies in any place within Mathura—a holy place, a home, or even a courtyard—certainly attains salvation. In this world Mathura is the best of all holy places beginning with Kashi."

Ayurvedic Medicine

According to the science of Ayurvedic medicine, by controlling your diet and taking herbal medicines, you can cure or avoid most diseases. Ayurvedic medicine aims not only to cure a disease's symptoms, but also to eradicate the cause of the disease. It takes into consideration that each person has a different bodily constitution and should be treated accordingly, even if the details of the disease are the same. People come under three basic categories: Kapha, Pitta, and Vata. Ayurvedic medicine is much more effective than other kinds of medical treatments for digestive diseases and many of the typical diseases of India. Ayurvedic medicine can cure hepatitis (jaundice); there is no cure according to conventional medicine practiced in the West.

You can also take Ayurvedic medicine to avoid illness. Many diseases in India are caused by the fact that a person's liver or digestive system does not work properly. You can take Ayurvedic medicine to tone your digestive system. This reduces the amount of undigested food in your system, a cause of illness. If your food is properly digested, you will have sufficient energy to fight disease. There are also Ayurvedic massages to help cure various afflictions.

The main problem with curative Ayurvedic treatment is finding a competent doctor to prescribe and administer it. I suggest you get recommendations before trusting your health to any particular doctor. Only if I have complete faith in an Ayurvedic doctor will I trust him to treat me for a serious disease.

Cows

A cow is considered the symbol of religion in Hinduism. Cows are sacred because they are dear to Lord Krishna. Also, the cow is important because she supplies the most important food, milk. Because of this, the cow is considered one of mankind's mothers. The main ingredients to perform a *Vedic yajna* (sacrifice) come from a cow—milk, yogurt, butter, and ghee (clarified butter). Ghee is offered into the fire at all *yajnas*. The cow is protected because she is helpless. It should not be misunderstood that Hindus worship cows as God, but cows are simply offered respect.

The urine and dung (stool) of the cow are considered pure and are used in worship. Scientific studies have revealed both to be antiseptic. According to Vedic culture, beef-eating is strictly forbidden and is considered extremely sinful. If a person must eat meat, he should eat the meat of animals other than the cow. Beef is never sold in the streets in India.

Daksha and Lord Siva Story

Daksha, the son of Lord Brahma and father of Sati, once performed a *yajna* (great sacrifice). When Daksha entered the assembly of great sages, philosophers, and demigods, all the participants in that great assembly, with the exception of Lord Brahma and Lord Siva, stood in respect. Daksha was offended to see Lord Siva not showing him respect. He considered Lord Siva his inferior because Siva was married to his daughter, Sati. Therefore he cursed Lord Siva: "The demigods are eligible to share in the oblations of the sacrifice, but Lord Siva cannot have a share." Daksha then returned home, and Lord Siva's followers counter-cursed Daksha's supporters. Lord Siva then left the assembly with his followers.

At the next *yajna* (sacrifice) that Daksha performed, he did not invite Lord Siva. Still, Sati decided to attend. When her father would not speak to her due to her connection with her husband, Sati was insulted and destroyed her body by meditating on the fiery elements (self-immolation). Hearing of his wife's death, Siva then created Virabhadra, a fearful black demon as tall as the sky, who had thousands of arms and was equipped with various weapons. Lord Siva sent Virabhadra and his followers to ruin the sacrifice and cut off Daksha's head. After fulfilling his assignment, Virabhadra threw Daksha's head into the sacrificial fire. Later, at Brahma's request, Siva restored Daksha to life, but because his head had been destroyed in the fire, he was given the head of a goat.

Dance

The object of Indian religious dance is to evoke different moods in the audience. Indian dances are usually done barefoot. The dance is composed of *mudras* (hand gestures), *abhinayana* (face and body expressions), and *gati* (footwork). There are four main Hindu dances: Bharata Natyam of Tamil Nadu, Kathakali of Kerala, Kathak of Uttar Pradesh, and Manipuri. There are also other types of classical and folk dance, although less well-known.

Bharata Natyam Dance

This is one of the main classical styles of South India temple dancing. Each gesture and movement has meaning. Dancers never turn their back to the gods they are honoring. *Devadasis,* or servants of God, traditionally perform this type of dance in temples. *Bharata* means India, and *natya* means dance.

Bharata Natyam is usually performed by a solo woman. It begins with *alarippu,* a gesture symbolizing that the body is an offering to the gods. The dancer then combines *nritya* (emotions) with *nritta* (pure dance), in which the dancers use heavy face and hand expressions. They are accompanied by musicians and a *nattuvanar.*

Bharata Natyam is mainly performed in Chennai, where there are regular performances at the Kalaksetra center, Music Academy, Raja Ananmalai Hall, Museum Theater, and at other places.

Kathakali Dance

Kathakali literally means "story-play." The performance is intended as worship, and it is performed only by men (boys play the parts of women). A vocalist and drummers accompany the dance. They tell stories of the *Mahabharata* and *Ramayana*. Dialogue is combined with the dance. The costumes are decorative, with huge skirts and headdresses, and the dancers wear heavy makeup. There is much movement of the limbs and eyes, and each gesture carries a specific meaning.

There are five primary characters, who are distinguished by their costumes and makeup. *Pacha* (green) represents the noble-hearted hero or god; *kathi* (knife) represents a mixture of nobility and evil (both have their faces painted green, but the *kathi* has a knife pattern on the cheek in red pigment and small white balls on the tip of the nose and the middle of the forehead). The other characters are *tati* (beard), *kari* (black), and *minukku* (polished). The bad guys usually have black faces with white spots on their cheeks or noses. They may also have red beards (*thadi*), a false nose, and a big frill. They place a *cunlappuva* seed inside their eyelids to turn the white part of the eyes red. Hanuman's face is red.

The orchestra consists of the *maddalam, edakka, chenta,* cymbals, and the gong. There is also a singer who directs the play; the actors take their cues from him.

Dances can last for hours. Originally, Kathakali was an all-night performance in temples during festivals. A typical performance would begin at 7 pm and end at 7 am. Dancers train for six to twenty years to learn the dance steps and movements. It demands extraordinary muscle control to contort the face and make the sudden leaps and spins. It takes four hours to prepare for a performance—to put on makeup, elaborate costumes, and head dresses. Everything is put on in a fixed order.

Chatunni Paniker and Guru Gopinath are considered two of the best dancers in India. Kochi in Kerala is the best place to see this type of dance, as there are daily performances at the Cochin Cultural Centre. The India Foundation and Art Kerala, both near Ernakulam Railway Station, have regular performances from 7 to 10:30 pm.

Other Dance Styles

Manipuri style dancing is considered a religious ritual. Many of the dances have themes based on Krishna's pastimes. Both men and women take part in the dance. A chorus of singers accompanies them. The dancers wear colorful outfits. Manipur is a hilly tract of land in the extreme northeastern part of India.

Krishnayattam is a predecessor of Kathakali, performed at the Guruvayur temple. The performances start around 10 pm from October through April.

Odissi is classical Orissan temple dancing. The dance is a ritual offering performed in temples. There are strict rules of position of feet, body, and hands. Jayadeva's *Gita Govinda*, which depicts Krishna's love for Radha, is a favorite subject of this style of dance.

Ganges and Yamuna Rivers

The Yamuna and Ganges Rivers are considered the most sacred rivers in India. The Yamuna begins at Yamunotri in the Himalayas; the Ganges begins near Gangotri, where it is called the Bhagirathi River. When the Bhagirathi meets the Alakananda River, it takes the name Ganges. The Ganges meets the Yamuna and the underground Saraswati in Allahabad (Prayag).

Several other important rivers meet the Ganges, such as the Gandhaki, Kosi, Son, and Karnali on their way to the Bay of Bengal. About 450 km before reaching the Bay of Bengal, the Ganges divides into several rivers. The widest river goes into Bangladesh, and another branch heads south through Mayapur and Calcutta before reaching the Bay of Bengal at Ganga Sagar. It is called the Hoogly when it passes through Calcutta. The numerous holy places along the Ganges include Gangotri, Haridwar, Kankhal, Prayag (Allahabad), Varanasi, Mayapur, and Ganga Sagar.

The *Srimad-Bhagavatam* (5.17.1) glorifies the Ganges with the following words: "Sukadeva Goswami said: My dear King, Lord Vishnu, the enjoyer of all sacrifices, appeared as Vamanadeva in the sacrificial arena of Bali Maharaja. Then he extended his left foot to the end of the universe and pierced a hole in its covering with the nail of his big toe. Through the hole, the pure water of the Causal Ocean entered this universe as the Ganges River. Every living being can immediately purify his mind of material contamination by touching the transcendental water of the Ganges, yet its waters remain ever pure. Because the Ganges directly touches the lotus feet of the Lord before descending within this universe, she is known as Vishnupadi. Later she received other names like Jahnavi and Bhagirathi."

The water of the Ganges is called *patita-pavani*, the deliverer of sinful living beings. Many sages, including Sankaracharya, have composed prayers in praise of the Ganges. Sankaracharya recommends that a little knowledge from *Bhagavad-gita* and the drinking of a little quantity of Ganges water can save one from the punishment of Yamaraja, god of death.

Ganges water does not become contaminated, even if stored for years. The purity of the Ganges has been documented by Mr. Henkin's research in the book *The Ganga Trail*. Water was taken from the mouth of a sewer as it emptied into the Ganges and after six hours, all the germs were dead. A corpse floating in the Ganges was towed to the shore and the water taken from next to the body was found to be swarming with cholera germs, but after six hours all the germs had died. When water was taken from a pure well and a few cholera germs were added to the water, the germs multiplied greatly.

Ganges Story

During Satya-yuga, King Sagar performed a horse sacrifice (Ashwamedha *yajna*) to prove his supremacy. Lord Indra, the leader of the demigods, became fearful over the results of the *yajna*, so he decided to steal the horse. He left the horse at the ashram of Kapila, who was in deep meditation. King Sagar's 60,000 sons (born of Queen Sumati) and his son Asamanjas (born of Queen Kesoni) were then sent to find the horse. When the 60,000 sons found the horse at Kapiladeva's ashram, they thought he had stolen it. When they prepared to attack the meditating *rishi* (sage), Kapiladeva opened his eyes. Because the sons of King Sagara had disrespected such a great personality, consequently, fire emanated from their own bodies, and they were immediately burned to ashes.

Later King Sagar sent his grandson Amsuman to retrieve the horse. Kapiladeva returned the horse and told Amsuman that the sons of King Sagar could be delivered if the Ganges descended to earth and bathed them in her waters.

King Sagar's great-great-grandson, Bhagiratha, eventually pleased Mother Ganga and asked her to come to earth. Mother Ganga told Bhagiratha that the force of the Ganges falling from heaven would be too great for the earth to sustain, and that she needed someone to break the fall. Bhagiratha then worshiped Lord Siva, who then agreed to accept the descending river upon his head.

King Bhagiratha then preceded the holy river with his chariot and ripped open a gorge in which the Ganges could flow. The river followed the King to Ganga Sagar at the Bay of Bengal, where Kapiladeva resides. The Ganges River then bathed the remains of the 60,000 sons and returned them to their eternal positions.

Jyotisha (Astrology)

Jyotisha encompasses both astrology and astronomy. Vedic Astrology is a very exact science and is taken seriously by most Indians. Until an astrological chart is drawn, a marriage will not be performed. It is said that Brighu Muni wrote an astrological horoscope for every person ever born or to be born in this world. There are a few astrologers in India who can provide readings from this book, known as the Brighu Samhita.

Kumbha-mela

Kumbha-mela is like a "Yogi Convention," where *yogis, sadhus* (saints), holy people, and pilgrims come from all over India—even from the most remote forests and mountain caves in the Himalayas.

Kumbha-mela takes place every twelve years at four different holy places in India: Prayag (Allahabad), Haridwar, Nasik, and Ujjain. The Kumbha-mela at Prayag (Allahabad) is the largest event in the world, with about fifteen million people attending. Many different sects of holy men gather for Kumbha-mela. There is a grand procession on the main bathing days. The Naga Babas (Siva worshipers) are famous because they walk around naked. They cover their bodies with ash and wear their hair in dreadlocks. They are always the first to bathe on major bathing days.

The time for Kumbha-mela is judged by the astrological positions of Jupiter and the Sun. In Prayag (Allahabad) the Kumbha-mela takes place during January-February, when Jupiter is in Taurus and the Sun enters Capricorn. Kumbha-mela takes place in Haridwar in April-May, when Jupiter is in Aquarius and the Sun is in Aries. In Nasik the Mela is in July-September, when both Jupiter and the Sun are in Leo. In Ujjain it is held in May-June, when Jupiter is in Scorpio and the Sun is in Aries.

Kumbha-mela lasts for one month while the Sun transits the particular zodiacal sign. During the month there are certain important bathing days, such as the Sankranti (when the Sun enters the next sign), Ekadasi, and Amavasya (dark moon). The most important bathing day is when the nectar actually falls from the sky. It is considered especially auspicious to bathe at a particular place at just the right time.

Kumbha-mela Story

The demigods *(devas)* and demons *(asuras)* once made a truce in order to churn the milk ocean to get the nectar *(amrita)* of immortality. Lord Vishnu advised the demigods to do this because the demons were becoming too powerful; the demigods were in danger of losing their position to the demons. They used Vasuki, the huge serpent as a rope, and Mandara Mountain as a churning rod.

As they were churning the milk ocean thirteen items were produced from the ocean. The first item was a poison *(halahala)* so strong it could kill all the people on earth. Lord Siva drank it and held it in his throat. The poison turned his throat blue, and since that time, Lord Siva has been known as Nila-kantha, or "blue-throated."

A *shankha* (conch shell), *surabhi* cow, horse named Uccaihsrava, the elephant Airavata, other elephants that could go in any direction, Kaustubha gem, *parijata* flower, *apsara* (the most beautiful women), Chandra (the Moon-god), and Lakshmi, the goddess of fortune were also all produced. Then Varuni, the goddess of drinking, appeared.

Eventually the physician of the gods, Dhanvantari, who is a partial incarnation of Lord Vishnu, appeared carrying a jug containing the nectar *(amrita)*.

The demigods *(devas)* entrusted the nectar pot *(amrita-kalasha)* to Brihaspati, Surya, Chandra, and Shani. These demigods ran from the demons with the *amrita-kalasha* because the demons were powerful enough to steal it for them. When the demons learned of the conspiracy, they became angry and chased the four demigods. The chase lasted twelve days in the life of the demigods (each demigod day is one year of our time), at which time the *devas* and *asuras* circled the earth. Drops of nectar fell at Haridwar, Allahabad (Prayag), Ujjain, and Nasik.

Another version of the story is that the demons snatched the jug of nectar from Dhanvantari and began to fight among themselves. During the fight, some of the nectar fell at these four places. Kumbha-mela is held in each of these four places every twelve years.

Eventually, the demons were able to get the nectar, but they then fought among themselves as to who should have the honor of drinking from the jug first. Suddenly, Mohini (a partial incarnation of Lord Vishnu) appeared as the most beautiful woman in the universe. Bewildered by her beauty, the demons submitted to her and allowed her to decide who would receive the first drop of nectar. She knew that the demons were unfit to drink the nectar. She cheated them and instead distributed it to the demigods.

Marriages

The initiative for the marriage should always come from the girl's side. Usually an intermediary (matchmaker) arranges a marriage. In the past, a priest or barber usually did this. Now usually a common friend of the families does it. A horoscope is drawn by a priest to see if the couple is compatible, and if not, the marriage will be canceled.

An engagement ceremony *(tilak)* is held in which the forthcoming marriage becomes finalized. Usually only relatives and close friends attend this ceremony. After fixing an astrologically auspicious time, a priest then fixes the exact date and time of the marriage.

On the day of the marriage, the groom is taken on a horse in procession to the bride's home. A brass band, relatives, and friends will often accompany him. The bride normally does not leave her house during the marriage period. The marriage is supposed to take place at the bride's home, but it is often held in a hall, a large pandal (tent), or a temple. The marriage area is decorated with flowers, auspicious items, and other decorations.

The bride and groom dress in elegant clothing, and the girl is often adorned with expensive jewelry. The couple sits next to each other cross-legged before a fire sacrifice, while the Brahmin priest chants various mantras. As they sit before the fire, someone ties one end of each of their clothes together to signify union. Then the bride's father places the bride's hand in the groom's hand while sacred prayers are chanted. They then hold their hands together, their hands are covered with a cloth, and a thread is wrapped around them. The bride and groom exchange rings in some weddings. As part of the marriage ceremony, the bride and groom throw rice and other grains, ghee (clarified butter), and other items into the fire. At the end of the ceremony, they place a banana into the fire, and the bride and groom walk around the sacred fire three to seven times (depending to which caste they belong).

The marriage usually takes a couple of days, but all the ceremonies involved can take more than a week. This is a typical marriage, but there are variations depending on the community and region.

Ekadasi

Ekadasi is a day of fasting. One is expected to fast from at least grains and beans, but one can also completely fast, even from water. There are two Ekadasis a month, one on the eleventh day after the new moon and one on the eleventh day after the full moon. *Ekadasi* means the "eleventh day." Ekadasi is broken the next day (Dvadasi) by taking food prepared with grains. The fast is supposed to be broken at a specific time. Fasting is done so one has more time to hear and speak about God.

Yugas

There are four *yugas:* First there is Satya-yuga (1,728,000 years), and then in order Treta-yuga (1,296,000 years), Dvapara-yuga (864,000 years), and Kali-yuga (432,000 years). Principles of religion work fully in the age of Satya-yuga; in Treta-yuga they are reduced by a fraction of one fourth; in the Dvapara-yuga they are reduced to one half, and in the Kali-yuga they are reduced to one fourth, gradually diminishing to the zero point, and then devastation takes place.

Satya yuga is characterized by virtue, wisdom and religion, there being practically no ignorance and vice. It is called the golden age. In this age people live for a hundred thousand years. It was very suitable for self-realization because people could perform prolonged meditation.

In Treta yuga vice is introduced. It is called the silver age and people live for ten thousand years. Self realization was achieved by performing great sacrifices.

In Dvapara yuga there is an even greater decline in virtue and religion, vice increasing. People live for one thousands years in this age and self realization is reached by worship of the Lord.

In Kali yuga there is an abundance of strife, ignorance, irreligion and vice, true virtue being practically nonexistent. The maximum duration of life in Kali-yuga is one hundred years and the recommended process of self-realization in this age is hearing and chanting the holy name, fame and pastimes of the Lord. At the present time about 5,000 years have passed in Kali-yuga, the present age.

In Kali-yuga vice increases to such a point that at the termination of the *yuga* the Supreme Lord Himself appears as the Kalki *avatara*, vanquishes the demons, saves His devotees, and commences another Satya-yuga. Then the process is set rolling again.

Yuga

A *kalpa* is a day and night of Brahma. Each *kalpa* is two thousand *Maha-yugas*. Each *Maha-yuga* is divided into the four *yugas*, which are Satya, Treta, Dvapara, and Kali. A *Maha-yuga* lasts for 4,320,000 years. A year of the demigods is equal to 360 years of human beings.

Brahma lives for 100 years. Each year of Brahma consists of 360 days. Brahma lives for 311 trillion and 40 billion earth years. This is 100 (years that Brahma lives) x 360 (days in Brahma's year) x 2000 (*Maha-yugas* in a *kalpa*) x 4,320,000 (years in a *Maha-kalpa*). By these calculations the life of Brahma seems fantastic and interminable, but from the viewpoint of eternity it is as brief as a lightning flash. Brahma and his creation are all part of the material universe, and therefore they are in constant flux.

At the end of Brahma's life is a Mahapralaya, which is when the universe is completely destroyed. At this time there is a new Brahma and creation begins again.

During the daytime of Brahma living entities receive various bodies for material activities, and at night they no longer have bodies but remain compact in the body of Vishnu. Then again they are manifest at the arrival of Brahma's day. When Brahma's life is finished, they are all annihilated and remain unmanifested for millions and millions of years, and when Brahma is born again in another millennium they are again manifest.

Foods

Prasada is food offered to the gods. It is sanctified food. Before eating any food many Hindus offer the food to one of the gods. In this way they are eating the remnants of the particular god they offer the food to, and therefore, they become purified. Depending on which god the food is offered to, the *prasada* may be known as: Krishna *prasada*, Vishnu *prasada*, Siva *prasada*, or Devi *prasada*.

There are three types of foods: Tamasic (in the mode of ignorance), Rajasic (in the mode of passion), and Sattvic (in the mode of goodness).

Tamasic food is prepared more than three hours before being eaten, food that is tasteless, decomposed and putrid, and food consisting of remnants and untouchable things. These types of foods cause one to be dull, sleepy and greedy.

Rajasic food is too bitter, too sour, salty, hot, pungent, dry and burning. Rajasic foods are meat, onions, hot peppers, garlic and very spicy foods. These foods cause distress, misery and disease.

Sattvic food is juicy, fatty, wholesome and pleasing to the heart. Eating sattvic food increases the duration of life, purifies one's existence and gives strength, health, happiness and satisfaction. Sattvic foods are grains, fruits, nuts, and vegetables that are freshly prepared.

Funeral Rites

There are many variations of exact funeral rites depending on the area of India and the social status. Someone who is religious wants to pass his last days in a holy place such as Varanasi, Vrindavana, Jagannatha Puri or Dwarka. It is said that a person dying on the bank of the Ganges at Varanasi is freed from all sins.

When a person dies their body is first bathed in Ganges water or in a sacred river and then wrapped in white cloth for a man and red cloth for a woman. They are then carried to the cremation site on a wooden stretcher. While this is going on everyone chants "*Ram Nam Satya Hai*" (Rama is Truth). A king or a *sadhu* is carried sitting up to the cremation site.

The nearest relative, usually the eldest son lights the funeral pyre. Whoever lights this fire is considered the legal heir. Brahmin priests chant Vedic *mantras* while the cremation is going on. Then the ashes are put in a sacred river such as the Ganges or Yamuna, and many times the ashes are taken to Haridwar, where the Ganges begins.

Depending on the caste of the person, a mourning period of about 14 days is observed. During this time all the furniture in the living (sitting) room is taken out and all the relatives sit on the floor. Relatives will also pay a condolence visit to the home of the mourning family.

Every year the relatives have certain days when they pay respects to their dead ancestors.

Music

Indian music is not divided into twelve-tone scales as is Western music, but into microtonal patterns that form a *raga*. A *raga* is a combination of five, six, or seven notes played in a melodious pattern. *Ragas* contain certain fixed notes, and this is how they are identified one from another. Each *raga* is meant to evoke a different mood, and therefore there are many different kinds of *ragas*. Certain *ragas* are played only at certain times of the day, and often particular *ragas* are identified with particular seasons. Indian classical music, not being based on a fixed scale, emphasizes improvisation, but only within the range defined by the particular *raga* being played. In that sense, even the improvisation is based on tradition.

There are two types of music in India, Hindustani and Karnatic music. Hindustani is North Indian and is influenced by Arabic and Persian cultures. Karnatic music is South Indian and has its roots in the Sama Veda, without outside influence. The musical notes are Sa, Ri, Ga, Ma, Pa, Dha and Ni. These musical notes combined form a *raga*. In Karnatic music, few instruments are used to accompany singing. Karnatic music usually means devotional songs sung for deities.

Musical instruments

Shankha: conch shell. It is used in worship and is blown when the door of a temple altar is opened. It is also used in folk music.

Sitar: a stringed instrument similar to a guitar. It has a long neck and a spherical gourd at the lower end. There are five main metal strings and two drones. It is now a popular instrument even in the West, but before the 18th century it was not used in classical music.

Tablas: a two-piece drum set consisting of the tabla and the dagga. The tabla is made of metal and is broader than the dagga at the top. The dagga is made of wood. The tabla can be tuned; the dagga cannot. The tops of the drums are held by leather straps, which can be tightened by moving round pieces of wood between the body and the leather straps.

Harmonium: a small reed organ with a bellow and an air chamber. Classical musicians do not use it.

Tanpura: a stringed instrument similar to the sitar, with four drone strings. Each of the strings are plucked one after the other to made a melodious sound. It provides background for other instruments or singing. The round bottom is usually made of a dried gourd or wood.

Sarod: a stringed instrument often used in classical music. It has four main strings, four subsidiary strings, and two drones.

Dholak: a two-headed drum used all over India. It is either held in a person's lap or suspended from the neck.

Mridanga: a two-headed drum used to play devotional music. It is especially used in *kirtan* (congregational chanting).

Karatals: small hand cymbals often used in devotional music.

Shehnai: a wind instrument often played in classical concerts. It is similar to a clarinet.

Sarangi: a stringed instrument played with a bow. It is used both in classical music and in folk music. There are four principal strings. It is about two feet high and has a wide body.

Namaste and Greeting

People also say *namaskar*. Saying *namaste* is the normal way people greet each other in India. People fold their hands and touch them to their foreheads. They also bow slightly when they say *namaste*. It means "I offer obeisance (bow down) to you." When people offer obeisance to one another, they are actually bowing before God, who is seated in everyone's heart.

PERSONALITIES

Caitanya Mahaprabhu

Caitanya Mahaprabhu appeared in Navadvipa, West Bengal, in 1486. He accepted the renounced order of life at twenty-four. He then left Navadvipa and went to Puri in Orissa. His spiritual master, Iswara Puri, was in the line of Madhavendra Puri, who was in the line of Madhvacarya.

Gaudiya Vaishnavas accept Sri Caitanya as nondifferent from Lord Krishna, in the form of a devotee. He taught that by chanting the holy names of the Lord, specifically the mantra, *Hare Krishna Hare Krishna, Krishna Krishna Hare Hare/ Hare Rama Hare Rama, Rama Rama Hare Hare*, one could attain transcendental devotion to God.

He taught the philosophy that the Supreme Lord and the individual souls are inconceivably and simultaneously one and different. He explained the direct meaning of the *sastras* (scriptures) as devotion (*bhakti*) to Lord Krishna.

Madhvacarya

Madhvacarya (1239–1319) was a Vaishnava (devotee of Vishnu) and devoted himself to defeating the impersonal philosophy. He named his explanation of the Vedas *dvaita-dvaita-vada* (pure dualism). He taught that there is the Supreme Lord, the individual souls, and the material world. He taught that the individual souls are superior to matter and are distinct from the Lord, as his servitors. He also taught that each person molds his own *karma*, and that by serving the Supreme Lord one can eliminate *karma* and return to his position of serving the Lord in the eternal spiritual world.

He possessed an unusually strong body and extraordinary intellectual power. It is said that there was no limit to his physical strength. He went to almost every sacred place of pilgrimage, where he defeated scholars of rival schools and won them over to Vaishnavism.

Madhvacarya traveled to the Himalayas to meet Srila Vyasadeva, and Vyasadeva gave him a *shalagram-shila* called Astamurti and approved his *Bhagavad-gita* commentary.

Ramanujacarya

Ramanujacarya was born in 1017 AD in a small village near Kanchipuram. He founded the Sri-sampradaya, one of the four main Vaishnava *sampradayas*. This *sampradaya* propounds the *visistadvaita-vada* philosophy, or qualified monism.

Mahapurna, a disciple of Yamunacarya, initiated him. He took the *sannyasa* name Yatiraja and lived the later part of his life in Sri-Rangam, a large temple located on an island by Tiruchirappalli. He established seventy-four Sri Vaishnava centers, and converted thousands of people, including several kings. Besides householders, his followers included 700 *sannyasis*, 12,000 *brahmacaris*, and 300 *ketti ammais* (ladies who have taken vows of renunciation). He left his body in 1137 AD, in Sri-Rangam at the age of 120.

He taught that there is a difference between the Supreme Brahman and the individual soul. By God's grace, the *jiva* (individual soul) can get out of the material world and attain the eternal abode of Lord Vishnu. Ramanuja accepts three classes of *jivas* (living souls): eternally liberated, forever bound, and those freed by devotion and devotional practices. He taught that we should serve God in Vaikuntha with awe and reverence. He always defeated any scholar who preached the impersonal school of thought.

Ramanuja initiated anyone regardless of caste. He established that the position of a Vaishnava surpasses all social considerations.

Sankaracarya (788–820)

When he was only eight years old, Sankaracarya completed his study of the scriptures and took *sannyasa* from Govinda, a *sannyasi* residing on the banks of the Narmada River. After accepting *sannyasa*, Sankaracarya stayed with his spiritual master for some days. He then took his permission to travel to Varanasi, and from there he went to Badrinath, where he stayed until his twelfth year. While there he wrote commentaries on the *Brahma-sutra*, ten *Upanisads*, and the *Bhagavad-gita*. He traveled widely all over India and died when he was thirty-two.

Sankaracarya wrote two major works, *Sariraka-bhasya* and *Vivekacudaani*. For many, his *Sariraka-bhasya* is the definitive rendition of Vedanta. He established four main maths in Puri, Joshimath, Dwarka, and Sringeri.

Sankara taught that the living entities are themselves the Absolute Truth and that there is ultimately no variety, individuality, or personality in spiritual existence. He said that the individuality of both the Supreme Being and the individual is false.

During his time, Buddhism had spread all over India. Sankara sought to reform and purify religious life by reinstating the authority of the Vedic scriptures, which Buddha had rejected. Since it would have been impossible to restore the Vedic literature's theistic conception just after Buddha's atheism, Sankara made a compromise to fit the time and circumstance. His interpretations resembled Buddhism, but unlike Buddhism, they were based on the authority of Vedic literature. The personal school of thought propounded by Ramanujacarya, Madhvacarya, and Sri Caitanya Mahaprabhu rejects his philosophy.

Sri Andal

Sri Andal wrote two works, *Tiruppavai* and *Nachiar Tirumozhi,* both of which express her burning love for God. There is a major temple dedicated to her in Srivilliputtur, and a shrine in the Srirangam Temple.

She was the daughter of Periya Alwar, also known as Vishnucittar, one of the Twelve Alwars. According to tradition, Periya Alwar used to care for the flower gardens at the Vishnu temple in Srivilliputtur. While tending the garden he found Andal as a baby and then raised her as his own. This was around the 8th century. When her foster father tried to find her a husband, she refused any mortal man and said she would marry only the Lord.

Periya Alwar used to make flower garlands for Lord Vishnu. One day he was shocked to find a human hair in the basket of flowers. The next day he watched and saw Andal standing in front of her dressing mirror wearing a garland. He scolded her and sent a fresh garland for the Lord. That night the Lord told him in a dream that he only likes the garlands worn first by Andal. He also requested him to bring Andal to Srirangam so he could marry her. When she saw the image of Sri Ranganatha, she became absorbed in him. The incarnation of the goddess of fortune known as Godadevi (Andal) was then married to the Deity, Sri Ranganatha.

A.C. Bhaktivedanta Swami Prabhupada

Bhaktivedanta Swami was born in 1896 in Calcutta. Bhaktisiddhanta Saraswati Maharaja later initiated him into the Gaudiya Vaishnava sampradaya (followers of Sri Caitanya Mahaprabhu). He traveled to New York in 1965. He is the Founder Acharya of the International Society of Krishna Consciousness (ISKCON) or the Hare Krishna movement, whose followers are found all over the world.

Between the years 1965 and 1977, Bhaktivedanta Swami Prabhupada spread the teachings of Krishna consciousness to every major city in the world and formed an international society comprising thousands of members. He established 108 temples spread over six continents and circled the globe twelve times.

He also translated, wrote, and published fifty-one volumes in twenty-eight languages, tens of millions of which have been distributed throughout the world. His followers know him as Srila Prabhupada.

Sadhu

A *sadhu* is a saintly person who has renounced the material world, giving up all possessions. He or she is an ascetic who has renounced personal possessions, social position, and family life, and who has become totally engaged in the Lord's service. A true *sadhu* is considered to be of the highest social order, and they are also known as *sannyasi* or *yogis*. *Sadhus* will often not be cremated, but are buried. Their burial site is then known as a *samadhi* tomb and is worshiped.

In India *sadhus* may be followers of Krishna, Vishnu, or Siva. We can distinguish between different types of *sadhus* by their dress and markings. Some Siva worshipers have long, matted hair, cover their body with ashes, and often remain naked. They mark their foreheads with three horizontal lines, and may also carry a trident and wear *rudraksha* beads. Such *sadhus* are normally seen in the Himalayas, Varanasi, or other holy places sacred to Lord Siva, or near Siva temples. They can also be seen wandering in different places in India.

Shaivites are worshipers of Siva. They are divided into several sects. The Dasanami sect has ten branches throughout India. The Naga Babas do not wear clothes and they carry tridents. They often smoke *ganja* (hashish) and follow a Tantric form of worship. The Aghori Yogis perform unusual rites involving dead bodies. Gorakhnathis wear large earrings.

A Vaishnava *sadhu* is devoted to Lord Vishnu or Krishna. There are several main schools of Vaishnava *sadhus*. They may have long hair, or their heads may be shaved. They may wear saffron or white. Vaishnavas wear vertical markings on their forehead, which will be slightly different depending on the sect represented. They also wear *tulasi* beads around their necks and carry a *tulasi* bead *mala* (chanting beads).

Samskara Purificatory Process

These processes are performed so that society produces a good population. They are not mere formalities or social functions, but they are for practical purposes.

Some *samskaras* are: **Garbhadhana**—ritual for conception, **Simantonnayana**—ritual to protect the fetus, **Jatakarman**—ritual at birth, includes an astrological chart, **Annaprasana**—feeding grains to the child for the first time, **Chudakarana**—first hair cutting ritual, **Upanayana**—giving the sacred thread and the boy becomes twice-born, **Viveha**—the marriage ceremony, **Anthyesthi**—the funeral ritual. After death the Sraddha ritual is performed for the departed relative. Also going to holy places is consisted an important ritual that a person should perform.

Mandala

It is a complicated Yantra. Mandala means "circle." A Mandala is made up of circles and lines, which are placed geometrically around the center, which is usually a dot (*bindu*). The patterns of a Mandala are scientifically placed and a Mandala has a certain effect. Mandalas may be carved on temples. It may be small, like the size of a page of a book or it can be the size of a temple hall. A Mandala might have many deities connected to it, while a Yantra usually has only one deity.

The word *mandala* may also refer to a "temple hall."

Manus

Manu means the "ruler." A Manu lives for a period called a "Manvantara." There are 14 Manus in a Kalpa (one day of Brahma). A Kalpa lasts for 8,640,000,000 years. After the dissolution of a Manu, the next Manu comes in order, along with his descendants, who rule over the different planets. In a lifetime of Brahma there are 504,000 Manus. A Manu lives for 311,040,000 years. Vaivasvata is the present Manu. It is said that the first Manu, Svayambhuva Manu, wrote the *Manu Samhita*.

The 14 Manus are 1) Svayambhuva Manu, 2) Svarochisha, 3) Uttama, 4) Tamasa, 5) Raivata, 6) Chakshusha, 7) Vaivasvata (the present age), 8) Savarni, 9) Daksha Savarni, 10) Brahma Savarni, 11) Dharma Savarni, 12) Rudra Savarni, 13) Deva Savarni, 14) Indra Savarni.

Moksha

Moksha means liberation from this material world of birth, death, old age and disease. This is not a negative stage, but is a stage which is reached when one is freed from *karma*. Someone who has attained *moksha* can still be performing activities, but he is fully engaged in the service of God internally. *Moksha* leads to *Nirvana*. *Moksha* means liberation from material consciousness.

A *guru* or a transcendentalist is called a *jivan-mukta*, or one who is liberated in this very life and is not attached to the world.

Nirvana

Nirvana means material cessation, and after this one reaches union with the Supreme Lord's desires. By practicing *yoga* one can reach the state of Nirvana. This means that you are free from birth, death, old age and disease, and you are completely engaged in the service of the Supreme.

Mudra

A *mudra* is holding the hand in a particular way to indicate a particular meaning. Most Hindu deities hold their hands in a *mudra*. Some of the more important ones are Abhaya Mudra, Sankha Mudra, Yoni Mudra, Gada Mudra, Padma Mudra and the Tattva Mudra. Many Hindu deities hold their hands in the Abhaya Mudra, which means "Fear not, I will protect you."

Padma (Lotus Flower)

The lotus is an aquatic plant in which only the leaves touch the water, but the flower remains above the water. Its stalks grows underneath the water connecting each plant with each other with roots that can spread across an entire lake. The white lotus is a symbol of purity. The lotus flower is considered pure because it neither touches the water or the mud from which it grows. Brahma appeared from a lotus that came from the navel of Lord Vishnu and it is the seat on which Lord Brahma creates the universe. Many gods either hold or are seated on a lotus. The lotus flower is considered the most beautiful flower and they are considered auspicious.

Rudraksha Beads

These beads are especially sacred to those who worship Lord Siva and they will often wear these beads around their neck. The trees on which *rudraksha* beads grow are found in the Himalayas. The seeds of this tree are often made into a necklace or rosary.

The beads are classified by the number of lines they have on them, which ranges from one to fourteen. The most common number of lines is five. Beads with one line are the rarest and it is considered auspicious to own one of these beads. Rudraksha beads are said to have different effects depending on the amount of lines they have. The seeds may be four different colors: white, red, golden, and black. The reddish color is the most common. The smaller the bead, the more potent it is and, therefore, it is usually more expensive. The beads are usually put on a string in numbers of 54 or 108.

Sacred Trees and Plants

Many trees and plants are considered sacred. The spirits that are within the trees are always female. The spirit within a plant may be worshiped by offering food, or cloth that is tied to its branches.

Tulasi is an extremely sacred plant and is considered worshipable. Almost every Vishnu temple has a *tulasi* garden. When food is offered to Lord Vishnu or Krishna, *tulasi* leaves are put on each preparation offered. Many people have a *tulasi* plant in their home. It is considered inauspicious to brush against a *tulasi* plant, even by mistake. *Tulasi* plants look like basil plants, but have smaller leaves.

Pipal is considered sacred both to the Hindus and the Buddhists. It is also known as a *bodhi* tree because Lord Buddha attained enlightenment under this tree. It is worshiped all over India.

The **Banyan** is also considered sacred. To mark the spot where sacred pastimes took place we may find a banyan tree. It is a very big tree, which has roots, which rise from the ground and then come back to the ground and appear to be additional trunks.

Trees that are considered sacred in relation to Siva are the **Ashoka**, **Champaka** and **Kesara**.

The **Kamala** is sacred to Lakshmi and the **Sriphala** is sacred to Parvati. The **Kaila** or plantain tree is considered sacred to a form of Kali. It is often used as decoration during festivals and marriages.

Kusha Grass and **Durva Grass** are considered sacred. Sages often sit on Kusha grass mats when they do their meditation. Durva Grass is said to be sacred to Ganesh.

Sacred Mountains

The Himalayas are considered to be a holy mountain range. Because there are many holy places and mountains in the Himalayas *sadhus* and holy men often go there to perform austerities to attain self-realization.

Some holy mountains are:

Meru is in the center of the three worlds and it is the pivot, which the universe goes around. Brahma has his abode on top of this mountain.

Mount Kailash is where Siva lives. This mountain is now located in Tibet and is very difficult to reach. Both Hindus and Buddhists consider this mountain very sacred.

Mount Kailash is a mountain 50 km in circumference, which rises about 6,608m (22,028 ft) above sea level. It takes two or three days to walk around

Mount Kailash. It is believed that if you go around Mount Kailash 108 times you attain *nirvana* (liberation).

Mandara is a sacred mountain located in the Himalayas. It was used as a churning rod by the demigods and demons to churn the milk ocean in order to get the nectar of immortality.

Govardhana Hill, located near Vrindavana, is considered a very holy hill because it is intimately connected to Krishna.

Himavan is a mountain that took the form of a man and became the father of Parvati.

Some other holy mountains are: Chitrakoot (Madhya Pradesh), Girnar (Gujarat), Shaktiman (Madhya Pradesh), Kamagiri (Assam) and Mahendrachal.

Temples

In India there are many temples dedicated to Lord Vishnu in his various forms, such as Govinda, Madhusudhana, Narasimha, Madhava, Keshava, Narayana, Padmanabha, Parthasarathi, and many others. The Lord expands himself into innumerable forms, but all of them are nondifferent from one another except in mood.

Lord Vishnu has four hands, and each hand holds a particular item—a conch shell, wheel, club, or lotus flower. Of these four emblems, the *cakra*, or wheel, is the chief. The Lord's *cakra* is the symbol of the power by which the Lord controls the universe. The spires of Vishnu temples are marked with the *cakra* so that people may have the chance to see this symbol from a long distance and at once remember Vishnu.

The purpose of building high temples is to give people a chance to see them from a distance. This system is carried on in India whenever a new temple is constructed, and it appears that this system is coming down from a time before recorded history.

The deities can be moving *(dhruvabera)* or unmoving *(achala)*. The unmoving deities are usually large and made of stone. The moving images are usually made of metal—bronze or an alloy of five metals *(pancaloha)*. The moving deity is taken out on festive occasions and is used for bathing, ritualistic worship, etc. A third type of deity is *cala-acala* (both moving and unmoving). This would be the case with Lord Jagannatha in Puri, who goes out once a year for a chariot ride (Ratha-yatra).

Important Temples and Deities

Each region has one or two favorite incarnations of Lord Vishnu, Lord Siva, or some other god. From Uttar Pradesh to Bihar they worship

Lord Rama, in Western India Lord Krishna, in Maharashtra and northern Karnataka Lord Vitthala, in Tamil Nadu Lord Vishnu, and in Andhra Pradesh Narasimha.

Each region has one or two important religious shrines. There are the Guruvayur and Padmanabha temples in Kerala; Sri Meenakshi (Madurai) and Srirangam in Tamil Nadu; Chamundeswari and Udupi in Karnataka; Tirupati in Andhra Pradesh; Pandharpur in Maharashtra, Dwarka in Gujarat; and Nathdwar in Rajasthan.

Throughout India, the Supreme Lord is worshiped in various forms. Vishnu is known by various names and at each temple, the Vishnu Deity is given a special name. In Tamil Nadu he is worshiped as Varadaraja Perumal in Kanchipuram, Ranganatha Swami in Sri Rangam, and Kallalagar in Madurai. In Andhra Pradesh he appears as Tirupati Balaji, in Kerala as Guruvayurappan, in Karnataka as the beautiful Udupi Krishna, in Gujarat as Dwarkadish, and in Pandharpur as Sri Vitthala. Often the names of the deity refer to specific pastimes the Lord performed.

Some places have become important pilgrimage sites because of the important temples located there. Such places are Tirupati, Thiruvananthapuram, Kanchipuram, and Pandharpur, all famous because of the Vishnu temples there. Kedarnath, Bhubaneswara, Madurai, and Rameswaram are famous for having important Siva temples.

Worshipers in a temple fall into three main groups: Vaishnavas (worshipers of Lord Vishnu or Lord Krishna), Shaivites (worshipers of Lord Siva), and Shaktas (worshipers of Durga, Kali, or Parvati).

Temple Design

The principles of temple design culminate in the vast and rich knowledge laid down by *sastra,* religious scriptures, such as *Silpa-sastra* and *Sthapana-veda.* A temple is traditionally designed by a *stapati,* a traditional Indian architect coming in a line of trained temple architects. The different stages of building a temple are started at auspicious times, calculated astrologically.

The most important part of the temple is the sanctum sanctorum, or *garbha-griha,* where the main deity of the temple is located. In a South Indian temple, this room is usually square with a low roof and no windows or doors other than the front door.

A tower is always built over the deity. In North Indian temples the tower is usually quite high; in South Indian temples the tower is usually of low or medium height. The main entrance to the temple is usually from the east.

Inside the *prakara* (walls surrounding the temple) there will usually be minor temples that contain deities connected to the main deity. In a Vishnu temple, these deities may include Sita, Lakshmi, Hanuman, or Garuda. In a Siva temple, these deities may include Parvati, Ganesh, or Karttikeya (Subrahmanya).

Dravidian Temple Design

The Dravidian style is typical of the South Indian style and is usually built from stone. The temple shape may be rectangular, square, star-shaped, or octagonal. These temples usually have *gopurams*, large towers over the entrances; a *vimana*, a tower over the *sanctum* (the Deities); and large, pillared halls and corridors. The *gopurams* were in the past always the tallest structures in town.

The most sacred place is the *pitha* (altar), or pedestal, of the Deity. The *pitha* is in the sanctum sanctorum (inner *sanctum*) called the *garbha-griha* (womb house). This is where the altar of the main deity of the temple is located. The *garbha-griha* of the main shrine is usually semi-dark and has no sculpture other than the deity. This part of the temple must be constructed first, and before construction begins there is a ceremony known as impregnating (*garbhadhana* or *garbha-nyasa*). There is usually a *pradakshina* path enabling pilgrims to circumambulate the deities.

The sanctum sanctorum (central shrine) is topped by a pyramidal tower several stories high called *vimana* or *sikhara*. It is crowned by a *cakra* in a Vishnu temple and a trident in a Siva temple.

The inner sanctum is surrounded by subsidiary shrines, *mandapas* (halls), and pillared corridors. *Mandapa* (*mantapa* in Kannada) means any roofed, open or enclosed pavilion (hall) resting on pillars, standing independently or connected to the sanctum of the temple. *Mandapas* are one or more entrance porches or halls that lead to the inner sanctum.

The inner sanctum and the pavilion in front of the main altar are connected by a vestibule or porch called *ardha mandapa* (or sometimes, *antarala*). There is a rectangular hall in front of the sanctum *(mukha mandapa)* where the devotees stand to view the deity. The *nityarchana mandapa* is where the daily worship of the small (moveable) representative of the main deity is performed. The flight of stairs connecting the first *prakara* with the sanctum sanctorum is called *sopana*. In front of these stairs is the main *mandapa*.

The subsidiary shrines or altars contain other deities, including the consort of the main deity (Lakshmi or Parvati). The shrine dedicated to the consort usually has her own sanctum *(garbha-griha)* and ambulatory pathway *(pradakshina-patha)*. In some larger temples, they also have their own halls and pavilions.

Many temples have several halls, such as *ranga-mandapa*—usually a large hall with intricately carved pillars used as a large audience pavilion; *yajna-sala*—hall for occasional sacrifices; *nrittya mandapa*—hall for dance recitals; *vahana-mandapa*—place where the festival vehicles are kept; *kalyana-mandapa*—marriage hall; *asthana-mandapa*—where the processional deity holds court; *alankara-mandapa*—where the processional deity is dressed before being taken on procession; *vasanta-mandapa*—hall in the middle of the temple tank used for festivals; and *utsava mandapa*—hall used on festive occasions. Temples will also usually have a treasury, a kitchen *(paka-sala)*, a store room *(ugrana)*, and a dining hall.

In the temple yard outside the main entrance of the inner sanctum is the flag post *(dhvaja-stambha)* and a platform for food offerings *(bali-pitha)*. Both of these are usually right next to each other and directly in front of the doorway. Nearby is the *vahana-mandapa* where the Deity's carrier *(vahana)* is located. This is Garuda in a Vishnu temple and Nandi in a Siva temple.

Each temple usually has a temple tank *(teppakulam)*, flower garden *(nanda-vana)*, and temple chariot *(ratha)*. On festival days, the processional deity is paraded around town on the chariot. Thousands of people join the festival.

This entire area is surrounded by high walls *(prakara)* with entrances through towering gateways *(gopurams)*. The gateway facing the sanctum is called *maha-dvara* and is usually the main entrance to the temple. These rectangular, pyramidal towers are often fifty metres high with intricate sculptures of gods, demons, humans, and animals. They may also be painted in bright colors.

Dravidian Temple Enclosures

The main area of the temple, plus the halls, tanks, and gardens may be surrounded by a single wall *(prakara)* or series of walls. This is especially true of South Indian temples. The *prakara* contributes to the security and beauty of the temple—even two hundred years ago, it was not uncommon for a temple to be attacked and destroyed.

The *garbha-griha* is encircled by the first *prakara*, called *antara-mandala*. This is a passageway; often narrow, permitting the devotees to circumambulate the sanctum in a customary act of devotion. The flight of stairs that connects the first *prakara* with the sanctum sanctorum is called the *sopana*. In front of the *sopana* is the main *mandapa*.

Around the main *mandapa* and *antara-mandala* is the second *prakara* (*antahara*). This forms a broad verandah with doorways on all four sides. The *antahara* leads out into an enclosure containing the main *bali-pitha*.

The next enclosure is called *madhyahara*. Beyond this and just outside the main *bali-pitha* is the flagstaff (*dhvaja-stambha*).

The fourth enclosure is called *bhayahara*. It forms the pathway for the processions within the temple. The fifth *prakara* (enclosure) is the *maryada* (limit), or last wall.

Vertical Construction of Temples

1. The lower part of the temple, basement, or foundation (*adhishthana, adhara*).
2. Stone walls with columns embedded in the walls and also projecting out.
3. Roof above the columns.
4. The molding.
5. The spherical top, a small tower over the molding (*sikhara*, also called *sirah* and *mundaka*) that covers the sanctum (altar).
6. The pinnacle and the spire.

The temple is divided into six main vertical divisions: The last three items constitute the tower over the *garbha-griha* called the *sikhara*. *Vimana* refers to the entire sanctum from the basement to the pinnacle. *Sikhara* commonly refers to the superstructure over the sanctum, not the superstructure over the entrances of the surrounding walls.

Andhra Pradesh Temples

In Andhra Pradesh the main deity is generally found in the center of the temple. The accessory buildings are usually inside a rectangular wall with high gopurams (towers) that can be seen from a distance. The eastern entrance is typically the main entrance and the deity usually faces east.

The tower over the main deity is called a *vimana*, and it is generally covered with sculptures from top to bottom. The deity room is called the *garbha-griha*, which is in a circular or square building surrounded by a *pradakshina-patha* (path) on which devotees can circumambulate the deities. In front of this area is the *ardha-mandapa*, which may be square or rectangular. The *maha-mandapa* is in front of the *ardha-mandapa*. It consists of a building held up with pillars, with an entrance, and space on three sides. There may be other *mandapas*, such as the *nrittya mandapa* and *kalyana-mandapa*.

Usually on either side of the main entrance of the *ardha-mandapa* are two *dwarapalakas* (carvings of temple guards). In front of the sanctum is located either Garuda (in a Vishnu temple) or Nandi (in a Siva temple).

In most temples there are usually two sets of deities: One is permanent and is called the *Mulabera;* the other is taken on processions and is called the Utsavabera. In some temples there are different deities for *abhisheka* (bathing) and *utsava* (festivals).

Kerala Temple Design

Most temples in Kerala face east, but some face west and a few south. The central shrine or altar is called the *srikoil,* and it may be square, oblong, or circular. It may be one or two stories high. Within it is the *garbha-griha,* the altar upon which the deity is installed. In front of the central shrine is a *namaskara-mandapa,* or hall from which the devotees view the Lord and offer obeisances. Surrounding this is a corridor or pillared hall called either the *nalambalam* or *chuttambalam,* the outer portico of which is called the *belikkalpura,* which contains the *belikkal* or platform for food offerings. In front of the *belikkal* is the *dwajasthamba* (flag-staff). Around the *nalambalam* could be the *vilakkumatam,* rows of lamps lit during festivals.

Outside this structure is a paved processional path. Normally the temple well is situated in the northeast corner of this area. The temple kitchen, *madappalli,* is usually in the *nalambalam*. There are often smaller shrines in the temple dedicated to the goddess of the temple and other deities.

Orissan-style Temples

The Orissan temple consists of two apartments. The *deul* corresponds to the *vimana,* or towered sanctum. It is a cubical inner apartment where the main deity is located, with a tower over it.

In some temples there is a *pradakshina-patha* or *bhrama* (circumambulatory path), which goes around the sanctum sanctorum (altar) so the devotees can circumambulate the deity.

In front of the sanctum is the *mukha-mandapa* or *mukhashala*. Sometimes it is called *ardha-mandapa* or *sukanasi,* depending on its size in relation to the sanctum. It is used as a passage and sometimes to keep food offerings on special occasions.

After this is the *antarala,* which connects the sanctum and *mukha-mandapa* to the *mandapa,* or pavilion hall. The *antarala,* which is usually square and has a pyramidal roof, is also called the *jagmohana* (world-delighter). In many cases the *antarala* is the same as the *mukha-mandapa*. Sometimes one or two pavilions are added in front of the *antarala*, such as the *nat-mandir* and the *bhog-mandir*.

A *mandapa* (*nritta-mandapa* or *navaranga*) is a large hall used for spiritual classes, singing, dancing, or chanting.

In front of these is the *dhvaja-stambha* (flagpost). The *lanchana* (insignia), which is made of brass or copper, is different depending on the deity in the temple. This is usually the deity's carrier. For Lord Vishnu it would be Garuda, for Lord Siva, Nandi, etc.

The *bali-pitha* (pedestal of sacrificial offerings), which is usually imprinted with the deity's footprint or a lotus, is near the *dhvaja-stamba*.

The entire temple is surrounded by a high wall (*prakara*), which usually has a main gate and three subsidiary gates opening in the four directions. Sometimes there is a *gopuram* (high tower) over the gate.

Inside the *prakara* there will usually be minor temples that contain deities related to the main deity. In a Vishnu temple, such deities may include Sita, Lakshmi, Hanuman, or Garuda. In a Siva temple, these deities may include Parvati, Ganesh, or Subrahmanya.

Within the temple's wall there may also be a kitchen, *yajnashala* (sacrificial arena), a well or tank (*puskarini*), flower gardens, a processional cart, and other buildings for worship or management of the temple.

North India Temples

The North Indian temple style is called *nagara*. The North India temple towers tend to be curved. The superstructure (tower) of a *nagara* temple is square from the base to the pinnacle *(stupi)*.

The parts of the temple are the *garbha-griha, prakara, upa-tirtha, khanda,* main *tirtha, kshetra, mandala* and/ or *desha*. The inner sanctum (altar) is called *deul*.

Temple Priests

The worship of deities in a temple is performed by priests *(archaka)* and their assistants *(paricharaka)*. These priests must be Brahmins to enter the altar room (inner sanctum) and to worship or touch the deity.

Most of the priests are born in Brahmin families, but some attained Brahminical status through initiation. In many places, attaining brahminical status through initiation is not accepted as authentic; there are those who believe that the status can be achieved only by birth in a Brahmin family.

Only the temple priest can enter the inner sanctum. None of the administrative staff or donors can enter. Even among the temple priests, not all of them are permitted entrance. Only the head priest and a few assistants can actually touch the deity.

Only a priest can clean the altar, and only qualified Brahmin priests can cook for the deity.

Temple Worship

Temple worship usually consists of bathing the deity in the morning, dressing, offering foodstuffs, *aratik,* taking the deity on processions, and holding festivals. The worship in the temple is called *puja (pooja),* and the priests who perform such worship are thus called *pujaris.*

In Sri Vaishnava Vishnu temples, *pujaris* follow the mode of worship established by Ramanujacarya called *pancharatra,* which was established according to such texts as the *Padma Samhita, Paramesvara Samhita, Sri Prasna,* and *Jayakhya Samhita.* The more ancient Vaikhanasa mode of worship is also used in some South Indian temples.

The fifteen most common forms of worship are: 1) offering a seat (*asana*) for the moveable deity (which represents the main deity); 2) welcoming (*svagata*); 3) offering water to wash the feet (*padya*); 4) water offering (*arghya*); 5) sipping of water (*acamana*); 6) bathing the deity (*snana*); 7) presenting garments and ornaments (*vasana-bhushane*); 8) offering sandal paste; 9) offering flowers; 10) offering incense (*dhupa*); 11) offering lamps (*dipa*); 12) offering food (*naivedya*); 13) offering water to rinse the mouth (*punar achamaniya*); 14) reciting prayers to the Lord; and 15) offering prostrated obeisances (*namaskriya*).

Other forms of worship are cleaning the altar, offering a mirror, offering *aratik* or various items to the Lord, offering instrumental music, reciting Vedic hymns, and offering the Lord food several times a day.

Worship of the Lord begins early in the morning (usually between 4 or 5 am) and continues throughout the day (usually until 9 or 10 pm).

The water that is distributed in the temple is usually the water that is used to bathe the deity in the morning. Bathing the deity is done every morning in an elaborate ritual. Various items such as milk, yogurt, ghee, sugar, honey (five items known as *panchamrita*), and water may be used to bathe the deity. Prayers are also recited during the bathing.

After the bathing, the deity is decorated with fresh clothes and ornaments, which may include valuable jewelry. Food is then offered to the Lord, and an *aratik* presentation of different items is performed.

Besides the daily worship, festivals are celebrated. There may be an annual Rathotsava festival in which the processional deity is brought out of the temple and pulled on a cart around the streets. Many festivals are on fixed dates and cannot be missed. In South India, the major festival of the year is usually called Brahmotsava.

Also, *yajnas* (fire sacrifices) are performed in temples during festivals, initiations, marriages and other special events. A special *yantra* is drawn on the altar to represent the deity being worshiped. During a *yajna*, priests chant Vedic hymns.

Main Deity's Consort

Usually next to the shrine (altar) of the main deity is a shrine for the deity's consort. In a Krishna temple, this could be Radharani or Rukmini; in a Vishnu temple, Lakshmi; in a Siva temple, Parvati. In Krishna temples, Radha could also stand next to Krishna; on the main altar of a Vishnu temple, Lakshmi could be at the Lord's feet or standing next to him.

Sometimes, as in Tirupati, the deity's consort could be in established in another temple some distance away. The consort of Sri Venkateswara, Sri Padmavathi, is in the town of Tiruchanur, 23 km from the main temple in Tirumala. Also, the temple dedicated to Rukmini, the wife of Sri Krishna, is located just outside the town of Dwarka, a few kilometers away from the temple dedicated to Krishna in Dwarka.

Varnasrama Dharma (The Caste System)

According to the Vedas, the system of *varnasrama-dharma* has existed since time immemorial. There are four *varnas* (social orders): *Brahmins*, or teachers and spiritual advisors; *ksatriyas*, or administrators and warriors; *vaisyas*, or farmers and businessmen; and *sudras*, or laborers and craftsmen. These *varnas* are neither political nor social factions; they are natural categories of propensity found in every human civilization.

The present system generally practiced in India is corrupt. People claim their caste simply by birthright and do not consider nature or qualification. At present, there is virtually no pure system of *varnasrama-dharma* to be found in the world.

There are also four spiritual orders: *brahmacarya* (celibate student), *grihasta* (married), *vanaprastha* (retired), and *sannyasa* (renounced).

Brahmacharya is practiced from birth to approximately age twenty-five by men. The *brahmacari* is trained to control his senses through austerity and service to the *guru*. School begins at age five, and a boy is expected to leave home to live with his teacher until the completion of his education. The *brahmacari's* main duty is to study and to perform menial service around the ashram. He is also taught the scriptures along with arts and sciences.

Grihasta, or the householder ashram, refers to marriage. During marriage, people are permitted to engage in some sense pleasure, but only in a regulated way. The goal of *grihastha* life, like *brahmacharya*, is spiritually purification. Upon finishing his education, a student returns home and accepts a wife. The wife is known as *ardhangini*, the man's second half. Without a wife's participation, religious activities cannot be performed. *Grihastas* are supposed to earn a living and to support the other orders of life. A *grihasta* is also expected to be hospitable and welcoming when guests arrive at his home.

Vanaprastha comes after *grihastha*. After living through a marriage, one is supposed to renounce family life to engage full time in spiritual life. The first stage of *vanaprastha* life is that husband and wife discontinue sexual relations but do not separate. Ideally, the couple travel together to places of pilgrimage such as Puri, Haridwar, Rishikesh, and Vrindavana.

Sannyasa is the forth and last order of life, the renounced order when all family connections are broken to become fully dedicated to the cultivation of spiritual life. Generally, a *sannyasi* travels to preach and engages in meditation and devotional service. He lives on what is given in charity and on fruits and leaves in the forest. Intimate relationships with women are forbidden—he is even forbidden to talk with a woman in a secluded place. Possession of wealth for sense gratification is also strictly forbidden.

108 Divya Desams & the Alwars

The Alwars were twelve Vaishnava saints (devotees of Lord Vishnu) in Tamil Nadu. There are 108 important temples glorified by hymns composed by the Alwars. If an Alwar praised a temple or Deity of Vishnu, whether in a single verse or even part of a verse, then that temple and Deity were regarded in a class apart from the rest. All these temples are considered special. Different Alwars have visited these temples and sung the glories of the presiding Deities. Alagia Manavala Dasa (also known as Divya Kavi Pillai), who was a devotee of Lord Vishnu and a Tamil poet, has compiled a list of 108 Divya Desams in his *108 Tirupati – Anthaadi*. This list is still accepted as authoritative.

The Divya Desam temples can be grouped broadly into six geographical locations: Thondai Nadu, which is in the Chennai and Chengalput area; Chola Nadu (Chozha Naattu); Nadu Naattu; Pandya Nadu; Vada Nadu; and Paraloka. Many times it is possible to visit several Divya Desam temples in one day. In the area of Kanchipuram there are fourteen different Divya Desam temples, which can be visited within one or two days.

The Twelve Alwars are Kulasekhara Alwar, Pey Alwar, Tirumalisai Alwar, Thirumangai Alwar, Tondaradippadi Alwar, Bhutatt Alwar, Poygai Alwar, Nammalwar, Periy Alwar, Andal, Tiruppan Alwar, and Madhurakavi. Four of the Alwars were born within 80 km of Kanchipuram.

Tirtha Yatra

The journey to a pilgrimage place is called a *tirtha-yatra*. A *tirtha* is a sacred place that is holy because a pastime of God took place there, it is a holy river, a temple of God is there, or a holy sage (saint) lived there. The confluence of two holy rivers is especially holy. *Tirtha* means "crossing place." A holy place is called a *tirtha* because it is a place where one can cross easily from the material world to the spiritual world. Some holy places are considered spiritual places in this world such as Varanasi, Puri, Dwarka and Vrindavana. *Yatra* means to "travel" or "to go on pilgrimage."

It is a general rule to shave your head at a place of pilgrimage. You can especially notice this at Tirupati, where even many of the women have their heads cleanly shaven. One is not supposed to take gifts when he goes to a *tirtha*, rather one is supposed to give religious charity. It is recommended that as far as possible one should go to a *tirtha* by foot.

Yantras

A *yantra* is a mantra or "mystical diagram" expressed in pictorial form. Often a *yantra* represents a particular planet or deity, or a number of deities. *Yantras* are two-dimensional, but are considered to have depth. *Yantras* may be drawn, painted, or etched onto metal plate. A *yantra* is an energy that gives a certain effect. People draw or purchase the *yantras* of particular planets, worshipping them in order to counteract adverse astrological effects or to increase good effects. *Yantras* and mantras are used together, and there is a mantra for every *yantra*.

Yantras are usually composed of a complex figure of geometrical forms drawn around a center point (*bindu*). They are often comprised of a series of triangles surrounded by a square. They are all based on mathematical formulas. There are over nine hundred different *yantras* representing deities such as Krishna, Siva, Durga, Vishnu, and Ganesh.

One of the most famous and powerful *yantra* is the Sri Yantra, or Sri Chakra. This *yantra* represents both Siva and Shakti, and it is often seen in Shakti temples. This *yantra* has a dot (*bindu*) surrounded by nine triangles (*tirkona*). Five face down and four up. The intersection of the nine triangles makes forty-three triangles in total. The triangles are surrounded by two circles, one possessing eight lotus petals and the outer sixteen. This figure is then surrounded by another three circles. On the outside of the *yantra* are four squares, each with openings in the middle of each side. The *yantra* on the front cover is the Sri Yantra The mantra chanted with this *yantra* : "*Om sharing Haring Kaling Haring Shri Mahalakshmaya Namaha.*"

It is best that a *yantra* be created by one qualified in yantric science, and the correct mantras chanted to give the *yantra* power. Most qualified yantric priests etch their *yantras* into gold, silver, copper, or stainless steel, although sometimes they draw them on paper.

Each planet has its own *yantra,* which can be worshipped to free oneself from those planets' negative effects. The *yantras* can also be used to increase the planets' beneficial aspects. It is best to have *yantras* prescribed by a qualified astrologer, and then installed by him. *Yantras* should be properly worshipped if the full effect is desired. It is important that the proper mantras be chanted while worshipping *yantras.*

Besides diagram *yantras,* there are "numerical *yantras.*" Each numerical *yantra* is based on a root number and contains nine divisions (three horizontally, and three vertically). Numbers go into each of the nine squares, and the planet's base number is set in the top middle square. The numerals in each direction total the same number horizontally, vertically, and diagonally.

Writing and Worshipping Yantras

Yantra design is a science. There are prescribed ways in which *yantras* should be drawn, and prescribed materials that should be used in the work, according to the *yantra*. These details may vary depending on the purpose for which the *yantra* is being drawn. Also, the order in which the lines are constructed is important. A *yantra* intended to bring a planet's positive effects should be drawn from east to west; a *yantra* drawn to help the worshipper overcome an enemy should be drawn west to east.

It is also important that the person drawing a *yantra* sits facing the correct direction. *Yantras* should also be drawn at particular auspicious times and days. Different times of the day are ruled by different planets, so it is important to begin the *yantra* at a time ruled by the particular deity one is hoping to propitiate.

Yantras should be worshipped by holding flowers with two hands and chanting the correct mantra over the *yantra*. Each *yantra* represents a particular deity, so one should meditate on this deity while worshipping. Holy water, ideally from a sacred river such as the Ganges, should be offered to the *yantra*. Sandalwood paste (*chandan*) should be placed on the *yantra* along with garlands of flowers, and unhusked rice. Then the worshipper should offer incense and a lamp, then fruit and betel nut, and finally, prayers.

Yoga

Yoga means to "unite." It implies the path that one has to perform to be able to unite with God. It is not just physical exercises, but is a mental discipline. The exercises are done to relax the body and mind. Pranayama (breathing exercise) is then performed. Often *mantra* meditation is done. There is Raja Yoga, Bhakti Yoga, Jnana Yoga and several other yoga paths to reach God realization.

Vedic Sciences

Much of the information of the sciences in ancient India comes from the Vedas.

Mathematics in India was well developed in 2,500 BC. Indian mathematicians developed the zero and the system of using a decimal point. Algebra was used in ancient astronomy. The Surya Siddhanta written around 2,000 BC contains a system of trigonometry and geometry.

Astronomy was very advanced in Indian even 5,000 years ago. Architecture has been highly developed in India for thousands of years. There were planned cities in India over 3,000 years ago with temples, garden, houses, palaces, tanks and forts. Many of the gigantic temples are over a thousand years old.

There was an ancient system of warfare that was developed thousands of years ago. In the *Mahabharata* there is much detail of tactical warfare.

Islam

Islam is the largest religious minority in India. Its followers are known as Muslims (Moslems). Islam means "submission to God." About ten percent of the Indian population is Muslim (about 110 million people). India has one of the biggest Muslim populations in the world. The holy book of Islam is the Koran.

The messenger Muhammad (570–632) founded Islam. He was born in 570 AD at Mecca, in Saudi Arabia. He had his first divine manifestation from Allah (God) in 610. He preached against idol worship, which at that time was popular in Mecca. Islam is considered to have been founded in 622 AD, which is when Muhammad and his followers were exiled from Mecca and made the *hijra*, or the "going to Medina" ("City of the Prophet") journey. Muhammad led his people into battles against the Meccans, under the *jihad* understanding that it was on behalf of God. This was the beginning of the concept of "holy war," which helped the Muslims expand Islam. Mecca surrendered to Muhammad in 630, and it then became the pilgrimage center for Islam.

To become a Muslim one simply has to declare, "*La illaha illa 'llah Muhammad Rasulu 'llah*": "There is no god but Allah, and Muhammad is his prophet." Muslims believe that the body is resurrected after death. They believe that if someone worships Allah, they will go to heaven at death, which is a place of pleasure; if one does not worship Allah, he will go to hell, a place of eternal suffering and torture.

The teachings of the Muslims closely follow the Bible's Old Testament. Moses and Jesus are considered to be Muslim prophets, but Jesus is not accepted as the son of God. Muslims believe that it is sinful to worship images of God

Muslims are expected to pray daily at dawn, noon, in the afternoon, sunset, and at night. They must give charity to the poor. They must try to go on pilgrimage to the Ka'aba in Mecca at least once in a lifetime (make the *hajj*—one who has undergone this pilgrimage is called a *hajji*). Muslims must fast during the month of Ramadan. Friday is the Sabbath, and the main mosque in a town is known as the Jama Masjid or Friday Mosque. The main worship is performed at noon on Fridays. Mosques usually have a round dome, a *mihrab* to indicate the direction of Mecca, high minarets, a balcony for women, a water tank, and a *mimbar* or platform from which the Friday prayer is led.

Muslims follows various prohibitions: no alcohol, no gambling, no eating of pork, and they are not permitted to charge interest for loans.

Islam split into two sects in the first century of its existence, now known as the Sunnis and Shi'is. Both sects believe in the holiness of the Koran, but they disagree both on Muhammad's successor and on the interpretation of certain verses in the Koran. The Sunnis are a majority in Southeast Asia. They believe that Muhammad did not appoint a successor, and that after his death, the first three *caliphs* (representatives) were Abu Bak'r, Omar, and Uthman, and that Ali, Muhammad's son-in-law, was the fourth *caliph*. The Shi'is believe that Ali was the first rightful *caliph*, and that Omar and Abu Bak'r were usurpers.

Sufi Muslims practice renunciation and self-denial for God's service. They use music and dance to come closer to God, which more orthodox Muslims would not use.

July 16, 622 AD is the first day of the Muslim calendar. This is the day that Muhammad moved from Mecca to Medina. Each year is divided into 12 lunar months, each lasting from twenty-nine to thirty-nine days.

Women in strictly orthodox communities usually wear a black *burqa*, an outfit that covers them from head to toe, and a face veil.

Islam is the major religion in most of the Middle East, Pakistan, Bangladesh, Indonesia, and Malaysia. Beginning in the 12th century and lasting for about six hundred years, most of Northern India was controlled by Muslim rulers. The Muslim Mughal Empire eventually spread over most of India. Despite their long rule, only about twenty-five percent of the population converted to Islam. Most of these people came from lower castes, as Islam provided them the opportunity to escape from their socially designated roles.

Buddhism

Buddhism is practiced in many countries all over Southeast Asia, but it was first established in India. Buddhism was a major religion in India two thousand years ago. The present number of Buddhists in India is approximately 6.5 million.

Siddharta Gautama, who later became known as the Buddha, appeared around 563 BC (the Mahabodhi Society accepts 624 BC) in a warrior caste. He was married when he was sixteen, and his wife had one son. He left home when he was twenty-nine in search of the answer to life. After about six years, he traveled to Bodh Gaya and sat under a bo tree. While meditating, he was tempted by the demon Mara, who offered him all the pleasures of the world. Not accepting the temptations, he became enlightened. These scenes have been depicted in Buddhist art and carvings throughout India. Buddha then went to Sarnath and preached his first sermon. Gautama Buddha was not the first Buddha but the fourth. Buddhists believe that everyone can become enlightened and reach the stage of Buddhahood.

There are two major schools of thought in Buddhism. Under the Theravada (doctrine of the elders) or Hinayana ("lesser vehicle") school of thought, Buddha's form cannot be displayed as a human, but is instead shown through symbolism—footprints, the wheel of life, the bo tree under which he sat to attain enlightenment, an elephant (his mother saw an elephant in a dream before he was born), and *stupas*. Mahayana ("greater vehicle") Buddhism, in which statues and pictures of Buddha are shown, became popular around 100 AD. Hinayana Buddhism started to decline at this time and lost popularity around 400 AD.

Buddha is often seen sitting on a lotus and wearing yellow cloth. His hands are in the protective and boon-giving positions.

Hinayana followers say that the path to *nirvana* is an individual quest. Mahayana followers believe that everyone can attain *nirvana,* and they aspire to reach the state of Buddhahood not for themselves, but in order to help other living entities.

There are four important places connected with Buddha's life: his birth site in Lumbini, Nepal; the site of his enlightenment in Bodh Gaya, Bihar; the site of his first sermon in Sarnath, near Varanasi; and the place of his death in Kushinagar, UP. When Buddha died, his body was cremated and the ashes given to people to whom he had preached. Some of these ashes were buried under *stupas* throughout India.

At Rajgir, Buddha converted King Bimbisara to Buddhism, and the First Buddhist Council was held there. At Vaishali, Buddha preached his last sermon and announced his approaching *nirvana.* At Nalanda are the remains of an ancient Buddhist University. These three places are all in Bihar near Patna. Other places in India are famous Buddhist places because of monuments, temples, or cave temples built there. The finest of these are at Ajanta and Ellora in Maharashtra, Sanchi in Madhya Pradesh, and Amaravati in Andhra Pradesh.

Buddha preached Four Noble Truths: (1) life is painful because nothing in this material world is permanent or reliable; (2) suffering is caused by desire, attachment, and ignorance; (3) there is a state beyond suffering called *nirvana;* and (4) *nirvana* is reached by following the eight-fold path of right understanding, right thought, right speech, right action, right livelihood, right effort, right mindfulness, and right concentration.

By following this path for a series of births, an aspirant eventually attains *nirvana* and freedom from the cycle of birth and death. Buddhists teach about the law of *karma* in which our actions in this life determine our next birth.

Lord Buddha is considered to be one of the ten major incarnations of Lord Vishnu by Hindus. He rejected the teachings of the Vedic scriptures and the Vedic gods in order to stop people's use of the *Vedas* to justify animal slaughter in the name of performing sacrifice. Thus even though followers of the *Vedas* accept Buddha as an incarnation of Vishnu, they reject his atheistic philosophy.

Buddhism spread over a good part of India during the time of Emperor Ashoka (272–32 BC), after the emperor's conversion. Ashoka sent people all over South Asia to preach Buddhist doctrine. He later sent his son to Sri Lanka to establish Buddhism there. From the 7th to 12th centuries AD, Buddhism began to decline in India due to the influential preaching of Sankaracharya, Ramanujacarya, and Madhvacarya, all of whom gradually reintroduced the Vedic conclusions. As a final blow to Buddhism, the Muslims carried out a large-scale slaughter of monks, destroying their monasteries and temples.

Sikhism

There are about eighteen million Sikhs in India, most of whom live in Punjab and Delhi. Sikhism was established by Guru Nanak (1469–1539) in 1497. He believed that God was one and that anyone could reach him. He emphasized three actions to understand God: meditating on God's name, giving charity, and bathing. He rejected the worship of the deity, and established communal meals that crossed caste boundaries. He was born in Talwandi, a village west of Lahore (now in Pakistan), into a Hindu *ksatriya* family.

The Sikh religion was originally intended to bring the Hindu and Islamic religions together. It is similar to Hinduism, but the Sikhs are opposed to caste distinctions and pilgrimage to holy rivers. They are not opposed to pilgrimage to holy sites. Sikhs do visit holy places. They believe in one God and do not believe in worshipping images. They believe that Sikhs should be honest, and they will give shelter to anyone who wants to stay in their *gurudwaras*. They believe in *karma* and the cycle of repeated birth and death *(samsara)*. They baptize their children and cremate their dead.

The holy book of the Sikh religion is called the *Granth Sahib*. Guru Nanak was the first of ten gurus. His disciple, Guru Angad, recorded Guru Nanak's hymns and added his own in a new script called Gurumukhi. Gurumukhi has formed the present-day Punjabi script.

Guru Ram Das (1552–1575) founded the city of Amritsar. Guru Arjan compiled the *Adi Granth*, a prayer book of the *gurus*. Emperor Jehangir executed him.

The last Sikh Guru, Gobind Singh (1666–1708), did not name a successor but said the Sikh holy book should be accepted as *guru*. The *Granth Sahib* consists of the teachings of the ten Sikh *gurus* along with the teachings of Hindu and Muslim saints. Guru Gobind Singh introduced a military inflection into the Sikh religion because the Sikhs were being heavily persecuted. This is when the Khalsa ("the pure") brotherhood was formed. Most Sikhs have the name Singh, "Lion."

Many Sikh homes have a room with a copy of the *Granth Sahib* in it. Members of the household start the day with private meditation, then read the *Granth Sahib* and recite verses written by Guru Nanak *(japji)*.

The Sikhs are supposed to wear the following five symbols (*kakkars*): a sword, *kripan;* a comb, *kangh;* short drawers, *kacha;* an iron ring on the right arm, *kada;* and long hair, *kesh.* Because Sikh men do not cut their hair throughout their lives, they are easy to identify. They cover their hair with a turban, and keep their beards long, sometimes twisting them up under their turbans. Sikhs have prohibitions against smoking, eating halal meat, and having sex with Muslims.

The Sikhs worship congregationally in temples called *gurudwaras* ("gateway to the *guru*"). A *gurudwara* usually has a dome on top and a yellow flag. The Golden Temple in Amritsar, built at the end of the 16th century, is the most important Sikh temple. There are no priests or fixed times for worship, but people normally come to the *gurudwaras* in the mornings and evenings. Many worshipers visit the *gurudwaras* on the first day of the year and on *Ekadasi* (eleventh day of the lunar month). Worship in a *gurudwara* consists of chanting verses from the Adi Granth.

Jainism

The word "Jain" comes from *jina*, the "conqueror." Jains are followers of the Conqueror, the first teacher, Adinath. There is a line of twenty-four great teachers, called *tirthankaras* or "finders of the path."

Vardhamma, who was known as Mahavir (599–526 BC) was the twenty-fourth teacher. Mahavir means "great hero." He was born near the border of India and Nepal, about 50 km north of Patna, into a *ksatriyas* family. He renounced his family life and all his possessions when he was thirty years old, and wandered as an ascetic. He died in 526 BC, so this religion is ancient.

Jain temples are dedicated to one of the *tirthankaras*. In their temples they offer prayers and worship to the images of the *tirthankaras,* as well as circumambulating them. They also offer rice, sandalwood paste, incense, and flowers. The Jain religion has about 4.5 million followers. A high percentage of Jains live in Gujarat. They are highly influential in business in many places throughout India.

Jains believe in *ahimsa* (nonviolence). They believe that every living entity, even insects and plants, has an eternal and indestructible soul *(jiva)* within it. Orthodox Jains are strict vegetarians and also avoid onions and garlic. Traditionally, they are not supposed to farm, so that they can avoid killing insects and small animals.

Jains do not accept the *Vedas*, but they do believe in *karma*, reincarnation, that the universe is infinite, and that one can eventually attain *moksha* (liberation) by following the path of the *tirthankaras*. They believe that to become free of *karma*—and therefore the wheel of birth and death—requires a life of meditation and austerity, the renunciation of attachment and of impure thoughts. The *tirthankaras* are the supreme object of worship. They do not accept the caste system.

Jains are pious. They are prohibited from lying or stealing, must avoid useless actions, talk, or thoughts, and must eat only pure food. Ideally, they should practice celibacy. Mahavir taught that one's state of consciousness was directly influenced by the food he eats. Jains must also give charity, either in the form of knowledge or money. Jains are good businessmen.

The Jains are divided into two sects, the Digambaras ("sky-clad") and the Svetambaras ("white-robed"), who are more numerous. They worship in different temples. The Digambaras monks are austere. They renounce all material possessions, even to the point of wearing clothes. The Sravanabelagola shrine in Karnataka is a Digambara temple. In this temple there is an 18m high sculpture of Gomateswara, which was built around 938 AD. Often Svetambara monks wear a white cloth to cover their mouths so that they will not accidentally swallow insects and thus commit violence.

Jains have constructed some of the most impressively carved temples in India. The temples they build are not usually so large, but the sculptures on the temples can be spectacular. They tend to build a complex of outstanding temples at a time. One of the most important Svetambara *tirthas*, Shatrunjaya, near Palitana in eastern Gujarat, has hundreds of temples located on a hilltop.

Zoroastrianism

Zoroastrianism was founded in Persia by the prophet Zarathustra around the 17th or 16th century BC (some say much later). He was from Mazar-i-Sharif, which is now in Afghanistan. At one time, Zoroastrianism was a major religion in the Middle East. Now followers of Zoroastrianism are found only in Mumbai in India, Karachi in Pakistan, and Shiraz in Iran. Its followers are known as Parsis.

There are about 100,000 Parsis in India; most live in Mumbai. The first Parsis arrived in India in 936 AD in Gujarat. They have a lot of influence in India because some of them are wealthy. Their numbers are continually decreasing in India because they do not believe in marriage outside their religion. When a mixed marriage does occur, the children are not considered Parsis.

They believe that there is an invisible and omnipotent God called Ahura Mazda. Their Scripture is the *Zend-Avesta,* which describes the struggle between good and evil. Good defeats evil by following the principles of *humata* (good thoughts), *hukta* (good words), and *huvarshta* (good activities).

Parsis wear a sacred thread *(kasti)* and a sacred shirt *(sadra)*. They worship fire as God's representative in their temples. There are eight main fire temples in India—four in Mumbai and one each in Udwada and Navsari, and two in Surat. Only Parsis can enter their temples. They do not bury or cremate their dead because this pollutes the elements consisting of fire, air, water, or earth. They leave the bodies of their dead on the "Tower of Silence," where they are eaten by vultures.

On Chanting Hare Krishna

Chanting the transcendental vibration Hare Krishna, Hare Krishna, Krishna Krishna, Hare Hare/ Hare Rama, Hare Rama, Rama Rama, Hare Hare is the sublime method for reviving our transcendental consciousness, or Krishna consciousness. As living spiritual souls, we are all originally Krishna conscious entities, but due to our association with matter from time immemorial, our consciousness is now polluted by the material atmosphere, called *maya*, or illusion. And what is this illusion? The illusion is that we are all trying to be lords of material nature, while actually we are under the grip of her stringent laws. When a servant artificially tries to imitate the all-powerful master, he is said to be in illusion. We are trying to exploit the resources of material nature, but actually we are becoming more dependent on her. This illusory struggle against material nature can be stopped at once by revival of our eternal Krishna consciousness.

Krishna consciousness is not an artificial imposition on the mind. This consciousness is the original energy of the living entity. When we hear and chant the transcendental vibration Hare Krishna, Hare Krishna, Krishna Krishna Hare Hare/ Hare Rama, Hare Rama, Rama Rama, Hare Hare, this consciousness is revived. This simplest method of meditation is recommended by learned authorities for this age. By practical experience also, one can perceive that by chanting this *maha-mantra*, or the Great Chant for Deliverance, one at once feels transcendental ecstasy coming through from the spiritual stratum.

In the material concept of life we are busy in the matter of sense gratification, as if we were in the lower, animal stage. A little elevated from this status of sense gratification, one engages in mental speculation for the purpose of getting out of the material clutches. A little elevated from this speculative status, when one is intelligent enough, one tries to find out the supreme cause of all causes, within and without. And when one is factually on the plane of spiritual understanding, surpassing the stages of sense, mind, and intelligence, one is situated on the transcendental plane. The chanting of the Hare Krishna mantra is directly enacted from this spiritual platform, and thus this sound vibration surpasses all lower strata of consciousness—namely sensual, mental, and intellectual.

There is no need, therefore, to understand the language of the mantra, nor is there any need of any mental speculation or intellectual adjustment for chanting this *maha-mantra*. It springs automatically from the spiritual platform, and thus anyone can take part in the chanting without any previous qualification and dance in ecstasy. We have seen this practically. Even a child can take part in the chanting and dancing. Of course, for one who is too much entangled in material life, it takes a little more time to come to the standard point, but even such a materially engrossed person is very quickly raised to the spiritual platform. When the mantra is chanted by a pure devotee of the Lord, it has the greatest effect on hearers, and therefore this chanting should be heard from the lips of a pure devotee of the Lord, so that immediate effects can be achieved. As far as possible, chanting from the lips of nondevotees should be avoided, just as one would avoid milk touched by the lips of a serpent because it has poisonous effects.

The Hara is a form of addressing the energy of the Lord, and the words Krishna and Rama (when mean "the highest pleasure eternal") are forms of addressing the Lord Himself. Hara is the supreme pleasure energy of the Lord, and when addressed as Hare in the vocative, She helps us to reach the Supreme Lord.

The material energy, called *maya*, is also one of the multienergies of the Lord, and we, the living entitles, are the marginal energy of the Lord. The living entities are described as superior to the material energy. When this superior energy is in contact with the inferior energy, an incompatible situation arises, but when the superior marginal energy is in contact with the spiritual energy, Hara, the living entity is established in his happy, normal condition.

These three words, namely Hare, Krishna, and Rama, are the transcendental seeds of the *maha-mantra*. The chanting is a spiritual call for the Lord and His internal energy Hara to protect the conditional soul. This chanting is exactly like the genuine cry of a child for its mother. Mother Hara helps the devotee achieve the grace of the Supreme Father, Hari or Krishna, and the Lord reveals Himself to the devotee who chants this mantra sincerely.

Therefore no other means of spiritual realization is as effective in this age of quarrel and hypocrisy as the chanting of the *maha-mantra*: Hare Krishna, Hare Krishna, Krishna Krishna, Hare Hare/ Hare Rama, Hare Rama, Rama, Rama, Hare, Hare.

Bhagavad Gita Verses

2-12 Never was there a time when I did not exist, nor you, nor all the kings; nor in the future shall any of us cease to be.

2-13 As the embodies soul continuously passes, in this body, from boyhood to youth to old age, the soul similarly passes into another body at death. A sober person is not bewildered by such a change.

2-14 The nonpermanent appearance of happiness and distress, and their disappearance in due course, are like the appearance and disappearance of winter and summer seasons. They arise from sense perception and one must learn to tolerate them without being disturbed.

2-15 The person who is not disturbed by happiness and distress and is steady in both in certainly eligible for liberation.

2-17 That which pervades the entire body you should know to be indestructible. No one is able to destroy that imperishable soul.

2-20 For the soul there is neither birth nor death at any time. He has not come into being, does not come into being, and will not come into being. He is unborn, eternal, ever-existing and primeval. He is not slain when the body is slain.

2-21 As a person puts on new garments, giving up old ones, the soul similarly accepts new material bodies, giving up the old and useless ones.

2-58 One who is able to withdraw his senses from sense objects, as the tortoise draws its limbs within the shell, is firmly fixed in perfect consciousness.

2-62 While contemplating the objects of the senses, a person develops attachment for them, and from such attachment lust develops, and from lust anger arises.

2-63 From anger, complete delusion arises, and from delusion bewilderment of memory. When memory is bewildered, intelligence is lost, and when intelligence is lost one falls down again into the material pool.

3-9 Work done as a sacrifice for Vishnu has to be performed; otherwise work causes bondage in this material world. There, O son of Kunti, perform your prescribed duties for His satisfaction, and in that way you will always remain free from bondage.

3-37 It is lust only, Arjuna, which is born of contact with the material mode of passion and later transformed into wrath, and which is the all-devouring sinful enemy of the world.

4-5 Sri Krishna said: Many, many births both you and I have passed. I can remember all of them, but you cannot.

4-6 Although I am unborn and My transcendental body never deteriorates, and although I am the Lord of all living entities, I still appear in every millennium in My original transcendental form.

4-7 Whenever and wherever there is a decline in religious practice and a predominant rise of irreligion—at that time I descent myself.

4-8 To deliver the pious and to annihilate the miscreants, as well as to reestablish the principles of religion, I Myself appear, millennium after millennium.

5-10 One who performs his duty without attachment, surrendering the results unto the Supreme Lord, is unaffected by sinful action, as the lotus leaf is untouched by water.

5-18 The humble sages, by virtue of true knowledge, see with equal vision a learned and gentle brahman, a cow, an elephant, a dog and a dog-eater (outcaste).

5-28 A person in full consciousness of Me, knowing Me to be the ultimate beneficiary of all sacrifices and austerities, the Supreme Lord of all planets and demigods, and the benefactor and well-wisher of all living entities, attains peace from the pangs of material miseries.

6-47 And of all yogis, the one with great faith who always abides in Me, thinks of Me within himself, and renders transcendental loving service to Me—he is the most intimately united with Me in yoga and is the highest of all. That is My opinion.

7-3 Out of many thousands of men, one may endeavor for perfection, and of those who have achieved perfection, hardly one knows Me in truth.

7-8 I am the taste of water, the light of the sun and the moon, the syllable OM in the Vedic mantras; I am the sound in ether and ability in man.

7-19 After many births and deaths, he who is actually in knowledge surrenders unto Me, knowing Me to be the cause of all causes and all that is.

8-7 Therefore, Arjuna, you should always think of Me in the form of Krishna and at the same time carry out your prescribed duty of fighting. With your activities dedicated to Me and your mind and intelligence fixed on Me, you will attain Me without doubt.

8-16 From the highest planet in the material world down to the lowest, all are places of misery wherein repeated birth and death take place. But one who attains to My abode, O son of Kunti, never takes birth again.

9-26 If one offers Me with love and devotion a leaf, a flower, a fruit or water, I will accept it.

9-27 Whatever you do, whatever you eat, whatever you offer or give away, and whatever austerities you perform—do that as an offering to Me.

9-29 I envy no one, nor am a I partial to anyone. I am equal to all. But whoever renders service unto Me in devotion is a friend, is in Me, and I am also a friend to him.

10-8 I am the source of all spiritual and material worlds. Everything emanates from Me. The wise who perfectly know this engage in My devotional service and worship Me with all their hears.

12-5 For those whose minds are attached to the unmanifested, impersonal feature of the Supreme, advancement is very troublesome. To make progress in that discipline is always difficult for those who are embodied.

15-7 The living entities in this conditioned world are My eternal fragmental parts. Due to conditioned life, they are struggling very hard with the six senses, which include the mind.

15-15 I am seated in everyone's heart, and from Me come remembrance, knowledge and forgetfulness. By all the Vedas, I am to be known. Indeed, I am the compiler of Vedanta, and I am the knower of the Vedas.

15-19 Whoever knows Me as the Supreme Personality of Godhead, without doubting, is the knower of everything.

18-51-53 Being purified by his intelligence and controlling the mind with determination, giving up the objects of sense gratification, being freed from attachment and hatred, one who lives in a secluded place, who eats little, who controls his body, mind and power of speech, who is always in trance and who detached, free from false ego, false strengths, false pride, lust, anger, and acceptance of material things, free from false proprietorship, and peaceful—such a person is certainly elevated to the position of self-realization.

18-55 One can understand Me as I am, as the Supreme Personality of Godhead, only by devotional service. And when one is in full consciousness of Me by such devotion, he can enter into the kingdom of God.

18-65 Always think of Me, become My devotee, worship Me, and offer your homage unto Me. Thus you will come to Me without fail. I promise you this because you are My very dear friend.

18-66 Abandon all varieties of religion and just surrender unto Me, I shall deliver you from all sinful reactions. Do not fear.

Vedic Astrology

In Sanskrit, astrology is called *jyothisha*, "the science of light." Astrology is the science which deals with the influence of the planets. Planetary influences on humankind can be classified into three categories: spiritual, mental, and physical. Astrology postulates that people are always under the influences of planetary rays and that those influences can be understood scientifically. The science of astrology has been used in India for thousands of years.

Vedic astrology accepts that a person takes a position in this birth according to the karma accrued in past births. According to Vedic astrology, people accumulate karma in every life based on their actions and desires. They are reborn at the moment the planets move into a particular configuration. That configuration can then be studied to discover whether a person's past activities were pious or impious, and what events are most likely to occur in a person's future as a result. The planetary positions at the time of birth thus reveals the events of a person's present life as well as his or her past and future lives.

The quality of a person's chart is judged by the position of the various planets in the zodiac—in the different signs and constellations. Each planet has a different influence over the person. Astrology can be used to examine all aspects of life, including finance, marriage, spiritual life, career, health, relationships, and even every day activities. Astrology can also give an indication of someone's personality. The placement of planets in a chart can enable an astrologer to predict short- and long-range situations and how best to meet them according to an individual's needs.

Planetary influences change quickly. We can see that even two people born within an hour of one another at the same place can have completely different karmas. Therefore, astrology has developed into an exact science, and when used properly, it can help oneself and others.

The planets influence every living being who takes birth on earth. Astrology can determine how and when the various influences will act, and whether their effects will be good, bad, or neutral. A qualified astrologer can give advice about how to adopt positive remedies to counteract negative planetary influences. If we have an indication of troubles ahead, we can choose to either protect or fortify ourselves against them, just as if we know it is going to rain, we can choose to carry an umbrella.

This book describes the sidereal system of astrology, used by Vedic authorities. It is the most correct system, and the most detailed, in its ability to predict the planetary influences on mind, intelligence, soul, and spiritual life. It is also the most complete in prescribing remedial methods to solve potential problems, and to better use the positive influences of stars and planets. Although each person is affected by karma, Vedic astrologers propound that karma is not eternal; adjusting the planetary influences can change it. Gemstones, for example, are one way in which the planetary vibrations can be appeased or changed for the better.

An ephemeris is a book that lists the position of the planets at any particular time. A number of Vedic astrologers have made their own ephemerises, but their calculations are sometimes incorrect. Many astrologers agree that the values in Lahiri's ephemeris (an Indian ephemeris) are correct. Another recommended ephemeris is the Rosicrucian ephemeris. Most Western (tropical) astrologers use Raphael's ephemeris.

An important point to note in reference to the difference between Vedic and Western astrology is the position of the Sun or Moon at the time of birth. In Vedic astrology when you see Aries and other signs discussed in newspapers and other places they are usually talking about where the Moon is located in a birth chart and not where the Sun is located in the birth chart. So if a person tells someone in India that they are an Aries, an Indian will often assume you are saying that the Moon was in the sign of Aries at the time of birth, while most Westerners are saying that the Sun was in the sign of Aries at the time of birth.

Prashna

Astrology can be used to answer questions about health, occupation, marriage, auspicious times to take journeys, and how to recover stolen items. When approaching an astrologer with an actual question (as opposed to simply drawing up a birth chart), the astrologer will draw up a *prashna* chart. The *prashna* chart is drawn according to the time the question was asked. An astrologer drawing up a *prashna* chart will find it helpful to know the position of planets in both the questioner's birth chart and his or her *navamsa* chart.

Prashna charts can help find thieves and indicate where the stolen goods may be located. They can also help, in cases of illness, to indicate whether a prescribed medication is beneficial, whether the afflicted person will recover, and whether the illness has even been diagnosed properly. When used to answer a question about marriage, the *prashna* chart can indicate whether a proposed match is proper, auspicious, and whether a person will get the mate of their choice.

The Zodiac

The zodiac is a band in the sky extending nine degrees on either side of the ecliptic. The ecliptic is the great circle formed by the intersection of the plane of the earth's orbit with the celestial sphere; the apparent annual path of the sun in the heavens. The sun passes exactly longitudinally through the center of the zodiac, and the planets run up to nine degrees on either the north or south sides of the ecliptic. The distance north of the ecliptic is known as the northern latitude, and the distance south as southern latitude. If a planet is situated directly on the ecliptic, it is said to be at zero latitude.

The zodiac measures 360 degrees and is divided into twelve equal divisions consisting of thirty degrees each. These divisions constitute the signs of the zodiac. Each degree is divided into sixty minutes, and each minute is divided into sixty seconds.

The zodiac begins at the fixed star, Ashwini. This star is located at 0°, and from this point to 30° is the sign of Aries. The next sign, Taurus, begins at 30° and ends at 60°. Each following sign takes up 30°, ending with Pisces, which goes from 330° to 360°. It takes the earth about one year to travel around the sun.

Since there is more than one star in the constellation of Ashwini, not all Vedic astrologers agree with what the 0° exactly means.

Tropical vs. Sidereal

There are two types of charts, Tropical (Western) and Sidereal (Vedic, or "Fixed"). The important things to take into consideration in both systems are the position of the planets in the zodiac signs and the exact birth time. Astrological charts can be drawn using either system, but it is important that the astrologer be competent.

The Tropical system is not based on the actual location of the stars. In the Tropical system, the zodiac, or birth signs, are based on the position of the Sun in relationship to the Earth and not on the position of the stars. Therefore, part of the Tropical sign Aries presently corresponds with the Sidereal sign Pisces.

There is a difference between Vedic and Western zodiacs of about 22 to 23 degrees. The difference in degree between the two zodiacs is called the AYANAMSA. The ayanamsa in the Rosicrucian ephemeris is considered correct by many astrologers. If in a chart the position of the houses and the planets have been taken from a Western ephemeris (such as Raphael's), about 23° have to be deducted from the tropical longitude to come up with the Vedic or Sidereal zodiac.

The first degree of the zodiac was originally similar in both systems. As time passed, however, and because of the peculiarities of the earth's orbit, the stars and constellations appeared to shift in relation to the Tropical zodiac. This is called the "procession of the equinoxes," or the Ayanamsha. This is the difference between where the vernal equinox (where the Tropical zodiac begins) is located now and where the constellation of Aries begins. At the present time, there are about 22° to 23° between the beginning points of both zodiacs. In 1950, many Western astrologers placed the Ayanamsha at 24°02'. Vedic astrologers placed it at between 21°40' and 23°10'. B. V. Raman placed it at 21°42' in the same year. The difference between the charts changes about nine minutes per ten years; that is, .9 minute is added per year. The change is about ninety minutes every one hundred years.

Thus if a person is born on January 1, a Western chart would place the Sun in Capricorn while a Vedic chart would place it at about 16° Sagittarius. If the Sun is said to be in Capricorn according to the Tropical system, it does not mean that the Sun is in the fixed sign of Capricorn. In actuality according to the Vedic system the Sun could be in Sagittarius. If a planet in a Vedic horoscope is at 15° Leo, it will be calculated at 5° or 6° Virgo in a Western horoscope.

Another difference between the two systems is the position of the cusp. In Vedic astrology, the cusp begins at the middle of the house and goes 15° in both directions. In Western astrology, the cusp starts at the beginning of the house and goes 30° in each direction. These are the main differences between the two astrological systems.

The first degree of the Western zodiac is calculated by where the Sun is positioned on the first day of spring, the vernal equinox (about March 21). The position of the equinoxes to the fixed stars changes over a period of time, because the Earth moves on its axis, causing the fixed stars to move backwards in the zodiac. It takes about 25,000 years for a complete circle to be made in the zodiac. About 2,000 years ago, when Western astrology was first developed, the two zodiacs coincided.

According to the sidereal system, the zodiac or birth signs are based on the position of the fixed constellations and stars in the sky. Sidereal means "pertaining to the stars." It is judged by where the constellations are actually located.

For instance according to the Western or Tropical dates the Sun sign of Aries is March 21 to April 19, while according to the Indian or Sidereal Sun sign the dates of Aries are April 14 to May 13. The Western or Tropical dates for the Sun sign of Pisces is February 19 to March 20 and the Indian or Sidereal dates for Pisces is March 14 to April 13.

Please note that this book will deal only with the sidereal (Vedic) system and that all signs are based on a fixed zodiac.

Planets

The planets, or *grahas*, that influence a person in sidereal astrology are: the Sun, Moon, Mars, Mercury, Jupiter, Venus, Saturn, and the two shadowy planets, Ketu and Rahu. The nine *grahas* are all called planets, but Ketu and Rahu do not actually have "bodies." Rather, they are subtle planets.

The word planet is defined as a "celestial or astrological point (property of attraction) called *graha*." The literal meaning of *graha* is "holding, grasping, or seizing." A *graha* is an entity with the power to hold, grasp, or seize, and since the planets are capable of this, they are known as *grahas*. The influence planets exert on a person can be examined according to their placement, dignity, and strength at the time of the native's birth.

The three planets Uranus, Neptune and Pluto, as well as other planets and stars, are considered to have very little influence on a person's chart in Vedic astrology. Uranus, Neptune, and Pluto are considered to have little influence because they are so far from the earth and move so slowly. These planets were discovered only recently, and are not mentioned in the ancient Vedic astrology books. They are usually not taken into consideration when drawing up a person's chart.

In Western astrology, ten planets are taken into consideration: the Sun, Moon, Mercury, Venus, Mars, Jupiter, Saturn, Uranus, Neptune and Pluto. Ketu and Rahu are also taken into consideration as the moon's nodes, but they are not usually considered to be as important in Western astrology as in Vedic astrology.

The most important planets in Vedic astrology are the two luminaries, the Sun and the Moon. Since the Moon is so close to the Earth, it bears great influence on a person's chart.

Next in importance are Mars, Jupiter, and Saturn, which are outside the orbit of the earth. Next are Mercury and Venus, which are within the earth's orbit and close to the Sun. The Lunar Nodes, Rahu and Ketu, are considered the least important.

The planets move at different speeds, and each planet influences people according to its nature. The planets' speeds decrease as the distance from the Earth increases. Mercury, which is close to the Sun, moves quite quickly. It usually moves within 28° of the Sun. Different forces influence planetary movement and cause them to move at different velocities.

Ketu and Rahu

When the Moon orbits the earth, the two points where it crosses the ecliptic are considered important. The point where the Moon crosses to the north is called its northern node, or Rahu, and where it crosses to the south, it is called the Moon's southern node, or Ketu. The south point is exactly 180° from the north point. In Western astrology the northern node is called Caput Draconic, or Dragon's Head, and the southern node is called Cauda Draconic, or Dragon's Tail.

Ketu (Dragon's Tail) and Rahu (Dragon's Head) are actually two subtle but powerful points in relationship to the Moon's movement around the Earth. These two planets are referred to as "shadow planets" (*chaya grahas* or *aprakasha*) because they do not have any mass or body. Rather, they are two sensitive points in the zodiac. In Vedic astrology they are assigned functions like the other planets.

Since Rahu and Ketu are shadow planets, they reflect the qualities of the signs they tenant. If Ketu is in Virgo, for example, the sign ruled by Mercury, an astrologer will look to see where Mercury is located and then predict the same influence for Ketu.

Some Western astrologers take Rahu and Ketu into consideration, but many do not. The northern node's position is listed in the ephemeris, but the southern node is rarely mentioned. However, we know that it is always situated 180° from Rahu. Rahu influences power and affluence in a person's chart; Ketu is connected to noble and spiritual issues.

Planets and the Days That They Rule

In Vedic astrology, the planets are listed in the order of the days they rule:

Planets	Hindi Name	Day of Week
Sun	Ravi	Sunday
Moon	Chandra	Monday

Mars	Kuja	Tuesday
Mercury	Budha	Wednesday
Jupiter	Guru	Thursday
Venus	Sukra	Friday
Saturn	Shani	Saturday
Dragon's Head	Rahu	
Dragon's Tail	Ketu	

Attribute of Planets

Sun–religious, charitable, learned, strong; **Moon**–rich, educated, studious; **Mercury**–educated, respected, happy, fortunate; **Venus**–long life, charitable; **Mars**–educated, energetic, princely, famous; **Jupiter**–respected, easily angered, leader among men, strong; **Saturn**–charitable, long life, opulent, talented; **Ketu**–wealthy; **Rahu**–wealthy.

Sun

Where the Sun is situated in a chart is considered very important, as it is the king of the planets and the cause of universal light. The Sun and Moon are both sovereigns. The Sun is generally accepted to be malefic, but can be benefic. The Sun is significant for royalty or high government or political position. The Sun's qualities: fire, masculine, and the color copper-red. The Sun's gem is ruby.

The Sun deals with the father, a person's external appearance, how he or her is seen by the public, and the way a person acts. It deals with the soul and the self. It affects philosophical tendency, health, political power, and the native's status and respect. The Sun can make one decisive and determined. A well-situated Sun can give optimism, good fortune, a positive outlook, a high position, first-class qualities, and success.

The Sun rules the heart. It represents the right eye for men and the left eye for women. Rain is caused by the Sun, and since rain affects crops and financial position, the Sun is considered important. The Sun governs bankers, gold smiths, doctors, government positions, churches and temples, and public positions.

Moon

Because the Moon is so close to the Earth, the Moon's position in a chart is considered very important. The Moon represents the mind and the mother. The Moon's qualities: feminine, womanhood, and the color white. In general, the Moon is benefic when waxing and malefic when waning. The Moon's gem is a white pearl.

The Moon deals with the mind, and affects both the way a person thinks and his or her thoughts. Thus it influences happiness and emotions. During a full Moon, lunatics become more active. The moon deals with feminine qualities. It rules things dealing with water and affects the ocean tides. It affects the body fluids, liquids, and occupations dealing with water.

The Moon deals with public business, fame, and popularity. An exalted Moon will give a person respect, wealth, good health, and mental stability. A debilitated Moon will cause the opposite. Depending on which planet is afflicting the Moon, various effects will result.

Mars

Mars is naturally malefic, masculine, and fiery. Mars deals with the brothers, land, immovable properties, warfare, science, fire, competition, courage, and determination. Red coral is the gem for Mars, and Mars's color is blood-red. Its metal is copper and number is nine.

A positively placed Mars gives a person strong energy, productivity, a powerful leadership position (such as army leadership), physical strength, strong character, successful material life, quick mental facility, good organization skills, strong determination, ambition, and enables one to act independently. When Mars is exalted, one has strong energy, courage, strength, is well educated, famous, and majestic. When Mars is powerfully placed, a person devotes his or her energy to positive endeavors and worthwhile causes.

A badly placed Mars can cause injury, disease, hostility, enemies, scandal, anger, and disagreements. An afflicted Mars may make one too sexually active, reckless, fanatically religious, extravagant, violent, destructive, and one may tend to steal. It can cause a loss of energy and the tendency to waste time when badly placed. An afflicted Mars may cause the blood to be impure causing boils, anemia, and bad blood pressure.

Occupations that deal with Mars are the military, ambassadors, public speaking, construction, real estate, flying, athletics, restaurant management, and cooking.

Mercury

Mercury governs intelligence and therefore rules such fields as education, literature, communication, the arts, public speaking, and advertising. It deals with maternal uncles, friends, intelligence, and childhood. Mercury's nature is fast-moving and youthful. A person influenced by Mercury can usually perform activities quickly, and can do several tasks at one time. Mercury's color is green, metal is brass, number is five and emerald is its gem.

Mercury enhances the ability to learn languages and the scriptures, improves memory, speaking ability, and business. If Mercury is exalted in the chart, the native will be educated, talkative, playful, fortunate, highly respected, enthusiastic, and energetic. It is associated with friendship, logic, leafy trees, discrimination, charms (amulets), travel, agriculture, the nervous system, vocation, speech, adaptability, and commerce. A badly placed Mercury can cause a person to lack energy, have speech and hearing impediments, and to be deceptive.

Some occupations in relation to Mercury are public speaking, astrology, the medical profession, publishing, writing, dancing, drama, education, middleman in business or politics, accountancy, the testing of precious stones, sculpture, and professions requiring skillful hands.

Jupiter

Jupiter is the most auspicious and benefic planet. A powerful and benefic Jupiter is a strong asset in a person's chart and can give great rewards. Jupiter rules the higher qualities of the mind and the elevation of the soul. It influences one to do good. Powerful and rich people often have strong Jupiter. The Sanskrit name for Jupiter is *guru*, or one who teaches and is respected. Its color is bright yellow, metal is gold, number is three, and it has a masculine quality. Jupiter's gem is yellow sapphire.

Jupiter deals with the sons, husband (for women), religion, finance, prosperity, truth, philosophy, teaching, wisdom, knowledge, charity, positive thought, happiness, intelligence, one's spiritual orientation, learning, superior persons, guru, and religious activities. It is associated with education, pilgrimage places, transcendental wisdom, scriptural understanding, treasury, fruit, and fruit trees. Jupiter rules over the liver, blood circulation, bodily fluids, body fat, thighs, and feet.

A person with an exalted Jupiter will be a leader, wealthy, powerful, respected, and influential. A person influenced by Jupiter is noble, optimistic, positive, dignified, joyful, benevolent, dignified, and able to concentrate deeply. He or she may also be prone to anger.

If Jupiter is afflicted, the native may be extreme and immoderate. If Jupiter is debilitated, it can cause unhappiness, egotism, legal problems, carelessness, vanity, infamy, overeating, over optimistic, pressure from creditors, bad speculations, debts, disputes, false hopes, childlessness, and gambling. An afflicted Jupiter may cause a person to be extravagant, over-generous, and excessive. A person with a badly placed Jupiter may have sexual problems, be dishonorable, act improperly, and act undignified.

Venus

Venus is a benefic planet. It deals with the wife (for a man), marriage, happy family life, a good home, vitality, love, sex, beauty, sensual pleasure, comfort, luxury, art, poetry, and material comfort. A person influenced by Venus is optimistic, charismatic, gives others happiness, and moves gracefully. Venus gives a person pleasure in life. Its color is a mixture of all the colors (rainbow), metal is silver, and number is six. Venus is a teacher. Diamond is the gem for Venus.

Venus is associated with flowers, jewelry, beautiful things, semen, sweet foods and flavors, tropical climates, makeup, cows, sexual activity, nice clothes, various sensual pleasures, pleasant scents, ornaments, and flowering trees. Venus rules singers, dancers, musicians, artists, craftsmen, actors, prostitutes, and entertainers. Salesmen, watery places, diplomats, and peacemakers are also ruled by Venus. Venus is said to rule over the eyes, reproductive system, kidneys, cheeks, chin, and throat.

A well-placed and unafflicted Venus makes a person wealthy and comfortable. Those with a strong Venus in their charts will tend to be attracted to the opposite sex at a young age. When Venus is exalted, one will become a humanitarian, have a long life, and have many good qualities.

An afflicted Venus may cause a delayed and/ or disturbed marriage, cause one to get a bad name, to become impotent or sterile, and age quickly. One may also tend to overeat and drink, indulge in sex, and contract sexual diseases. People with a powerful Venus often have problems with the excretory system because of over-indulgence in food and drink. A badly placed Venus may cause bad eyes, anemia, and mucous disorders.

Saturn

Saturn is malefic by nature. Saturn's influence is powerful and is usually negative in a person's chart. It is often feared. Saturn rules death, disease, and old age. Saturn influences philosophy and *vairagya* (detachment). Saturn is the furthest planet from the Sun and has little light. It is a cold, defensive, dry, hard, barren, and binding planet. If a person is under Saturn's influence, they tend to be lazy, lethargic, and prone to gambling. Its color is blue, and blue sapphire is Saturn's gem. Its metal is iron and number is eight.

Saturn represents hardship, hard work, toil, misery, loss, theft, gambling, immoral activities, longevity, obstruction, limitation, disrespect, detachment, unrighteous activities, adversity, poverty, cruelty, lameness, and the problems of life.

It influences a person's work and employment, and the problems one must overcome to become successful. Saturn deals with laborers, thieves, foreign lands, foreigners, learning foreign languages, foreign travel, agricultural production, oil, gas, minerals, iron, servants, dangerous substances, hunters, and yoga practice.

Saturn stays in each sign for 2½ years and takes thirty years to go through all the signs. It moves very slowly. Because of its slow movement, it symbolizes delay. Saturn causes delay, can deny, and will often cause disappointment. Saturn's negative effects are difficulty, dejection, disharmony, differences, dispute, and despondency. If Saturn and Rahu influence marriage, they will cause a delayed marriage, and if really malefic, one may not be able to marry at all.

A well-placed Saturn can produce great results. The beneficial effects of Saturn are stability, prudence, patience, perseverance, endurance, self-control, economy, industry, sense of duty, the ability to become a positive public figure, thrift, and compassion. When Saturn is exalted, a person will live a long life, be charitable, efficient, and be loving toward their mate.

A badly placed Saturn may cause wind diseases and can cause sexual problems. If Saturn afflicts a particular house in a person's chart, the part of the body ruled by that house will also be afflicted. Diseases that may be caused by a badly placed Saturn are fevers, headaches, paralysis, epilepsy, fainting, jaundice, deafness, anxiety, dumbness, insanity, depression, bad teeth, and a bad right ear.

Rahu

Rahu is by nature a malefic planet. It often intensifies the effect of the house it tenants. People usually fear the influence of Rahu and Ketu. According to the *Vedas,* Rahu is a demoniac planet and will attack the Sun and Moon, causing eclipses. Many authorities say that Rahu acts like Saturn. The gemstone for Rahu is Gomedha. Its number is four.

Rahu influences the paternal grandfather, prosperity, abuse of alcohol and drugs and the use of intoxication in general, strong pain, theft, corruption, frustration, problems with ghosts, uncleanliness, renunciation, psychic disturbances, epidemics, harsh speech, gambling, traveling, wickedness, widowhood, disease, epidemics, supernatural phenomena, and suicidal impulses. It represents fear, snakes, snakebites, and problems from past bad activities.

Persons with an exalted Rahu are wealthy and fortunate. Rahu can make one powerful and influential over the public. An afflicted Rahu causes mental and bodily problems, dysentery, cholera, and may increase the tendency to commit suicide.

Ketu

Ketu is normally a malefic and restrictive planet. It usually afflicts the house it tenants, except when it is exalted or connected to a benefic planet. It tends to perform like the ruler of the sign that it tenants. Many astrologers say that Ketu acts like Mars. It often causes poverty and obstruction to a person's endeavors. Cat's Eye is the gemstone for Ketu. Its number is seven.

Ketu deals with the maternal grandfather, pain, suffering, causing trouble to enemies, poison, fever, injury, pride, death, negation, enmity, and selfishness. On a positive side, it deals with religion, philosophy, knowledge, salvation, spiritism, liberation, and psychic ability. An exalted Ketu can protect one from evil and make one wealthy.

If Ketu is weak or badly placed in a chart, it can cause poverty, fatal disease, a tendency to gamble, and be the cause of obstructions in life. Ketu is associated with material suffering; therefore, it can have a good effect on a person's spiritual life. An afflicted Ketu may cause accidents, paralysis, skin problems, dropsy, ringworm, and colic pains.

Karakas

Each planet is a Karaka, or indicator (significator), of certain matters, events, characteristics, and occurrences in a person's life.

Planet	Karaka
Sun	father
Moon	mother
Mercury	maternal uncle, friends
Venus	wife or husband
Mars	brother
Jupiter	children, sons, elder brothers, guru
Saturn	servants, life duration
Rahu	paternal relations
Ketu	maternal grandfather

Signs

In Sanskrit, a sign is called a *rashi*. The zodiac consists of twelve signs. Persons born under a particular sign often have the qualities of that sign. The dates listed below are approximate. When it says that Aries begins on April 14, it can actually change by a day or two depending on the year.

The signs are:

English Name	Indian Name	Degrees		Sidereal Dates
Aries	Mesha	0°	to 30°	April 14 to May 13
Taurus	Vrishabha	30°	60°	May 14 to June 13
Gemini	Mithuna	60°	90°	June 14 to July 15
Cancer	Karaka	90°	120°	July 16 to Aug. 15
Leo	Simha	120°	150°	Aug. 16 to Sept. 15
Virgo	Kanya	150°	180°	Sept. 16 to Oct. 16
Libra	Tula	180°	210°	Oct. 17 to Nov. 15
Scorpio	Vrischika	210°	240°	Nov. 16 to Dec 14
Sagittarius	Dhanu	240°	270°	Dec. 15 to Jan. 13
Capricorn	Makar	270°	300°	Jan. 14 to Feb. 12
Aquarius	Kumbha	300°	330°	Feb. 13 to March 13
Pisces	Meena	330°	360°	March 14 to April 13

Appearance of Signs

1. Aries–ram
2. Taurus–bull
3. Gemini–twins, a man and a woman holding a trumpet and a harp
4. Cancer–crab
5. Leo–lion
6. Virgo–a virgin, a woman holding a lamp and a corn cob
7. Libra–the balance, a man holding in his hand a balance
8. Scorpio–scorpion
9. Sagittarius–body of horse and face of a human, holding a bow and arrow
10. Capricorn–crocodile
11. Aquarius–water carrier, man holding a water pot
12. Pisces–two fishes

Qualities of the Signs

Aries–movable, masculine, fiery, odd, cruel, of short ascension, rising by the hinder part

Taurus–fixed, feminine, earthy, mild, fruitful, of short ascension, rising by the hinder part

Gemini–Common, masculine, airy, barren, odd, cruel, of short ascension, rising by the head

Cancer–movable, feminine, watery, even, mild, fruitful, of long ascension, rising by the hinder part

Leo–fixed, masculine, fiery, cruel, odd, barren, of long ascension, rising by the head

Virgo–common, feminine, earthy, mild, even, of long ascension, rising by the head

Libra–movable, masculine, airy, cruel, odd, of long ascension, rising by the head

Scorpio–fixed, feminine, watery, mild, even, of long ascension, rising by the head

Sagittarius–common, masculine, fiery, cruel, odd, of long ascension, rising by the hinder part

Capricorn–movable, feminine, earthy, even, mild, of long ascension, rising by the hinder part

Aquarius–fixed, masculine, airy, cruel, odd, fruitful, of short ascension, rising by the head

Pisces–common, feminine, water, even, mild, of short ascension

Parts of the Body

Parts of the body relate to different signs.

1.	Aries	head
2.	Taurus	face (also the neck)
3.	Gemini	chest and arms
4.	Cancer	heart, breast, area above stomach
5.	Leo	stomach, area above navel
6.	Virgo	area below navel and above basti
7.	Libra	basti
8.	Scorpio	genitals and anus
9.	Sagittarius	hips and thighs
10.	Capricorn	back and two knees
11.	Aquarius	legs and calves
12.	Pisces	feet

Aries

Aries is a fire sign ruled by Mars. It is symbolized by two rams butting heads, which indicates an adventurous, challenging mentality. It is a movable sign, and indicates wandering.

An person under the influence of Aries tends to be heroic, a leader, competitive, aggressive, active, dynamic, proud, adventurous, have initiative, a martial nature, be independent, is always on the move, and likes to walk. They tend to initiate projects, be impulsive, instinctive, opinionated, or critical. Good at logic and research, those under Aries may be impulsive and manipulative. They may try to push their ideas on others, become easily angered but easily pleased. Aries people usually don't resort to violence.

They eat quickly and sparingly, like vegetables and spicy food. They often have round eyes, weak knees, a slightly copper complexion, and prominent veins.

Taurus

Taurus is an earth sign and fixed in nature. It is ruled by Venus, and is symbolized by the bull. It represents the laboring class.

Taurus people may be artistic, lucky, stubborn, productive, and prosperous. They may work hard and be willing to sacrifice. They tend to have good memories, communicate well, and be poetic. They tend to acquire, maintain, and improve.

They tend to enjoy comfort and luxury. They become angry slowly, but are also slow to forgive. They may be cruel to those outside their circle of influence and tend to be sentimental. They often have more daughters than sons. They maintain permanent friendships.

A Taurean may be a businessman, banker, or property owner. They tend to consider marriage important and have happy family lives. Romantic and devotional, they believe in true love. They may be good at agricultural, and own cattle.

Taureans often have a pleasant appearance, with a broad face and thighs. They tend to be attractive and like to decorate themselves. They often have a good digestion.

Gemini

Gemini is an air sign ruled by Mercury and symbolized by two lovers. It represents the vaisyas or merchants. Geminis often prefer to stay indoors.

Geminis are often skillful at a variety of things, and are learned, talkative, jovial, nervous, and restless. They are quick thinkers and speak nicely. They can often understand people's intentions. Sometimes they can become fixed on an idea and can pursue it even if no conclusion is in sight. They are often changeable and indecisive.

Geminis enjoy food, singing, and dancing. They may be attached to many women, and can be sexually oriented. They tend to marry more than once or have several partners. They may make improper and useless friends. They can be tricky.

Because they are intelligent and well-spoken, they tend to become writers, computer programmers, scientists, or secretaries. They are often good ambassadors and skilled artisans. They often work too hard and exhaust themselves.

They tend to have an attractive appearance, curly hair, dark eyes, and a prominent nose.

Cancer

Cancer is a watery sign and is movable. The Moon rules Cancer. Its symbol is the crab, and people influenced by Cancer prefer to live near water. Cancer is represented by the brahminical or spiritual nature. They enjoy astrology and may even become astrologers. Their fortunes often change.

Cancers are often emotional, intelligent, popular, sympathetic, gentle, and have sensitive natures. They like to have intimate and personal exchanges of feelings. They may be defensive or cowardly. When fixed on a project, they often have confidence and initiative. They also usually have good imaginations. They are easily persuaded by women. They tend to complain.

They tend to be of a shorter stature and to have broad waists and wide necks.

They have many friends, and people tend to visit them. They like to cook and take care of visitors. Cancer people understand the public and can use this skill in politics and to gain recognition. They love their countries and societies, and usually own houses. They usually have few sons.

Leo

Leo is a fire sign and represents the military nature. It is fixed in nature. Leos are noble, and like sunny, forested, and mountainous places. Leo is symbolized by the lion, which represents heroism. It is ruled by the Sun.

Leos are often leaders, have notable appearances, endurance, and are showmen. They tend to be heroic, courageous, ambitious, brave, determined, noble, proud, and to prevail over others. They enjoy recognition, attention, respect, and honor, and they like to have a high social position. They often have good character.

They can also become easily angered, and their anger is not easily pacified. They take things personally and may overreact. They like to talk about themselves and to be the center of attention. They may dominate others. They have high opinions of themselves, and if they do not come up to their own standards, they may become depressed.

Leos are often their mother's favorites. They often do not give their children enough independence, which may harm their relationships with their children. They often do not make good partners. They may try to subordinate their partners.

They often have large faces, prominent chins, yellowish eyeballs, and may have teeth problems.

Virgo

Virgo is an earth, worker, and feminine sign. Its symbol is the virgin, which represents purity. It is ruled by Mercury, and is the negative sign of Mercury.

Virgos tend to be able to express themselves well, be humorous, and give attention to detail. They are happy, orderly, comfortable, shy (especially when young), religious, clean, truthful, intelligent, have good memories, and possess a good command of language. They usually get the facts straight. Their knowledge is usually practical and not theoretical. They may be philosophical and live in foreign countries.

They tend to be good at arts and crafts as they have a good sense of detail. They may be good teachers, doctors, and healers. They may be good at hatha-yoga, and they often make good athletes. Because they can discipline their expression and project emotion, they also make good actors. Being good workers, they may tend to overwork.

Because they have changeable minds, they can become neurotic. They may suffer from nervous disorders. Shoulders and arms tend to droop.

They may gain pleasure from the wealth of others, and they often have more daughters than sons.

Libra

Libra is an air sign. It is a movable, merchant sign ruled by Venus, and is the positive sign of Venus. Its symbol is the scale, which signifies justice and balance in life.

Libras tend to be successful in a partnership.

Libra people have good judgment, can examine things properly, and can judge things fairly. They believe in justice, truth, and harmony. They tend to be intelligent, religious, wealthy, clean, to like beauty, and to live a good life. They may be active and enjoy travel. They may also be fanatical and idealistic.

Libras may enjoy fame, recognition, and like an audience. They are often political, and can influence the masses. Therefore, they can be leaders, generals, revolutionaries, prophets, and reformers. They prefer administrative positions, where they can control others. In business they are good at buying and selling. Their wealth and status tends to increase only at the end of life. They are often successful because they are sociable.

They are often attractive with tall, lean bodies. They may have prominent noses. They may also tend to have health problems, but they recover quickly. The problems are often in their arms and legs.

Scorpio

Scorpio is a water sign. A brahminical or spiritual sign, it is fixed in nature. Its symbol is a scorpion. Scorpio is ruled by Mars, and is the negative sign of Mars.

Person's ruled by Scorpio often desire excitement, are passionate, and have a good position in life. They may be intense, introverted, secretive, and sexually attached. They may work to overcome negative forces and be respected by the government. They may experience the loss of their father or other elders early in life.

They are often policemen, soldiers, and athletes. They can often use force and sometimes can be cruel. They may also become violent, and may become criminals or deal with vices.

They are often intelligent. They do not usually like to show what they are thinking. They tend to be good public speakers and debators. They may be good artists, poets, or actors, because they can express their sentiments and emotions. They tend to be good at research and investigation, and may be surgeons or chemists.

They often have a broad chest, big eyes, and round thighs, calves, and knees. They like to exercise and are often muscular. They tend to be sick when they are children.

Sagittarius

Sagittarius is a fire sign and a sign for the ksatriyas or warrior caste. It is ruled by Jupiter, which represents those seeking a higher goal in life. It is the positive sign of Jupiter. Its symbol is the archer, which indicates vigor and the ambition to complete a goal.

Sagittarius people are often religious, good speakers, friendly, dramatic, enthusiastic, philosophical, and active workers. They often have a positive viewpoint about life. They believe in law and justice, and are willing to sacrifice for others. They can be brought around by persuasion, but not by force. They love nature and the outdoors. They like to have a good time, but may overdo it. They may not be able to settle down easily.

On the negative side, they may be too moralistic or self-righteous. They may not get along well with relatives. They may also be too critical.

They tend to be lawyers, businessmen, religious leaders, or athletes. Things often come easy for them, and they may receive an inheritance.

They tend to have large heads and necks, prominent noses and ears, bent shoulders, big teeth, and bad nails.

Capricorn

Capricorn is an earth sign. It is ruled by Saturn, and is the negative sign of Saturn. Its symbol is the crocodile. It is a movable sign, a sign for laborers.

Capricorns are often committed and slow-moving. They will often work for themselves, and are ambitious, resolute, affluent, hardworking, fortunate, have strong stamina, and are willing to take good advice. Therefore they can often accomplish great tasks. They may start a task slowly, overcome obstacles, and attain long-range success.

The negative effects of Capricorn are that they may take themselves too seriously, be lazy, cruel, shameless, and have narrow goals.

In reference to accomplishment, a Capricorn person can reach the lowest or highest levels. They may be farmers or businessmen who invest for the future.

They often have good eyes, thin waists, and more developed lower bodies. Often they do not like cold weather.

Aquarius

Aquarius is an air sign ruled by Saturn, and is the positive sign of Saturn.

Its symbol is a woman carrying a water pot, which indicates that a person under its influence is carrying a heavy burden or serves others.

Aquarius people have pleasant, scattered, unstable, eccentric personalities. They enjoy pleasant fragrances and flowers. They can work hard, but their fortunes often come and go. They are not usually wealthy, but put their money to good use. They may work for others, be humanitarians, and protect the oppressed and troubled. They may also take long, hard journeys.

They are often interested in mystical things. Because they have faith and devotion they can be successful as teachers or religious leaders. They are not usually good political leaders because they lack charisma.

They may not protest wrongdoings aimed at them. They may accept subservient positions and be influenced by their peers. They often do what they have been advised against doing, and do not avoid negative people, which may cause them harm.

Aquarius people often have large bodies, large ears with hair in them, and rough body hair. They tend to have bodies shaped like pitchers and have prominent veins.

Pisces

Pisces is a water and brahminical or spiritual sign. It is ruled by Jupiter, and is the negative sign of Jupiter. Its symbol is two fish swimming in opposite directions.

Some attributes of Pisces: enthusiasm, compassion, education, gratitude, emotion, and intuitive. They are often imaginative, but may need to control it. They tend to engage in sacrifice and ceremony. Pisces are often friendly and communicative, and relate well with other people. They like good clothes and often drink large amounts of water. They enjoy music, and can be good musicians. They may get wealth without much effort, sometimes by transporting goods overseas.

They are not usually good leaders, but can be good followers or promoters. They like to influence others, but are just as easily influenced themselves. They are impressionable and often sentimental, moved easily by emotion regardless of whether or not it is genuine. They are also sympathetic. They often lack good discrimination.

Pisceans may have problems with intoxication, sugar addiction, indecision, and lack initiative or self-confidence. They are often attached to their spouses, and can come easily under their influence. They may suffer from emotional disorders, because Pisces is a mutable and emotional sign.

They often have beautiful eyes, attractive bodies, large heads, proportionate limbs, and prominent noses. Their digestion and nervous systems may be weak.

Twelve Houses

Each house signifies certain events, characteristics, matters and occurrences in a person's life. By studying the twelve houses, an astrologer can understand a person's destiny in the various areas of life.

After the ascendant is ascertained, then the order of the houses is known. The ascendant is always located in the first house; the rest of the houses proceed around the twelve signs of the zodiac.

The houses and signs are basically the same, but the signs always begin with Aries, whereas the houses always begin with the ascendant. If we say that a planet is in the first sign, it is in Aries, Virgo is the sixth sign, and Pisces the twelfth. In reference to the houses, if the ascendant is in Virgo (the sixth sign), Virgo would be the first house, Aries would be the seventh, and Leo would be the twelfth.

There is a difference between South and North Indian astrological systems concerning what the different houses rule. For example, education is ruled by the fourth house in the South and the fifth house in the North. In the South Indian system, the father is ruled by the ninth house and in the North by the tenth house.

The two most important things to consider when reading a chart are the houses and the position of the planets. For example, to understand a person's marital position, both the seventh house and Venus's placement are examined. To understand a person's intelligence, an astrologer will examine both the fifth house and Mercury. By understanding the nature of planets, houses, and signs—and how they combine, it is possible to interpret a chart. Aside from these major points, astrologers also examine the various planetary aspects, the lords of each house, etc.

Significance of the Twelve Houses

First House—bodily appearance, build, health, head, mentality, personality, character, childhood, environment, self, general life direction, and the horoscope as a whole.

Second House—property, wealth, finances, vision, family, source of death, speech, food, optimism, philosophical understanding, dealing with gems, eating habits, writing ability, face, right eye, and upper throat.

Third House—brothers, sisters, cousins, heroism, determination, communication ability, writing, intelligence, arms, shoulders, and lower throat.

Fourth House—mother, friends, education, home life, general happiness, land and properties, vehicles, residential house, inherited properties, transportation, education, inner feelings, heart, chest, breasts, shoulders, and neck.

Fifth House—fame, children, son, daughter, grandfather, intelligence, sports, quality as student, romantic life, entertainment, past birth, prayer tendencies, emotions, and stomach.

Sixth House—enemies, uncles, deity worship, diseases, misery, debts, distress, disappointments, foreign countries, and navel area.

Seventh House—death, spouse, partner, marriage, marital happiness, diplomacy, sexual relationship, sexual disease, business, business partner, public dealings, energy, general happiness, short journeys, and talent.

Eighth House—longevity, delays, gifts, unearned wealth, legacies, inheritance, death, cause of death, disgrace, fear, things buried in the ground, problems, money from death, money loaning, psychological position, previous and future births, legacies, genitals, anus, and excretory system.

Ninth House—God, guru, father (South Indian system), grandchildren, religion, righteousness, charity, fame, piety, travel, shipping goods, general prosperity or affluence, all-around happiness in life, government, family, long journeys, leadership, religion, hips, and thighs. This is an important house because it rules over a person's *dharma* or religious position. A strong ninth house gives a person great fortune, while an afflicted ninth house does the opposite.

Tenth House—karma, father (North Indian system), occupation, profession, self-respect, social status, economic development, reputation, dignity, philosophical knowledge, foreign travel, honor from government, temporary honor, activity, back, and knees.

Eleventh House—profit, elder brother, friends, house of gain, freedom from misery, capability to influence people, income, pets, enjoyments, sense enjoyment, calves. An afflicted eleventh house may cause the loss of brothers, friends, wealth, and may bring unhappiness and bad news.

Twelfth House—liberation, loss, expenditure, confinement, transcendental knowledge, spiritual renunciation, extravagance, waste, afterlife, sleep, dream life, sympathy, teeth, left eye, feet, and sexual enjoyment.

Constellations

The constellations or stellar points are used to identify particular points on the zodiac. Each constellation has a certain character that makes it appropriate for the performance of certain activities. There are millions of stars in the sky, but the constellations that are of interest are located on the zodiac, along the ecliptic. The ecliptic, or zodiac, has twenty-seven constellations that are used for astrological purposes. There are many more constellations than these twenty-seven, but they are not used for predictive purposes. Ptolemy and other ancient astrologers listed the constellations.

The constellations are divided into 13 1/3 (13°20') degrees of longitude, beginning at 0° Aries. The constellations are different sizes, but they are all considered to be 13° 20' for predictive purposes. This number is arrived at by dividing 360° by 27, the number of constellations.

The beginning point of both constellations and signs is the 0° longitude of Aries. By knowing the planets' longitude, an astrologer can calculate in which constellations they are located. Different constellations are considered auspicious for different purposes. Some are good for beginning journeys, some for marriages, some for elections, some for waging war. The shape of the constellation is not important in calculating predictions, but the shape does help identify the constellations' position in the sky.

Constellations	Degree Minute	Degree Minute	Shape	Number Of Stars	Lord
1. Ashwini	0-0	13-20	face of a horse	3	Ketu
2. Bharani	13-20	26-40	yoni	3	Venus
3. Krittika	26-40	40-0	curved	6	Sun
4. Rohini	40-0	53-20	cart	5	Moon
5. Mrigashira	53-20	66-40	deer face	3	Mars
6. Ardra	66-40	80-0	jewel	1	Rahu
7. Punarvasu	80-0	93-20	house	4	Jupiter
8. Pushya	93-20	106-40	arrow	3	Saturn
9. Ashlesha	106-40	120-0	circular	5	Mercury
10. Magha	120-0	133-20	house	5	Ketu
11. Purva Phalguni	133-20	146-40	raised seat	2	Venus
12. Uttara Phalguni	146-40	160-0	small cot	2	Sun
13. Hasta	160-0	173-20	hand	1	Moon
14. Chitra	173-20	186-40	pearl	1	Mars
15. Swati	186-40	200-0	coral	1	Rahu
16. Vishakha	200-0	213-20	arched doorway	4	Jupiter
17. Anuradha	213-20	226-40	wrinkle	4	Saturn
18. Jyeshtha	226-40	240-0	circular earring	4	Mercury
19. Mula	240-0	253-20	lion's tail	3	Ketu
20. Purva Shadha	253-20	266-40	elephant tusk	11	Venus
21. Uttara Shadha	266-40	280-0	raised seat	2	Sun
22. Shravana	280-0	293-20	airplane	3	Moon
23. Dhanishtha	293-20	306-40	*mridanga*	4	Mars
24. Shatabhisha	306-40	320-0	elliptic	100	Rahu
25. Purva Bhadra	320-0	333-20	raised seat	2	Jupiter
26. Uttara Bhadra	333-20	346-40	twins	2	Saturn
27. Revati	346-40	360-0	a type of drum	32	Mercury

Signs	Constellations in the Signs
1. Aries	Ashwini, Bharani, ¼ Krittika
2. Taurus	¾ Krittika, Rohini, ½ Mrigashira
3. Gemini	½ Mrigashira, Ardra, ¾ Punarvasu
4. Cancer	¼ Punarvasu, Pushya, Ashlesha
5. Leo	Magha, Purva Phalguni, ¼ Uttara Phalguni
6. Virgo	¾ Uttara Phalguni, Hasta, ½ Chitra
7. Libra	½ Chitra, Swati, ¾ Vishakha
8. Scorpio	¼ Vishakha, Anuradha, Jyeshtha
9. Sagittarius	Mula, Purva Shadha, ¼ Uttara Shadha
10. Capricorn	¾ Uttara Shadha, Shravana, ½ Dhanishtha
11. Aquarius	½ Dhanishtha, Shatabhisha, ¾ Purva Bhadra
12. Pisces	¼ Purva Bhadra, Uttara Bhadra, Revati

Lunar and Solar Year and Month

There are twelve lunar ("moon") months in a year. A lunar month is calculated by the time it takes the Moon to travel through all twelve signs of the zodiac, or from full moon to full moon. The Moon is the quickest moving planet. A solar ("Sun") month lasts thirty to thirty-one days, and is calculated by the time it takes the Sun to move through one sign of the zodiac.

The Moon's placement at birth is considered important. In popular astrology columns in Indian newspapers, predictions are made by the Moon's placement at the time of birth. Western newspapers base their predictions on the Sun's position.

There are thirty lunar days, or *tithis,* in a lunar month. The average lunar month lasts twenty-nine days, twelve hours, and forty-four minutes. A tithi is a lunar day. The period extending from the new moon to the full moon is called Shukla Paksha, the bright fortnight of the lunar month. It lasts fourteen days. The fifteenth *tithi* is called Purnima, full moon. The period that extends from the full Moon to the new moon is called Krishna Paksha, the dark fortnight of the lunar month, and it also last fourteen days. The thirtieth *tithi* is called Amavasya, new or dark moon.

The fourteen names for lunar days are listed below. They are used both for dark and bright halves of the lunar month. Since the fourteen names are used for both halves of the lunar month, each *tithi* is also labeled with "Shukla" or "Krishna": Shukla Pratipat for the first day of the bright half of the month, and Krishna Pratipat for the first day of the dark half of the month.

When the Moon waxes, it becomes fuller, and when it wanes, it becomes dark. Therefore the period of the waxing Moon happens when the moon grows from new moon to full moon. Similarly, the period of the waning moon takes place when the full moon gradually shrinks to the new moon.

The lunar year lasts about 354 days, and the sidereal year lasts about 365 days, 6 hours. Because there is a difference between the two years, Vedic astrologers add an extra month every three years. This extra month is known as Adhika-masa.

Hindu Tithis (Days)

1. Pratipat
2. Dwiteya
3. Tritya
4. Chaturthi
5. Panchami
6. Shashthi
7. Saptami
8. Ashtami
9. Navami
10. Dashami
11. Ekadashi
12. Dwadasi
13. Trayodashi
14. Chaturdashi

Influence of the Planets

Different planets have different influences on a person's chart. Benefic planets tend to bring good influence, although they can also sometimes bring harm. Benefic planets usually elevate, increase, further, expand or bring the fulfillment of the effects of the signs, planets, and houses they influence.

Malefic planets usually have a negative influence on a person's chart, although sometimes their influence can be lessened. Malefic planets usually impede, decrease, harm, destroy, limit, or ruin the effects of the signs, planets, and houses they influence. They can cause disease, delay, poverty, pain, difficulty, separation, and conflict.

A natural benefic can sometimes become a malefic. For example, Jupiter can become a malefic if it is the lord of an angle. A natural malefic can also become a benefic if it is the lord of an angle *(kendra)*.

The Moon is usually a benefic. It is strongly benefic if it is almost full. It is more benefic when waxing. It is strongly malefic when it is dark in nature and near the Sun. It is more malefic when waning. Some authorities say it is malefic when it is within 72 degrees of the Sun; others say it is malefic if it is within 60 degrees of the Sun. If the Moon is well aspected and in a good sign, however, it can be benefic even when it is situated close to the Sun.

Natural Tendencies of Planets

Benefic		Malefic	
Great	Jupiter	Great	Saturn & Rahu
Good	Venus	Good	Mars & Ketu
Medium	Moon & Mercury	Medium	Sun

The natural benefics are Jupiter, Venus, the bright Moon, and Mercury (when it is not under the influence of a malefic). The natural malefics are the Sun, Mars, Saturn, Rahu, Ketu, and the waning Moon. Some authorities believe that the Sun is not a natural malefic. Whether a planet is a benefic or malefic can change depending on which sign the *lagna* (ascendant) tenants.

Positive Effect
1. A benefic planet in exaltation or in its own house has fully good effects.
2. A benefic planet in a friend's house has three-fourth good effects.
3. A benefic planet in an enemy's house has half good effects.
4. A benefic planet in debilitation has one-fourth good effects.

Negative Effect
1. A malefic planet in exaltation or its own house has one-fourth of the bad effects.
2. A malefic planet in a friend's house has half the bad effects.
3. A malefic planet in an enemy's house has three-fourth of the bad effects.
4. A malefic planet in debilitation has fully bad effects.

Relationships between Planets

Relationships between planets can either be permanent or temporary. If a planet does not counteract the rays of another planet, they are considered friends. Planets found in the 2nd, 3rd, 4th, 10th, 11th, and 12th houses from another planet become that planet's temporary friends. The planets in the other signs (1st, 5th, 6th, 7th, 8th, and 9th houses) from a planet become temporary enemies.

To discover the strength of the influence, combine a planet's temporary influence with its permanent relationship. If a permanent enemy is also a temporary enemy, expect the effect to be strongly inimical.

There are two basic categories of friend: the Sun, Moon, Mars, and Jupiter are usually friends, and Saturn, Mercury, and Venus are usually friends. Planets in each category are usually enemies with planets in the

1. A permanent friend with a temporary friend creates a strong friendship.
2. A permanent friend with a temporary enemy is neutral.
3. A permanent enemy with a temporary friend is neutral.
4. A friend in one and neutral in the other is a friend.
5. A permanent enemy and a temporary enemy creates a strong enemy.
6. A neutral in one and an enemy in the other is an enemy.

Table of Friend and Enemy Planets

Planet (Graha)	Friend (Mitra)	Neutral (Sama)	Enemy (Satru)
Sun	Moon, Mars, Jupiter	Mercury	Venus, Saturn
Moon	Sun, Mercury	Venus, Mars, Jupiter, Saturn	None
Mercury	Sun, Venus	Mars, Jupiter, Saturn	Moon
Venus	Mercury, Saturn	Mars, Jupiter	Sun, Moon
Mars	Sun, Moon, Jupiter	Venus, Saturn	Mercury
Jupiter	Sun, Moon, Mars	Saturn	Mercury, Venus
Saturn	Mercury, Venus	Jupiter	Sun, Moon, Mars
Rahu & Ketu	Mercury, Venus, Saturn	Mars	Sun, Moon, Jupiter

Relationship Between Planets and Signs

There are four types of relationships between planets and signs: ownership (ruler), exaltation, debilitation, and moolatrikona.

Ownership

The Sun rules Leo; the Moon rules Cancer; Mars rules Aries and Scorpio; Mercury rules Gemini and Virgo; Venus rules Libra and Taurus; Jupiter rules Pisces and Sagittarius; and Saturn rules Aquarius and Capricorn.

A planet located in its own sign has a powerful and benefic influence. The ownership of a good or bad house can modify the natural good or bad effect a planet may have. Natural benefics, such as Jupiter, the Moon, or Venus, can be transformed into malefics if they own bad houses.

Some authorities on Vedic astrology do not assign ownership of a sign to Rahu or Ketu. Other authorities, however, say that these subtle planets represent the lords of the sign in which they are located.

Exaltation

A planet is exalted when it is in a particular sign. When a planet is exalted, it has a greater influence to do good than when it is in its own sign. When a planet is at a particular point in that sign that makes it exalted, it is said to be at its maximum exaltation. When an exalted planet is in retrograde motion, however, it usually brings inauspicious results.

Debilitation

When a planet is debilitated, it brings the opposite result of an exalted planet. Astrologers find the point of debilitation by adding 180° to the point of exaltation.

The seventh sign from an exalted sign is a debilitated sign.

Moolatrikonas

A moolatrikona is a favorable position for the planets. A planet in Moolatrikonas is considered to be strong and positive and in a better position than if it were in its own sign. This placement, however, is not as powerful as exaltation.

Some authorities say the Moolatrikonas are slightly different than in the chart below. Rather than the ones listed below they say they are instead: Sun–Leo 0° to 20°; Moon–Taurus 4° to 20°; Mars–Aries 0° to 12°.

Planet	Sign of Exaltation	Degree of Highest Exaltation	Sign of Debilitation	Degree Greatest Debilitation	Moolatrikonas
Sun	Aries	10°	Libra	10°	Leo 0°-10°
Moon	Taurus	3°	Scorpio	3°	Taurus 4°-30°
Mars	Capricorn	28°	Cancer	28°	Aries 0°-10°
Mercury	Virgo	15°	Pisces	15°	Virgo 16°-20°
Jupiter	Cancer	5°	Capricorn	5°	Sagittarius 0°-10°
Venus	Pisces	27°	Virgo	27°	Libra 0°-15°
Saturn	Libra	20°	Aries	20°	Aquarius 0°-20°
Rahu	Taurus			Scorpio	
Ketu	Scorpio			Leo	

Different Angles

The planets in *trines* are very strong, in angles are usually strong, in succeedents are fairly strong, and in *cadents* totally weak.

Kendras (angles or quadrants) are the 4th, 7th, and 10th houses.
Panaparas (succeedent houses) are the 2nd, 8th, and 11th houses.
Trikonas (trines) are the 1st, 5th, and 9th houses.
Apoklimas (cadent houses) are the 3rd, 6th, and 12th houses.

Planetary Avasthas

An *avastha* is the state of existence planets experience when they occupy a position in a chart.

Deeptha or exaltation–respect for elders, wealth, good children, gains.
Swastha or own house–happiness, fame, position, land.
Santha or auspicious divisions–happiness, strength, courage.
Muditha or friendly house–happiness, pleasure, good wife.
Sakta or retrogression–reputation, courage, wealth.
Peedya or residence in the last quarter of a sign–criminal tendencies, evil nature, jail.
Bheetha or in acceleration–torture, vicious habits, loss.
Vikala or combustion–disgrace, disease, problems with children.
Deena or unfriendly house–sickness, degradation, mental problems.

Conjunction

A conjunction occurs when two planets are close together. This usually means the planets share a sign or are within 10° of one another.

Combust

When a planet is too close to the Sun, it becomes combust, or burnt up. A combust planet is weak and has no power. Therefore, planets generally have more effect if they are situated some distance from the Sun. This is especially true of the Moon, Mercury, and Venus. The Sanskrit word for combust is *"asta."*

The Moon is said to be combust if it is within 12° of the Sun; Mars is said to be combust if it is within 17° of the Sun; and Mercury is said to be combust if it is within 14° of the Sun when it is direct and 12° if it is retrograde. Jupiter is combust at 11° and Saturn at 15°. According to different authorities on astrology there can be some changes in these distances. For instance some authorities say that Venus is combust at 10° if direct (8° if retrograde), and other say it is combust if it is within 4° of the Sun.

Planetary War

Two planets within one degree of one another are considered at war. The planet with the lower longitude wins. If a benefic defeats a malefic, it is strengthened. If a malefic defeats a benefic, however, the benefic's effects weaken. This does not count for the Sun or the Moon. For the Sun, follow the rule of combust.

Drishti or Aspect

An aspect is defined as the effect a planet has on another planet when it is a particular number of houses away. If one planet aspects a house or another planet, it influences that planet or house. The planetary aspects in a chart are considered very important in judging a chart.

An aspect can be positive or negative depending on the relationship between the aspected planet and the planet that aspects it. If a planet is aspected by a benefic, it has a positive effect. The conjunction or aspect of benefics increases the good effects and decreases the bad effects. If a planet is aspected by a malefic, it will have a negative effect. The conjunctions or aspects of malefics decreases the good effects and increases the bad effects.

All planets aspect the house and planet that are in the seventh house from them. Mars, Jupiter, and Saturn also have special aspects. Mars has a full aspect on the 4th and 8th houses, Jupiter on the 5th and 9th houses, and Saturn on the 3rd and 10th houses.

For example, an astrologer will look at a chart to see the location of a particular planet. Depending upon how many houses other planets are from that planet the effect of that planet may be affected. The location of other planets in relation to the planet under study will determine what influence the planet under study carries in the chart. If a planet is seven houses away from a particular planet it will have a full or powerful influence on the planet it aspects. If a planet is aspected by another three or ten houses away the original planet will carry a 25% effect, or a much reduced effect on the aspected planet, except if that planet is aspected by Saturn. If a planet is aspected by Saturn three or ten houses away, Saturn will have full, or 100% power, in affecting that planet.

Aspects are judged differently according to the Vedic and Western systems. The Vedic system judges aspects from sign to sign; the Western system judges aspects from degree to degree.

Aspecting Planet	3rd or 10th	4th or 8th	5th or 9th	7th
Sun	25%	75%	50%	100%
Moon	25%	75%	50%	100%
Mars	25%	100%	50%	100%
Mercury	25%	75%	50%	100%
Jupiter	25%	75%	100%	100%
Venus	25%	75%	50%	100%
Saturn	100%	75%	50%	100%

Ascendant or Lagna

The ascendant *(lagna)* is the sign on the eastern horizon at the time of birth. It is called the ascendant because it literally ascends. The ascendant sign changes approximately every two hours, and all twelve signs rise within a twenty-four-hour period one after the other. The ascendant or rising sign is considered very important in Vedic astrology, just as the Sun sign is treated with importance in Western astrology.

Technically the ascendant is the exact degree on the eastern horizon, but actually the ascendant is judged to be the sign that the ascendant is in. If the ascendant is in Aries, then Aries is considered to be the ascendant.

The sign ascending at the time of birth becomes the first house in the birth chart. For example, if Leo is ascending, the first house is Leo, the second Virgo, the third Libra, and on through the other signs in order: Scorpio, **Sagittarius,** Capricorn, Aquarius, Pisces, Aries, Taurus, Gemini, and **Cancer.**

Janma Rashi (Moon Sign)

Janma Rashi is the sign *(rashi)* that the Moon is in at the time of birth *(janma)*. The Moon sign and the ascendant sign are both given great importance in a chart.

Hemming

If a planet is situated with two planets on either side of it, it is considered hemmed in. If two malefic planets hem in a benefic planet, the benefic's effects are weakened. Similarly, if two benefic planets hem in a malefic planet, the malefic's effects are weakened.

Predictions

Six sources of strength and weakness may be determined for each planet. These sources of strength can be measured numerically. A full description of these can be found in *Graha & Bhava Balas,* by B. V. Raman.

1. **Sthanabala**—the strength achieved by residing in a friendly, *moolatrikona*, exalted house or own sign in the birth horoscope, Navamsa chart, or other subdivisions.
2. **Digbala**—literally, "directional strength." The Sun and Mars receive directional strength in the 10th house. Mercury and Jupiter get strength when they are in the Ascendant. The Moon and Venus get strength in the 4th house. Saturn gets strength in the 7th house.
3. **Chestabala** or Motional Strength—the Sun and Moon get motional strength in Capricorn, Aquarius, Pisces, Aries, Taurus, and Gemini, which make up Uttarayana or the summer solstice (when the sun travels in the north). Mercury, Venus, Mars, Jupiter, and Saturn in retrogression or in conjunction with the full Moon get motional strength.
4. **Kalabala** or Temporal Strength—the Sun, Venus, and Jupiter receive strength during the day. The Moon, Mars, and Saturn receive strength during the night. Mercury is always strong. Benefics are powerful during the bright half of a lunar month. Malefics are powerful during the dark half of a lunar month. Planets are more powerful during their day, month, and years.
5. **Drukbala** or Aspect Strength—aspects of benefics gives strong aspects strength. Aspects of malefics give weak aspects strength.
6. **Naisargikabala**—each planet produces a certain strength all the time, regardless of where it is situated. The Sun is the most powerful, then the Moon, then Venus, Jupiter, Mercury, and Mars. Saturn has the least strength.

Yogas

Yoga means "link" or "connection." A planetary yoga refers to a combination of influences in a person's chart; that is, when one planet or sign is situated in relation to another by way of aspect or conjunction. Different yogas give different effects, and there are both benefic and malefic yogas. Some important benefic yogas are Raja yoga, Dhurdhura yoga, Gajakesari yoga, Shubhakartari yoga, and Pancha Mahapurusa yoga.

If there are benefics on both sides of the ascendant, this combination is known as a Subhakarthari yoga. If the ascendant is sandwiched by malefics, it is known as a Papakarthari yoga, which is malefic. Raja yogas bring fame, wealth, good name, and great power.

It is important to see whether the ascendant and its lord are powerful, well-associated, and free of malefic aspect. The Moon must similarly be examined for similar associations.

Specific Situations

The Ascendant and the strength and weakness of the Ascendant determines a native's appearance and character. If a masculine planet rules the 5th house or the house of children during conception, then a male child will be born.

Education is usually judged from the 4th house, its lord, and where Jupiter, the lord of education, is placed.

Astrology can help determine the best occupation. Occupation takes into consideration the 10th house, its lord, and the planets in the 10th house. If there are no planets in the 10th house, then an astrologer will look at the Navamsa chart to determine occupation.

The 4th house rules the mother and the 9th house the father. The indicator of the mother is the Moon; the Sun is the indicator of the father.

When dealing with marriage, look at Venus, the spouse's lord, the 7th house, and the lord of the 7th house.

Time of Special Influence of Different Planets

Each planet has it greatest influence on a person during certain periods of his or her life. Below are the time periods accepted by many authorities.

Moon	Birth to 4th year
Mercury	5th year to 14th year
Venus	15th year to 22nd year

Sun	23rd year to 41st year
Mars	42nd year to 56th year
Jupiter	57th year to 68th year
Saturn	69th year to 108th year

Age of Planets

Different planets have a greater influence on a person's life at different times in a person's life. A strong Jupiter will give a good effect in the middle age. A strong Saturn will give wealth and a good position in old age.

Mars	child (some astrologers say 16 years old)
Mercury	boy (some astrologers say 20 years old)
Venus	16 years old (some say 7 years old)
Jupiter	30 years old
Sun	50 years old
Moon	70 years old
Saturn	100 years old
Rahu	100 years old
Ketu	100 years old

Major Periods (Mahadasha) and Sub-Periods (Antardasha)

The different major periods and sub-periods help to determine when certain things will happen in a person's life. A major period is known as a Mahadasha (*maha* means "great" and *dasha* means "period"); a sub-period is known as an Antardasha. Different planets rule different major periods in a person's life.

The timing of events can be ascertained through these periods. These periods show transitions in a person's life and how we experience periodic changes in life. When a major or even minor period changes, our lives may take new directions.

During a period influenced by a negative planet, a person is more likely to go through an adverse situation. Conversely, if a positive planet is influencing a period, a person is more likely to be going through something good.

The influence of different periods may only have a relative effect. For example, if the possession of wealth is strong in the overall chart, it is unlikely that when they are in a weaker period in relation to wealth that they will suffer abject poverty. Rather, there may be some suffering in relation to finances.

Because there are nine planets, there are nine Mahadashas. Each major period is divided into sub-periods called Antardasha, and there are also nine of them in each Mahadasha. Each sub-period lasts a proportionate amount of time according to how long that planet would rule a major period. Sub-periods are further divided into minor periods (Pratyantardasha).

How to Calculate the Periods

All the Mahadashas added together make up 120 years. Few people, however, live that long, so almost no one experiences all twelve major periods.

The location of the Moon at the time of birth is taken into account when calculating the first Mahadasha. Each constellation has a lord, one of the planets. The first dasha (period) is determined by the constellation that the Moon is tenanting at the time of birth. For example, if the Moon is in the constellation Chitra, the order of the Mahadashas are Mars, Rahu, Jupiter, Saturn, Mercury, Ketu, Venus, the Sun, and the Moon. The calculation begins with Mars, because Mars rules Chitra. How long the first major period lasts is determined by how far the Moon has moved through the particular constellation it is tenanting at the time of birth.

Each sub-period begins with the planet that is lord of the Mahadasha period. The rest of the planets in a sub-period follow in the same order as the Mahadasha periods. For example, in the Mahadasha of the Sun, the first sub-period begins with the Sun. The Sun is followed by the Moon, Mars, Rahu, Jupiter, Saturn, Mercury, Ketu, and Venus.

Length of Mahadashas (Major Periods)

Lords	Years	Constellations
Sun	6	Krittika, Uttara Phalguni, Uttara Shadha
Moon	10	Rohini, Hasta, Shravana
Mars	7	Mrigashira, Chitra, Dhanishta
Rahu	18	Ardra, Swati, Shatabhishta
Jupiter	16	Punarvasu, Vishakha, Purva Bhadra
Saturn	19	Pushya, Anuradha, Uttara Bhadra
Mercury	17	Ashlesha, Jyestha, Revati
Ketu	7	Magha, Mula, Ashwini
Venus	20	Purva Phalguni, Purva Ashada, Bhari

TABLE OF SUB-PERIODS

Sun Mahadasha
6 Years

Sub-periods	Year	Month	Day
Sun	0	3	18
Moon	0	6	0
Mars	0	4	6
Rahu	0	10	24
Jupiter	0	9	18
Saturn	0	11	12
Mercury	0	10	6
Ketu	0	4	6
Venus	1	0	0

Moon Maha dasha
10 Years

Sub-periods	Years	Month	Day
Moon	0	10	0
Mars	0	7	0
Rahu	1	6	0
Jupiter	1	4	0
Saturn	1	7	0
Mercury	1	5	0
Ketu	0	7	0
Venus	1	8	0
Sun	0	6	0

Mars Maha dasha
7 Years

Sub-period	Years	Months	Days
Mars	0	4	27
Rahu	1	0	18
Jupiter	0	11	6
Saturn	1	1	9
Mercury	0	11	27
Ketu	0	4	27
Venus	1	2	0
Sun	0	4	6
Moon	0	7	0

Rahu Maha Dasha
18 Years

Sub-period	Years	Months	Days
Rahu	2	8	12
Jupiter	2	4	24
Saturn	2	10	6
Mercury	2	6	18
Ketu	1	0	18
Venus	3	0	0
Sun	0	10	24
Moon	1	6	0
Mars	1	0	18

Jupiter Maha Dasha
16 Years

Sub-period	Years	Months	Days
Jupiter	2	1	18
Saturn	2	6	12
Mercury	2	3	6
Ketu	0	11	6
Venus	2	8	0
Sun	0	9	18
Moon	1	4	0
Mars	0	11	6
Rahu	2	4	24

Saturn Maha Dasha
19 years

Sub-period	Years	Months	Days
Saturn	3	0	3
Mercury	2	8	9
Ketu	1	1	9
Venus	3	2	0
Sun	0	11	12
Moon	1	7	0
Mars	1	1	9
Rahu	2	10	6
Jupiter	2	6	12

Mercury Maha Dasha
17 years

Sub-period	Years	Months	Days
Mercury	2	4	27
Ketu	0	11	27
Venus	2	10	0
Sun	0	10	6
Moon	1	5	0
Mars	0	11	27
Rahu	2	6	18
Jupiter	2	3	6
Saturn	2	8	9

Ketu Maha Dasha
8 Years

Sub-period	Years	Months	Days
Ketu	0	4	27
Venus	1	2	0
Sun	0	4	6
Moon	0	7	0
Mars	0	4	27
Rahu	1	0	18
Jupiter	0	11	16
Saturn	1	1	9
Mercury	0	11	27

Venus Maha Dasha
20 Years

Sub-period	Years	Months	Days
Venus	3	4	0
Sun	1	0	0
Moon	1	8	0
Mars	1	2	0
Rahu	3	0	0
Jupiter	2	8	0
Saturn	3	2	0
Mercury	2	10	0
Ketu	1	2	0

Harmonic and Navamsa Chart

A harmonic chart is drawn when each sign is divided into various divisions or "*amsas.*" In Vedic astrology, two charts are usually done, the birth chart (Rashi Cakra) and the Navamsa or Harmonic Ninth. There are sixteen major Harmonic or *amsa* charts, but the Navamsa is usually considered the most important. Astrologers usually place the main consideration on the birth chart and give extra consideration to the Navamsa chart.

Navamsa means "ninth part." A Navamsa chart divides a sign into nine equal divisions of 3° 20'. A Navamsa chart identifies in what part of a sign a planet is located, and whether its position is positive or negative. Each navamsa is a pada, or one-fourth of a constellation. Each sign contains 2¼ constellations. Divided into nine, it makes up one-fourth of a constellation.

The Navamsa chart can be used like the birth chart to read a person's entire life. The Navamsa chart is often used to determine marriage and relationships. By doing a couple's Navamsa chart, material and spiritual compatibility can be determined. A person's spiritual life can also be determined. If a planet is in the same sign in both the birth and Navamsa chart, it is strong, whether for the positive or negative.

Besides the Navamsa chart, other harmonic charts may be calculated, such as the Harmonic First, Second, Third, Fourth, Seventh, Tenth, Twelfth, Sixteenth, Twentieth, Twenty-fourth, Twenty-seventh, Thirtieth, Fortieth, Forty-fifth, and Sixtieth. The most important are the ninth, third, twelfth, twentieth, twenty-fourth, twenty-seventh, and thirtieth. Sometimes seven or even sixteen harmonic charts can be drawn.

As doing harmonic charts can be time-consuming, it is best to use a computer to do the calculations.

When doing a Navamsa chart, the Ascendant's placement is important. Because of the subtle differences possible if a birth time is not entirely accurate, it is best not to rely on the Navamsa chart for the most reliable reading. If the birth time is even ten minutes off, the Ascendant's position can change. A chart drawn with a wrong Ascendant is useless.

Transits or Movement of the Planets

The transit of a planet consists of its movement through the signs of the zodiac. Because of different cosmic influences, the speed of the planets change. The planets usually move through the signs and constellations in a forward motion, but sometime they seem to move in reverse or retrograde. For example, if the Sun is in Virgo, it is said that the Sun is transiting Virgo. The speed of each planet gets slower as their distance from the earth increases. As the planets move through different signs, they have different effects. The transits of the Sun, Moon, Jupiter, and Saturn are considered to be the most important.

1. The Sun moves about one degree in one day, and takes about 365 days and six hours to travel around the zodiac. The Sun spends about a month in each sign.
2. The Moon takes about one hour forty-eight minutes to go one degree of the zodiac. The Moon completes a cycle of the zodiac in twenty-seven to twenty-nine days.
3. Mars takes about one and half days to go one degree of the zodiac, or forty-five days to travel thirty degrees.
4. Mercury spends about one month in each sign. Since Mercury is always close to the Sun, Mercury's speed changes frequently. Sometimes Mercury moves in front of the Sun, and sometimes the Sun moves in front of Mercury. Mercury is never more than twenty-eight degrees in either direction of the Sun.
5. Jupiter stays in most signs for about a year, but stays in some signs for less than a year. Jupiter completes a cycle of the zodiac in about twelve years. Because Jupiter spends a long time in each sign, it is quite influential.
6. Venus spends about a month in each sign. Venus moves about one degree a day, or takes about 360 days to travel around the zodiac.
7. Saturn takes about 2½ years, or thirty months to travel thirty degrees, or one sign of the zodiac. Saturn takes about one month to move one degree of the zodiac. Saturn spends about two and a half years in each sign, or about thirty years to travel through all the signs of the zodiac. The transit of Saturn in a chart is usually unfavorable, unless it is transiting its own house or it is the lord of the ascendant when Capricorn or Aquarius is rising. When Saturn passes through the 12th, 1st, and 2nd houses, the native is generally considered to be in a bad period and should not expect peace of mind. This period lasts for 7½ years and is called Sadhe Sati, which literally means "seven and a half years."
8. Rahu and Ketu move in a reverse direction and take eighteen years to travel around the zodiac.

Times the Planets Spend in each Sign

Sun	1 month
Moon	2¼ days
Mars	45 days

Mercury	around 1 month
Jupiter	1 year
Venus	1 month
Saturn	2¼ years
Rahu	1½ years
Ketu	1½ years

Retrograde Motion

Retrograde is when a planet appears to move in a reverse or backward direction. Rahu and Ketu always move in a retrograde motion. The Sun and the Moon never move in a retrograde motion. The other planets sometimes go forward, sometimes backward, and sometimes remain stationery.

The planets become retrograde when they are a particular distance from the Sun. Otherwise, they move in a forward direction. It is said that the planets never actually go backward but only appear to do so when seen relative to the earth.

Judgment of a Horoscope

Many things are taken into consideration when judging a horoscope. At least two major charts are done, the birth and Navamsa charts, but other harmonic charts can also be done. Certain things should be examined when doing a horoscope: the native's age, sex, status, position, place of residence, and culture.

The position of the planets and their relationship to one another has to be considered. To judge certain things, often several houses have to be considered. To see what will happen to the native's children, an astrologer would examine the 5th house (the house for children), and also the 2nd, 7th, and 10th houses. For health, an astrologer will examine the 6th, 8th, and 11th houses. For material pleasure, the 4th, 7th, and 12th houses should be examined. To judge wealth, examine the 2nd house, which is for accumulated wealth, the 4th house for immovable property, the 8th, the 9th for prosperity, and the 11th for income.

Things to be Taken Into Consideration

1. The position of the Lagna (Ascendant or rising sign), and the lord of the rising sign in both the birth and Navamsa charts are the first things to be examined. For example, if Leo is on the ascendant, an astrologer will look at the Sun's position, which is Leo's Lord. If the Sun is in a sign of exaltation, its own sign, in the sign of a friend, or a trine, it will have a

beneficial effect.

2. Where the Moon is situated at the time of birth is considered important in Vedic astrology. If the Moon is in Leo, the sign ruled by the Sun, then the sign and house position of the Sun is also taken into consideration. A different planet rules each of the constellations. The ruler of the constellation in which the Moon is tenanting at the time of birth will affect the native.

3. The general placement of planets and how each of them is aspected by other planets.

4. The strengths, conjunctions, aspects, and the position of the lord of the house are all important.

5. Whether a planet is exalted or debilitated affects the chart.

6. If any planet is in moolatrikona or trine.

7. A planet in a friendly sign will have a beneficial effect.

8. Each house has to be taken into consideration.
   a. The house, its lords, what planets are in particular houses.
   b. Their *karakas* or indicators.
   c. If the lord of a house is friendly, an enemy, neutral, exalted, or debilitated.
   d. The position of the *karakas* or indicators of each house.
   e. The strengths, conjunctions, and aspects of the lords of the houses.
   f. Exaltations or debilitations of the lords of the houses.
   g. Planets in the various houses.
   h. Whether any yogas influence the houses.

9. The Mahadasha periods and the sub-periods.

10. The placement of the planet ruling the Mahadasha.

11. Ownership of the sign. A planet in its own sign will have a beneficial effect.

Marriage Selection

In India, an astrological chart is almost always drawn up to arrange compatible marriages. After compatibility has been established, astrology is used to select an auspicious time and date for the marriage. The time, date, day of week, planetary positions, and constellations should be auspicious when deciding when to marry.

The lunar days considered good for marriage are the 2nd, 3rd, 5th, 7th, 10th, 11th, and 13th of the bright half of the month. Days of the week considered more auspicious are Monday, Wednesday, Thursday, and Friday.

The lunar months of Magha, Phalguna, Vishakha, and Jyestha are considered auspicious, Karttika and Margasira are considered average, and the other months are considered inauspicious. Auspicious constellations are Rohini, Margashirsa, Magha, Uttara Phalguna, Hasta, Swati, Anuradha, Mula, Uttara Shadha, and Revati.

Judgment by

1st House and Sun	character, health
2nd House and Jupiter	wealth
3rd House and Mars	skills
4th House and Moon	mother
4th House and Venus	house and car
5th House and Jupiter	children
6th House and Sun	health
6th House and Jupiter	legal affairs
7th House and Venus	marriage
7th House and Mercury	business
8th House and Saturn	longevity
9th House	religious nature
10th House and Saturn, Mars, Mercury	occupation
11th House and Jupiter and Venus	opulence
12th House	one's next life

Remedial Measures

To help alleviate the effects of weak planet, certain remedial measures can be taken. One can perform sacrifice or austerity, one can wear gems, certain colors, worship certain deities, chant mantras, change one's lifestyle, or perform other positive activities. A good remedial measure is to give in charity. If a person wants a particular effect, a particular gem can be prescribed. Also, worshipping planetary yantras can improve the effects planets have in a chart.

The planets indicate a person's karma. If a person performs spiritual activities, he or she can overcome all karmic effects and thus all planetary influences. Worshipping God overrides the effects of karma because God is more powerful than material reactions.

Potential Problems with Time of Birth

There is a difference of opinion among astrologers on what constitutes the actual time of birth. Some say birth occurs as soon as the child's head first appears from the birth canal, others say that the head must be fully out, others insist that birth has occurred when the child takes its first breath (proven by a baby's first cry), and still others say that birth has truly occurred when the umbilical cord is cut. Not knowing the exact time of birth can alter the accuracy of the birth chart, as the first house of a birth chart reveals which planet was on the ascendant (on the horizon) just at the time of birth. The planets move along the horizon every two hours.

Even knowing how to decide the exact time of birth is often not enough to draw up an accurate chart if the parents do not record the actual time right at the birth. In many hospitals, birth times are not recorded accurately but at the convenience of the doctor or nurse. They can be as much as ten or fifteen minutes off. Therefore, many birth charts are based on approximate birth times.

Different Styles of Charts in India

There are three basic chart designs in India: the North Indian style, the South Indian style, and the East Indian style.

In the North Indian style, the signs are denoted by numbers, with Aries being 1, Taurus 2, Gemini 3, and so on in order for the rest of the signs. The sign at the top center of the chart is the ascending sign; the balance of the signs go in order counter-clockwise.

The South Indian style is a square chart with twelve divisions. The sign of Aries is marked with an asterisk. The signs then go clockwise starting with Aries, then Taurus, Gemini, and the rest the signs in order. The rising sign is marked by "Asc" for ascendant or "L" for Lagna, or a diagonal line may be drawn across the sign.

The chart drawn by the East Indian system is similar. The area with an asterisk is the sign of Aries. The signs then go in order, counter-clockwise. The rising sign or ascendant is marked with an "L" for lagna. Also, numbers are written next to the planets to indicate the constellation the planet is tenanting.

Some astrologers also use the Western style chart, which is drawn in a circle. The ascending sign is on the left, and the signs go in order counter-clockwise.

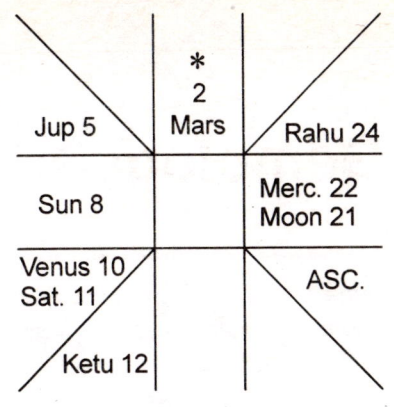

East Indian

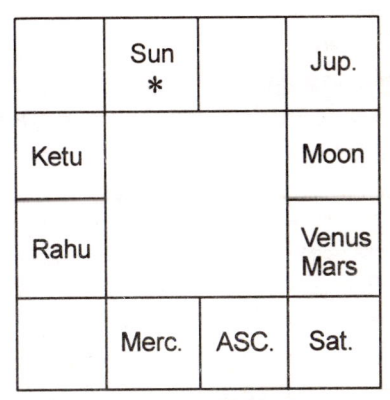

```
          *
          2
 Jup 5   Mars    Rahu 24

                 Merc. 22
 Sun 8           Moon 21

 Venus 10
 Sat. 11         ASC.

    Ketu 12
```

South Indian

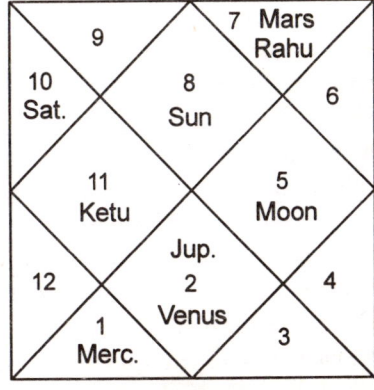

	Sun *		Jup.
Ketu			Moon
Rahu			Venus Mars
	Merc.	ASC.	Sat.

North India

```
           9          7 Mars
                        Rahu
     10         8
     Sat.       Sun        6

           11          5
           Ketu       Moon
                Jup.
     12          2          4
                Venus
             1
             Merc.      3
```

Vedic Gemology

Gems are used in Eastern astrology to avert the negative influence of various planets or to increase their positive effects. The use of gems has been mentioned in the Vedic literature—the *Brihat Samhita*, *Bhava Prakash*, *Ayurveda Prakash*, *Guruda Purana* and the *Rasa Ratna Samuchaya*. The gem therapy described in this book is based on the Vedic (Indian) or sidereal system of astrology.

Each sign of the zodiac is ruled by a planet, and each planet gives off a cosmic vibration and rules, or is related to, certain gemstones. The gems absorb or reflect the planets' vibration, or rays. Wearing the proper gem can increase a planet's positive effect on the wearer because the gem acts as a filter that allows only positive vibrations to have influence.

Gems surround their wearer with an electromagnetic field. If a person is receiving a planet's negative rays, wearing the correct gemstone can counteract those bad effects and allow only the planet's positive effects to work on the person. Wearing a gemstone to counteract the malefic effects of a planet is like carrying an umbrella to avoid getting wet; the gemstone actually deflects a planet's negative rays.

It is important to note, however, that wearing the wrong gemstone can have a negative effect on the wearer. Wearing the wrong gems short-circuits the subtle body's energy fields. Thus physical or mental problems may result. Great care should be taking when using a gemstone of a naturally malefic planet to counter act its bad effects, as instead, it may increase the bad effects of the malefic planet.

To have maximum effect, the gemstone chosen should be of good quality. The better the gem's quality, the more powerful its effect. Do not wear cracked or chipped gems, as they can have a very detrimental effect. Thoroughly inspect gems for defects before purchasing them.

The gem's size is also important. It is best that a precious stone be at least one carat; two or more carats are better. The minimum size for gems is determined by the type of gem. The less valuable the gem, the larger the stone should be to have the full effect.

It is sometimes not advised to wear gems that magnify the strength of planets already benefic to the wearer. The gem may make the planet's effect more powerful than the wearer can bear.

When choosing to wear a gemstone, it is important to consider one's overall astrological chart and to understand the synergy between the various planets. It is best to have a qualified astrologer prescribe the gem. Sometimes more than one gem will be prescribed. Gems sometimes have more effect when worn on one day than on another. To receive a gemstone's effect, the gem must actually be worn; simply owning it is not enough.

Astrological Remedial Measures

Gems help to improve the effects planets have on us. To counter the malefic effects of a planet, one can also chant planetary mantras, perform sacrifices and worship, and give charity along with wearing the gem. These other activities also increase the gemstone's effect.

In general, gemstones should be worn to strengthen weak planets as calculated by the astrological chart. It is best to strengthen benefic planets when they are weak. Care should be taken when attempting to strengthen naturally malefic planets, such as Saturn and Ketu, and gems used for this purpose should definitely be prescribed by a qualified astrologer.

Gems for Health

Gemstones can be used to cure diseases caused by afflicted planets, according to Ayurveda. To find the most effective gems for one's particular illness, one should be diagnosed and appropriate remedies prescribed by an Ayurvedic doctor. To make such medicines, the gems are powdered (*pishti*) or from the ashes (*bhasma*).

High quality gems can also be placed in a solution of diluted alcohol and set in a dark place for between twelve hours and seven days. The gemstones are then removed and the alcohol solution used as medicine. This gem tincture can be kept in storage; it does not quickly lose its potency. The gemstone itself is also reusable. To store such medicine, place it in a box the same color as the gem used. This will protect the tincture's potency. The usual dosage is about ten drops in half a cup of water, and then drunk. Some authorities believe that alcohol should not be used because it is not a pure substance.

Gems can also be tinctured in water, which is considered by some authorities to be a purest system. Place a gem in a glass of water in the sun for two to four hours or overnight. If overnight, the tincture should be drunk the next day; water tinctures quickly lose their potency.

Wearing Gems

Ideally, gems should be worn on the correct finger, should be set in the correct metal, and should be the correct weight. They will have the best effect if they are also worn on the correct day and at the correct time of day. At least the installation of the gems should be performed on the correct day, and proper mantras should be chanted when they are first put on. It is best if the gem's wearer, him or herself, chants the mantras.

It is important to clean gems before wearing them. They can be cleaned by running water over them for six to eight hours, by burying them overnight in the earth and then rinsing them with clean water in the morning, by placing them in a candle flame, or by placing them in direct sunlight. They can also be purified by being placed next to a crystal quartz.

Power of Colors

Seven colors radiate from the body: red, orange, yellow, green, blue, purple and indigo. Astrological gems are used in relation to these seven colors. Gems work by absorbing particular colors. Colors can have a subtle effect on a person's mood, situation, behavior, and destiny. Gemstones have the most condensed form of concentrated color of all elements in the world.

The colors that we wear as well as the colors we choose to paint our walls, have an effect upon us. Bright colors tend to brighten our mood, and they indicate the luxuries in and pleasures of life. Dull colors tend to make us more somber. Shades of red represent passion and energy. Light blues and light greens represent peace and calm. White represents purity, innocence, and peace. Light colors are more conducive to sound sleep; bright or dark colors can cause sleep to be restless.

Thus each gem and each planet emit particular colors and vibrations. Negative planetary vibrations can be averted, and positive planetary vibrations attracted, by wearing gems of particular colors. Gems have stronger or weaker effects depending on the color emanated and the rate of absorption. The wavelength of the red light emanating from the Sun is the same as the wavelength of the red light emanating from a ruby. Therefore, rubies can help solve afflictions arising from a weak sun in the native's birth chart.

The planets and colors are: **Sun** - Golden, dark yellow, orange; **Moon** - White; **Mars** - Red; **Mercury** - Green; **Jupiter** - Yellow; **Venus** - Rainbow; **Saturn** - Black, indigo; **Rahu** - Red, honey; **Ketu** - Purple.

Relation of the Planets

There is a gem stone that relates to each of the nine planets. These nine stones are called Navaratnas (nine gems). Five of them are categorized as Maha Ratnas, and are considered superior. These are diamond, ruby, emerald, blue sapphire, and pearl. If the better quality stones are too expensive, it is all right to wear a good quality substitute, but the higher the stone's quality, the stronger the effect.

Planet	Primary Gemstones	Secondary Gemstones	Zodiac Sign
Sun	Ruby	Red Spinel, Red Garnet, Red Zircon, Red Tourmaline	Leo
Moon	White Pearl	Moonstone	Cancer
Mars	Red Coral	Carnelian, Pink Coral, Red Jasper, Bloodstone	Aries, Scorpio
Mercury	Emerald	Green Jade, Peridot, Green Zircon, Green Tourmaline	Gemini, Virgo
Jupiter	Yellow Sapphire	Yellow Topaz, Citrine Quartz, Yellow Beryl (Heliodor)	Sagittarius, Pisces
Venus	Diamond	Clear Zircon, Quartz, Sapphire, Turquoise, White coral, White Topaz	Taurus, Libra
Saturn	Blue Sapphire	Lapis Lazuli, Amethyst Blue Spinel	Capricorn, Aquarius
Rahu	Hessonite Garnet	Golden Garnet, Orange Garnet, Spesserite, Orange Zircon	
Ketu	Chrysoberyl Cat's Eye	Other types of Cat's Eye, Tiger Eye, Beryl	

Setting in a Ring

Astrological gems are usually set either in a ring or a pendant. The gem's effect is stronger if the setting has a hole in its back by which the gemstone can actually touch the wearer's skin. Gemstones should be set in such a way as to allow light to pass through the stone into the body. Pendants are best worn over the heart or throat chakra.

Different gems should be set in different metals. Gemstones should be set in metal that naturally transmits the gem's potency. Rubies, yellow sapphires, red coral, and their substitutes should all be set in yellow gold. Diamonds, blue sapphires, emeralds, cat's eyes, and hessonites can be set either in white or yellow metals, but usually the white metals (silver, platinum, and white gold) are better. Pearls should always be set in silver, because silver has a cooling effect, which is good for the mind, while gold has a heating effect.

According to some authorities, the metals ascribed to the planets are: gold for the Sun, silver for the Moon, brass for Mercury, silver for Venus, gold for Jupiter, and iron or steel for Saturn. According to other authorities, it is copper mixed with gold for the Sun and Mars, silver for the Moon, Mercury, and Venus, gold for Jupiter, steel for Saturn, and an alloy of eight metals (Ashta Dhatu) for Ketu and Rahu. According to Western astrologers, silver is the best metal in which to set all gems.

Primary gemstones should be worn as rings or necklaces; secondary gemstones can be worn as rings, necklaces, bracelets, or earrings.

Fingers

It is best to wear primary gems as rings, so that the gem's energy can be transmitted through the finger's nerve. Each finger is governed by a specific planet, and is also related to certain parts of the body. Gemstones have more effect if they are worn on the proper fingers. If a particular gemstone is prescribed, and the planet that rules that gemstone is not related to a particular finger, then the gemstone should be worn on a finger ruled by a friend of that planet. The gem for one planet can be worn with the gem of another planet if the two planets are friendly.

For example, diamond, ruled by Venus, should be worn on the fingers of Venus's friends—the middle finger (controlled by Saturn), or the little finger (controlled by Mercury). Cat's eye and hessonite (gomedha) should be worn on the middle finger, because the planets that rule these two gemstones, Ketu and Rahu, are Saturn's friends, and Saturn controls the middle finger. Many astrologers say that the right hand is the hand for men and the left for women.

When a qualified astrologer prescribes a gem, it is important to ask him or her what finger it should be worn on.

Index finger—Jupiter controls the index finger (the finger next to the thumb). Yellow sapphire should be worn on this finger. Pearl, topaz, coral, and moonstone can also be worn on this finger. This finger relates to the stomach or respiratory system.

Middle finger—Saturn controls the middle finger. Blue sapphire, gomedha, and cat's eye should be worn on this finger. Sapphire, moonstone, and white pearl can also be worn on this finger. The middle finger relates to the brain, mind, intestines, and liver.

Ring finger—The Sun controls this finger. Ruby, pearl, moonstone, red coral, and yellow sapphire should be worn on this finger. This finger relates to the stomach, blood circulation, kidneys, and respiratory system. This finger is next to the little finger. The gems for the Moon and Mars are also worn on this finger, as both the Moon and Mars are friends with the Sun. It is also said that Mars rules the thumb, and should be worn on the thumb.

Little finger—Mercury controls this finger. Wear emerald, green jade, diamond, and zircon on this finger. It relates to the legs, feet, and genitals.

When and Where to Wear

If one wears gems to gain general good effects, they can be worn at any time, but in general the best times are in the morning (before noon) during Shukla Paksha (the bright half of the lunar month). If one is wearing a gem in order to offset the bad effects of planetary configurations, here are some suggested times as to the most effective times to wear the gems. Read the chart according to this example: for general luck, red coral should be worn within one hour of sunrise on a Tuesday, during the phase of Mars. In the list, the first finger refers to the index finger, the second finger to the middle finger, the third finger to the ring finger, and the fourth finger to the little finger.

Installation of Gems

1. First wash the gem in water (if possible Ganges water).
2. Then wash the gem in milk.
3. Then wash the gem again in water.
4. Then place the gem on an altar or sacred place before a picture of the deity of the planet that is related to the gem being installed. For instance, the gem should be placed before the deity of Surya or a *yantra* for the Sun if the planet that the gem is for is the Sun.
5. Incense should be offered.
6. The mantras for the planet should be chanted.
7. The ring should be placed on the hand.

Gemstone	Metal	Weight of Gemstone in Carats	Finger to Wear On	Auspicious Time to Wear
Ruby	Gold	2½	3rd	Sunday (4.30 pm – 6 pm)
Pearl	Silver	2	3rd	Monday (7.30 – 9 am)
Dark Red Coral	Gold	6	1st or 3rd	Tuesday (1.30 – 3 pm)
Emerald	Gold or Silver	3	4th	Wednesday (12 noon – 1.30 pm)
Diamond	Gold or Silver	1½	2nd & 4th	Friday (10.30 am -12 noon)
Yellow Sapphire	Gold	3	1st or 3rd	Thursday (3 – 4.30 pm)
Topaz	Gold	4	1st	Thursday (3 – 4.30 pm)
Blue Sapphire	Gold	4	2nd	Saturday (9 – 10.30 am)
Cat's Eye	Gold or Silver	5	2nd	Thursday 12 pm – 12 midnight
Gomedha Hessonite	Gold or Silver	6	2nd	Saturday 12 pm – 12 midnight

Testing for Positive Effect

It is usually best to test a gem before wearing it. Some gems are unlucky or not auspicious to wear, even if they are flawless. It is best to first test gems by placing them under your pillow at night, or wearing them on your arm wrapped in a cloth of the same color for three or four days. If the gem has a bad effect during the test period, it should not be worn. Blue sapphire should especially be tested, as the wrong stone can have a very negative effect.

Diamond (Hiraka)
Hardness 10, specific gravity 3.5, refractive index 2.42, dispersion 0.044.

Diamonds are the hardest substance on earth. They are four times harder than corundum (rubies and sapphires are transparent varieties of this mineral), the next hardest mineral. Diamonds can be cut because they possess cleavages. A diamond's cleavage is perfect in four directions, making it an octahedron. Diamonds have the highest refractive index of any gem. They also have one of the highest dispersions of any colorless stone; it is this dispersion that gives them the play of color known as "fire." Diamonds are 3.5 times as heavy as water, making them one of the heaviest minerals. Their optic character is singly refractive, and their crystal system is cubic.

Diamonds are composed of crystallized carbon, like graphite, the soft mineral used in pencils. What makes the difference between the two is how they bond chemically—the chemical bonding in diamonds is strong, in graphite, weak.

Nowadays, diamonds are most often found in Australia, South Africa, Zaire, Botswana, and Russia. About ninety percent of the diamonds on the market come from one of these five places. Australia and Zaire are the biggest producers, but only about five percent of the diamonds mined in these places are of gem quality; the rest are used industrially. The expensive pink diamonds are mined in Australia. South Africa was once first in world diamond production, but now it ranks fifth. About half the gems mined in Botswana are gem quality. Other places in Africa where diamonds are mined: Sierra Leone, Lesotho, Ghana, Angola, and Tanzania. Diamonds are also found in Brazil, Venezuela, and Guyana.

India and other parts of Asia were once major diamond producers, but they no longer rank among the world's larger producers. Asia is an important center for cutting and polishing diamonds. Many gems are processed in Thailand and Hong Kong, although other places in China are also becoming popular.

Diamonds can be white, yellow, red, pink, black, green, blue, purple, or a rosy color. Colorless diamonds are usually considered the best, unlike with other gems. The color in a diamond is caused by tiny amounts of nitrogen (mostly yellows) or boron (blues) in the mineral deposit that becomes a diamond. The diamonds generally used to make jewelry are both colorless and flawless. The clearest, whitest diamonds are considered most valuable, but less than one percent of all diamonds mined are this color. Blue-white stones are also highly regarded. Most diamonds have a yellow or brown tint to them, which is usually not considered good.

Color and clarity are considered more important than weight when considering a diamond's value. Flawless diamonds with stronger colors are known as "fancy diamonds," and are sometimes more valuable, because it is rare to find a flawless diamond of certain colors. The bright red ones are the most expensive. A valuable diamond can go for as much as

US$20,000 per carat. It is important to note that diamonds color enhanced by irradiation or heat treatments should be marked as such and should not be used for astrological remedies.

To ascertain a diamond's color, look through its side against a white background; artificial light can mask a diamond's true color, so always examine a diamond in sunlight. A good quality diamond is ascertained by its hardness: no other gem or metal should be able to scratch it.

Because larger diamonds are rare, a diamond's value usually more than doubles when it doubles in size. A one-carat diamond may cost about $1,000; the same quality two-carat diamond will cost about $3,000.

The quality of the cut also increases the diamond's value. Diamonds may be cut into round, pear, oval, or emerald shapes. The round cut is the most popular. It is also known as the "brilliant" cut.

The bright luster of a diamond is caused by light reflecting from its hard crystal faces or facets. Diamonds both reflect and refract light from their facets. A facet is a flat, polished face. The average diamond has 58 facets. Luster is increased by light within the diamond because of strong refraction, which causes internal reflections.

A diamond is considered flawless if no inclusions are visible though a lens or loupe with 10x magnification. A diamond is considered to have flaws if it possesses dots or droplet-shaped impressions.

If a jeweler vaporizes inclusions with a laser, or files a fissure to make them less visible it has to be disclosed to the buyer. These processes usually make a diamond unsuitable for use in astrological remedies.

Astrological Effects of Diamond

Diamonds are one of the most powerful gems and can give quick results to their wearers. Diamonds strengthen a weak Venus, enhance the color indigo, and are related to the number 6. Diamonds effect water and our sense of taste, and work with the Vishuddhi chakra (base of the neck).

Venus rules diamonds. Wearing diamonds is good for those for whom Venus is lord of an auspicious house in the birth chart (that is, with a well-placed Venus). Diamonds will help to neutralize the bad effects if Venus, as the lord of an auspicious house, is badly disposed or afflicted. Some authorities say that diamonds are good for those with Taurus rising, or for those with Leo or Aries on the ascendant.

A flawless diamond will benefit the wearer greatly. A flawed stone, however, can bring great misfortune. Only rulers should wear fancy yellow or pink-tinted diamonds. Such diamonds will bring others misfortune. But if a ruler wears a high-quality diamond, that diamond will enhance their ability to rule and help them to gain wealth. Usually, diamonds bring women unhappiness.

A diamond is believed to have beneficial effects if it shines through water like a ray of light, is glossy (shiny), has a luster like lightning, and has fire like a rainbow. A colorless diamond with a blue tint that sprays blue and red rays, and which does not have black dots, is the most auspicious to wear.

Flawed diamonds should not even be kept in the house. Diamonds have a negative effect if they are scratched, have double facets, are discolored, have dirt in the middle or in their corners, are covered in bubbles, mixed with colored substances, have fractured edges, have rough surfaces, are lusterless, split at the points, perforated, or are oblong. If a diamond has dots that resemble the shape of a crow's claws, it is considered particularly inauspicious and will cause the wearer to die. If a diamond has a dot or what resembles a drop of water, consider it badly flawed. Black dots are inauspicious, and red dots are very inauspicious. White dots are considered less so. Those who wear diamonds with red spots or that reflect a reddish glimmer can lose all their wealth and become ruined.

A defective diamond causes great trouble to the wearer. If a white diamond is flawed with a white, island-shaped mark, it destroys wealth and happiness. If the island-shaped mark is black, wealth will be destroyed. Diamonds with fractures, dark flaws, or discolorations are inauspicious. Defective diamonds destroy peace of mind, and cause disease and disasters. If the only diamonds available are flawed, better to wear one of the less expensive substitutes.

Varaha Mihir states that a triangle-shaped diamond, or a diamond shaped like a buttock, will help a woman conceive a son.

Wearing diamonds promotes material happiness, life span, prosperity, comfort, good harvests, artistic ability, creativity, marital happiness, physical and mental purity, patience, fearlessness, and good manners. Diamonds also create good feelings in social and family life, help the wearers make proper decisions, help alleviate legal difficulties, build determination, help the wearers to move up in the world and to not waste time. They make wearers successful, ambitious, and able to live a luxuriant life. They bring influence that helps wearers control their enemies for good causes, create feelings of loyalty, pleasantness, and innocence. Wearing diamonds also protects against evil spirits, curses, a snakebite, and Tantric curses. A good diamond can protect wearers from thieves, fire, floods, and poisons.

Diamonds make the wearers loyal to their mates, and increase the ability to feel love and devotion toward others. The diamond signifies faithfulness between lovers. Diamonds can support successful marriages. Sometimes, if a person is living an indulgent lifestyle, wearing a diamond may have too powerful an influence on the person, thus bringing on disease and other problems.

Diamonds and other colorless gems transmit indigo as their cosmic color. Indigo influences the body's watery elements, such as sperm and mucous. Thus diamonds work with the lymph system, hormones, semen and mucous. Diamonds also work with the bones and the reproductive system. They help one develop a lustrous complexion, and are good for diseases of the skin, genitals, uterus, and for diabetes.

It is recommended that actors, dancers, artists, and singers wear diamonds to attain success and popularity. They are also good for those interested in the arts and music.

Some authorities say that if a woman wants to be blessed with having a son, she should wear a good white diamond with a slightly blackish tint. Other authorities, however, say that women should never wear this type of diamond.

According to some authorities there are three types of diamonds—male, female, and eunuch (neutral), and that the male is the best, the female next best, and the eunuch inauspicious. Also, some authorities say that there are four types of diamonds—Brahmin, Kshatriya, Vaishya, and Shudra.

A male diamond has six or eight angles, is free of dots and lines, is round but clearly shows all eight faces, is lightweight but looks large, and when it is reflected on water, it displays the seven colors of the rainbow.

A female diamond has dots and lines, is slightly elongated, but otherwise has the qualities of a male diamond.

A eunuch diamond is large, round, is heavy, and has only three angles, which are turned.

A Brahmin diamond is white (colorless) and is flawless. One who wears a Brahmin diamond will be a scholar of the religious scriptures and receive great respect from others. Such a person will be born a Brahmin for his or her next seven births. It is good for those who perform spiritual, religious, and public activities to wear Brahmin diamonds.

A Kshatriya diamond is white with a slight red tint. Those who wear Kshatriya diamonds will be good political leaders, good soldiers, competent diplomats, and good administrators. Thus such diamonds are good for kings, political leaders, and leaders in any high position to wear.

Vaishya diamonds have a yellow hue. Businessmen who wear Vaishya diamonds will become wealthy and taste luxury. Businessmen or bankers who wear Vaishya diamonds gain success.

Sudra diamonds have a black tint, and those who wear them become intelligent and prosperous.

Depending on a person's occupation, different tints of diamond—yellow, blue, pink—can be worn. Priests, teachers, scientists, and intellectuals should wear white. Rulers, soldiers, and administrators should wear pink. Businessmen, bankers, and farmers should wear yellow. Laborers, artisans, and servants should wear black or blue.

The diamond chosen should not be less than one carat, but it is better if it is more than 1½ carats. The diamond should be set in silver, platinum, or white gold (some include yellow gold in this list), as a ring, and worn on the little (this finger is ruled by Mercury) or middle finger of the right (some say the left hand for women) hand. The diamond should be worn for the first time on a Friday morning during the bright half of the lunar month (when the Moon is waxing), and put on an hour before sunrise.

The ring should be made when Venus is exalted in Pisces, in Taurus, in a friendly sign, in its own sign, or when it is in a constellation favorable to Venus.

To install a diamond, the following mantras should be chanted: *Om shum shukraya namah om*. And for Mercury: *Om budhaya namah*. The stotra of invocation for a diamond or its substitutes: *Om hima kunda mrida labham, daityanam paramam gurum, sarva sastra pravantaram, bhargavam pranamami aham*. These mantras should be chanted on a Wednesday or a Friday.

If one cannot afford or find a suitable diamond, then white zircon, white sapphire, white spinel, natural turquoise, white topaz, beryl (goshenites), or white tourmaline may be substituted, but the gem chosen should not weigh less than three or four carats. Rock crystal quartz can also be used, but it should weigh at least eleven carats.

As Venus in not compatible with the Sun and Moon, diamonds or their substitutes should not be worn with rubies or pearls or their substitutes. Some authorities say that diamonds should also not be worn with yellow sapphire or red coral. Exception: when one is wearing a Navaratna ring (consisting of all nine planetary gems).

Certain demigods rule over certain tints of diamonds. White diamonds are ruled by Varuna, the lord of the oceans. Indra, the king of heaven, rules yellow-colored diamonds. Surya, the Sun god, rules over green-tinted diamonds. Agni, the fire god, rules over brown-tinted diamonds. The Maruts, the wind gods, rule over copper-colored diamonds.

Ruby
Hardness 9, specific gravity 4.03, refractive index 1.64–1.76, dispersion 0.018.

A ruby is a corundum, which is a crystalline form of an oxide of aluminum. It is infused with a small amount of chromium, which gives ruby its red color. A ruby is a beautiful red stone and is usually expensive. Rubies usually occur in crystals of six-sided prisms and are second in hardness only to diamonds. The mineral is chemically stable and has virtually no cleavage. Rubies are transparent to translucent. The crystal system is hexagonal, and the optic character is double refractive.

Perfect rubies are less common than perfect diamonds, and are usually much more expensive. Large rubies are unusual, so their value increases as the carat size increases more than with other precious gems. In Sanskrit, the ruby is known as *ratnaraj*, the "king of gems," and as *ratnanayaka*, the "leader of gems." Rubies with a vivid crimson color to a slightly purplish red (the color, they say, of pigeon blood) are the most valuable.

The best rubies come from the Mogok district in Upper Myanmar (Burma). This is where the pigeon-blood-colored rubies come from. A large ruby from Myanmar can sell for millions of dollars. Rubies are also mined in Sri Lanka, Thailand, Vietnam, and Cambodia. India mines some rubies, but they are not usually of good quality. Siamese rubies are usually darker than Burmese ones. The ones from Sri Lanka are usually pale and partially colored. Most rubies are brought to Thailand for processing.

A perfect ruby is a rich, even red; its color is pure. It is cold to the touch, clear, lustrous, brilliant, radiant, smooth, and transparent. Because rubies have less brilliance and sparkle, and are more opaque, than diamonds, they are cut differently. They are not faceted, but cut in such a way as to accent their color.

To check whether what you are holding is a genuine ruby, hold it along with a known ruby of the same size. This tests the specific gravity (its weight). A ruby can also be scratch-tested with a known ruby. Only another corundum or a diamond can scratch a ruby.

Astrological Effects of Ruby

The Sun transmits red. Since ruby is ruled by the Sun, if the Sun is the lord of an auspicious house in the birth chart, wearing a ruby will be beneficial. Rubies are often prescribed to offset a weakly placed (afflicted) or badly placed Sun, or to increase the power of a well placed Sun. A ruby worn mistakenly can increase the Sun's effect on mental and physical imbalance. Ruby is often recommended for one who has Virgo as their solar sign.

It is rare to find a flawless ruby. The qualities of a ruby that will have a good astrological effect: it is bright red, sparkles, has a fine shape, internal brilliance, is smooth, has lustrous rays, is heavy, it sprays out red rays in the early morning, and it glows in the dark. If a ruby is put in milk a hundred times, and afterwards the rays of the ruby can still be seen after it is taken out of the milk, it is considered to be high quality.

One who wears a defective ruby will have great trouble. A defective ruby can also cause trouble to the wearer's relatives. The qualities that make a stone have a negative astrological effect: if it has many scratches or inclusions, breaks, internal cracks, is dull, is an off-color, has depressions, is brittle, cracks on the outside, is mixed with other minerals, is lusterless, feathery, dirty, unattractive, possesses no fire, has a rough surface, has a sandy look, is without brilliance, if the colors are not homogenous or are ambiguous, and if it has a bluish or coppery tint. The ruby may also have black or white spots, silky inclusions, a cloudy appearance, and be too dark around the edges. A ruby is considered flawed if it is honey-colored or has spots of honey color in it. Flawed rubies bring disease and bad luck.

If one wears an unflawed ruby the wearer will become wealthy, have good children, happiness, courage, a respected position in society, high honor, prestige and property. The wearer's will-power and determination will also be strengthened. Rubies support the development of will power, courage, and vitality. They also help one have a proper spiritual view and to see truth, as well as helping to improve one's status in life. The wearer will develop a royal life, and be protected from problems, fear, misfortune, and disaster. He or she will be fortunate, successful, optimistic, authoritative, intelligent, and will receive social status.

Wearing rubies is good for persons in authority, politicians, and for people trying to get a high position in the country. They protect the wearer from the jealousy of others, from deadly enemies, and from their competitors. They strengthen administrative skills, managerial abilities, and initiative. Astrologers, artists, judges, gem experts, sculptors, architects, lawyers, and engineers can use rubies to support their work. Rubies also help cure learning problems.

Since red color waves are hot, red gemstones are useful for curing health problems caused by too much cold and moisture in the body. Ruby and the Sun effect fire, the eyes, and bones. Rubies therefore deal with blood circulation, including low blood pressure and heart problems. They help protect against colds and flu.

Wearing rubies will protect one from diseases caused by imbalances in the bodily functions. Rubies work with digestion, metabolism, rheumatism, fever, gout, headaches, bones, indigestion, and stomach ulcers. They can also help with eye problems, and have been known to help with cancer. Rubies can help develop general good health, and prevent unhealthiness.

Since rubies are so powerful, they can cause trouble when worn by the wrong person. If the sign of Capricorn, Virgo, or Pisces are on the ascendant (rising), it may be better to use the substitute gem for ruby; the ruby itself may be too powerful.

It is said that if a ruby fades in color, the wearer will be a victim of disaster. When the problem has passed, the wearer will notice the gem regain its color. It is said that a ruby's color will fade if it is near a poisonous substance. If a ruby's color becomes deeper, this indicates danger for the wearer.

If a ruby has many flaws, it may cause death. A smoky stone attracts lightning to the wearer; a dusty stone may cause childlessness and stomach disorders. If there are white, black, or honey-colored spots on a ruby, the wearer will be defamed and have his or her life span shortened, lose wealth, and will suffer in other ways. A ruby with four spots will create anxiety about attack by a weapon. If there is a depression in the stone, the wearer will suffer from bad health and be physically weak. A milky stone causes one's cattle to be destroyed.

It is not recommended that a married woman wear ruby because this may give her the power to dominate her husband. Working women, on the other hand, can use a ruby to good advantage.

A ruby should not have any inauspicious flaws and should be at least 1½ carats (some say two carats). The larger the ruby, the better—three to five carats is good. Rubies should be set in gold or gold mixed with copper, and should be worn on a Sunday, Monday, or Thursday on the ring finger of the right hand. The ring should be first worn just after sunrise (within one hour of sunrise) on a Sunday of the bright half of the lunar month (when the Sun is waxing). Ideally, the gem should be put on when the Sun is in Leo in the constellation of Pushya. It could also be put on during Sagittarius. It should be put on when the Sun is in its own sign or is exalted. It is also good if it is installed during a constellation ruled by the Sun, such as Uttara Phalguni, Karttika, or Uttarashadha.

Before wearing the gem, place it in unboiled milk or Ganges water. It should then be worshipped with incense and flowers. The Sun's mantra is: *Om hring hamsa suryaya namaha*, or, *Om grinih suryaya namah*. Some "name" mantras dedicated to the Sun are as follows: *Om suryaya namaha; Om ravaye namaha; Om savitra namaha;* and *Om adityaya namaha*. The Sun mantras should be chanted 108 times per week (best at sunrise, noon, and sunset on a Sunday).

The stotra of invocation: *Om japa kusuma samkasam, kasaya peyam maham dvitim, tamoran sarva papagnam, pranato smi divakaram*.

If one cannot afford a ruby, there are substitutes that can be worn, such as Pyrope red garnet (Arizona or Cape ruby—should be at least three carats; over five carats is better), Star ruby, red spinel (Balas ruby), red tourmaline (Siberian ruby), pink topaz (Brazilian ruby), rubellite, a red zircon, or other naturally red or pink transparent crystals.

A ruby or its substitutes should not be worn with a diamond, blue sapphire, cat's eye, or hessonite (gomedha) or their substitutes. This is because Venus, Saturn, Rahu, and Ketu are not compatible with the Sun, and these are the gems in relation to those planets. Using these gems in a Navaratna (Nine Gems ring or pendant) is the exception to this rule.

Depending on a person's occupation, different colors and tones of rubies should be prescribed. A priest, teacher, scientist, or intellectual should wear pink-red (women should also wear pink). A ruler, soldier, or administrator should wear blood red. A businessman, farmer, or banker should wear orange-red. A laborer, artisan, or servant should wear purple-red.

A good quality ruby should not be worn with a flawed gem or a gem with which it is not astrologically compatible.

Ruby deals with the fifth chakra, Manipura. The color to be enhanced for the Sun is red. The number relating to ruby is one.

Sapphire
Hardness 9, Specific gravity 3.96–4.03, Refractive index 1.76–1.78.

A sapphire is a corundum, a crystallized oxide of aluminum. It contains traces of titanium and iron, which are what give sapphires their blue color. If other mineral traces are also present, a sapphire may have a color other than blue, such as yellow, pink, orange, violet, or green. A corundum gem that is not red or blue is known as a "fancy sapphire."

Sapphires have strong refraction, which favors the use of the same brilliant cut that is used on diamonds. Sapphires have a moderate dispersion. They do not have as strong a dispersion as diamonds, and thus they do not share the diamond's "fire."

Rubies and sapphires, both corundum, are basically the same gem, except that rubies are always red and sapphires can be various colors. But sapphires have the same hardness, specific gravity, and refractive index as rubies. Both sapphires and rubies are second in hardness only to diamonds.

Sapphires are mined mainly in Australia, Myanmar (Burma), Kashmir, Sri Lanka, Thailand, Vietnam, Afghanistan, Pakistan, and Cambodia. Some of the best sapphires come from Sri Lanka. Australian sapphires are deep blue to nearly black. Montana, USA, has metallic blue sapphires.

Many of the best blue sapphires come from Kashmir, but production has dropped off greatly due to political strife in that area. Kashmiri sapphires do not change color under electric lights, while sapphires from other places take a navy blue tint under electric lights. Small, needlelike inclusions called rutile silk often deepen the blue and soften the Kashmiri sapphires. Rutile silk often increases the quality of a gem, although it can sometimes cause the gem to lose brilliance, making them of little value.

Sapphires usually occur in crystals of twelve-sided prisms. Most sapphires have faults, and some have silky-looking internal patches.

It is believed that about ninety percent of sapphires and rubies are heat-treated to increase the quality of their color. This treatment is accepted as bona fide in the gem business, and it is unlikely the trend will change. Slight flaws are also sometimes burnt out of the gems.

If a blue sapphire is to be used astrologically, it should not have been heat-treated but should be natural. The gem's astrological potency is reduced when treated with heat, often to the point of making it useless. Darker stones usually do not have a good effect astrologically. One who wishes to purchase a sapphire should trust the seller to disclose information such as whether the stone in question has been treated or is in its natural state.

A sapphire, especially a blue one, should first be worn only after trial. Even a perfect sapphire is sometimes unlucky and will cause trouble to the user. To test a blue sapphire one can wear the gem wrapped in a blue cloth bound around one's arm for a week. One can also place it under his pillow for three nights. If there is any bad effect, the sapphire should be rejected.

Blue Sapphire (Neelam)

Cornflower-colored sapphires are considered the most valuable. Blue sapphires without flaws, with evenly distributed color, that are well-cut and brilliant, are the best. Astrologically, blue sapphires and rubies have the same effect, but the value of a blue sapphire is about one fourth the value of an equal quality ruby. Blue sapphires transmit the color violet. In Sanskrit, blue sapphire is known as *sauriratna*, "sacred to Saturn."

Blue sapphires are less valuable if they are tinted green, light sky blue, dark blue, or purple. Sapphires that are very dark, very light or colorless, have inclusions, external blemishes, internal feathers, or black spots are not good.

Astrological Effects of a Blue Sapphire

Blue sapphires are the gemstones for Saturn. An ill-placed Saturn in a birth chart can cause poverty and suffering. Wearing blue sapphires can be advantageous for those for whom Saturn is the lord of an auspicious house. If Saturn, as lord of an auspicious house, is afflicted or ill disposed, blue sapphire may help to neutralize its effect.

Blue sapphires bring good effects if the right person wears them; if the wrong person wears them, his or her life can be ruined. Blue sapphires are touchy gems; even when they are worn by the proper people, they can bring negative effects on occasion. This is because some gemstones are unlucky. Therefore, blue sapphire should always be worn for a trial period to ascertain whether the particular stone you have purchased will do harm.

It is believed that blue sapphires will change color to warn against an enemy's attack.

A good sapphire is brilliant, radiant, and transparent. Its rays should spread out from within, and it should not reflect any color other than its own. A good sapphire is solid. Such a stone will bring the wearer wealth, fame, a good name, health, happiness, prosperity, a long life, mental peace, and good children. Wearing a blue sapphire protects against danger, travel problems, terror, thieves, accidents and problems from storms, fire, or natural disasters. It can cause financial fortunes to change for the better, help with a person's career, and make the wearer rich. It can free one of mental anxiety. It helps make one detached, and protects against envy. It can be worn for good luck and for protection against evil spirits.

Since Saturn rules the nervous system, blue sapphires help problems of the nerves—tension and neuroses—diseases caused by an afflicted Saturn. Because Saturn is the slowest moving planet, it tends to cause chronic disease.

Wearing a blue sapphire may help cure bad blood, mental problems, headache, vomiting, deafness, fainting, and may make the bones stronger. It can be worn to protect against heart problems, or by a person suffering from alcoholism.

But beware of flawed sapphires. A cracked gem may attract accidents. A stone with a depression may cause ulcers or boils. A milky stone may cause poverty. If a stone is two-colored, there may be trouble from an enemy. If it is dull or opaque, it may cause family problems. If it is marked with white lines, it may cause eye troubles. If it has red dots, it can cause poverty.

Those who choose to wear blue sapphires should choose stones that are at least two carats—and ideally at least five carats. Such stones should be set in rings made of steel (iron), and if necessary, *ashta dhatu*, an alloy of eight metals, which are gold, silver, copper, tin, zinc, mercury, lead and iron. They can also be set in rings of gold and silver. The proper rituals should be performed to install the gem. The ring should be worn on the middle of the right hand on a Saturday, two hours to two hours and forty minutes before sunset. A ring should be made when Saturn is in its exalted, well-placed sign—Libra—or in a friendly constellation. The gem should not be worn if Saturn is debilitated in the birth chart. Blue sapphires can be worn during an eclipse.

The mantra to be chanted for blue sapphire: *Om sham shanaischaraya namaha* (chanted 108 times). It is also good to chant *Om shanti shanti shanti*. The stotra of invocation: *Om nilanjana samabhasam, ravi putra yama agrajam, chaya martanda sambhratam, tam namami sanaiscaram*.

The substitutes for blue sapphire are: blue zircon, blue tourmaline, amethyst, indicolite, blue spinel and lapis lazuli. If lapis lazuli or amethyst are used, the stones should be at least five to ten carats—as they are weaker than blue sapphire.

Because Saturn is not compatible with the Sun, Moon, and Mars, blue sapphire and its substitutes should not be worn with ruby, pearl, or red coral. Some also say a blue sapphire should not be worn with a yellow sapphire. The exception is when the setting includes the Navaratna (Nine Gems).

The cosmic number relating to blue sapphire is eight. Sapphire deals with air, touch, skin, and the nervous system. It is related to the fourth chakra, Anahata (lower chest). Black cloth, a black thread, a black pearl, and the number eight can also sometimes help ease an afflicted Saturn.

Yellow Sapphire

A good quality yellow sapphire should be flawless, have a lemony color, have no spots, feel smooth when touched, be evenly colored, feel heavy when held in the palm, and should look clean, solid, without layers, and have a good shape. A light-colored, transparent yellow stone will have a good effect. A good quality gem looks better when it is rubbed on a testing stone.

If a yellow sapphire is dull, does not possess a yellow radiance, looks dried up, has a blackish or brownish tinge to its yellow color, or is a mixed red and yellow or a whitish yellow, is not symmetrical, or when touched, feels rough like sand, it is not considered a good gem. Also, if the yellow sapphire has black, droplike spots on it, it is best not to purchase that stone.

Good quality yellow sapphires come from Brazil, Sri Lanka, Thailand, Myanmar (Burma), Cambodia, Australia, Africa, Tasmania, Japan, and Mexico. Sri Lanka and India (selling Sri Lankan stones) are generally the best places to purchase natural, untreated yellow sapphires.

Astrological Effects of a Yellow Sapphire

Yellow sapphire is the gemstone for Jupiter and is ruled by Jupiter. Wearing a yellow sapphire attracts Jupiter's blessings. If Jupiter is lord of an auspicious house, then yellow sapphire will be useful. An astrologer may prescribe yellow sapphire for those who have a weak but well-placed Jupiter. They are good for persons born under the solar sign, Sagittarius. If in a birth chart, Jupiter is in any constellation that the Sun is transiting, such as Kritika, Phalguni, or Ashada, a yellow sapphire may be recommended.

Yellow sapphires are often heat-treated to make them a darker golden yellow. While this makes them more saleable, it makes them basically useless for astrological purposes.

A good quality yellow sapphire gives the wearer happiness, fortune, prosperity, intelligence, fame, good name, wealth, comfort, good health, a long life, and blesses women with good children. There can be an immediate financial change for the better shortly after putting on a yellow sapphire. Yellow sapphires can also give one a more philosophical attitude toward life, and aid meditation and concentration.

Yellow sapphire protects its wearers from evil spirits. It is believed that if a woman having difficulty getting married or with marriage problems wears a yellow sapphire, the obstructions to her happiness will be removed. Yellow sapphires can also help women to become pregnant. Yellow sapphires are recommended for those taking part in business, and those interested in spiritual pursuits, such as preaching, yoga, meditation, and study.

It is good to wear yellow sapphires when taking long journeys or if one travels often.

Yellow sapphires transmit the color light blue. This is a cold color, and thus it helps improve diseases concerning the glands, liver, and endocrine system. Yellow sapphires can help improve pancreas problems, jaundice, the fat systems in the body, and cerebral problems. They can also strengthen the immune system, and help one gain needed weight. Yellow sapphires affect the ears and body fat.

A defective gem will cause the wearer trouble. If the gem is milky, the wearer may receive an injury; if it has red dots, he or she may lose wealth; if it is cracked, one might suffer a theft; if it has webs, it may cause stomach problems; if it has a depression, it causes anxiety and mental disturbance. If the gem lacks luster or is opaque, one may suffer from family problems or at the hands of one's enemies.

Depending on one's occupation, different colored yellow sapphires should be worn. A priest, teacher, scientist, or intellectual should wear a whitish yellow stone. A ruler, soldier, or administrator should wear rosy yellow. A businessman, farmer, or banker should wear yellow. A laborer or servant should wear blackish yellow.

Yellow sapphire should not usually be worn if according to the birth chart, Jupiter is lord of the sixth, eighth, or twelfth house.

A yellow sapphire should be set in a gold ring on a Thursday. It is advised not to use a gem of less than two carats, but avoid gems of exactly six, eleven, or fifteen carats. Best is a gem of either seven or thirteen carats. The proper rituals should be performed to install the gem, and the following mantra chanted: *Om brim brihaspataye namaha om*. The ring should be worn on the index finger (Jupiter's finger, next to the thumb) or the ring finger of the right hand. It should first be worn on a Thursday morning of the bright half of the lunar month (when the moon is waxing), within an hour before sunrise. It is best to first put on the ring when Jupiter is in its own sign, in Cancer, in an exalted or friendly sign, or in the constellations of Pushya (best), Vishaka, Purvabhadrapada, or Punarvasu. Some authorities say it is best if Jupiter is at a favorable angle or in the same house as the Moon.

The substitutes for yellow sapphire are yellow zircon, yellow topaz, yellow pearl, heliodor, citrine quartz (should be at least five carats), and yellow tourmaline.

Because Jupiter is not compatible with Mercury and Venus, yellow sapphire should not be worn with emerald or diamond. Some authorities also say that yellow sapphire should not be worn with blue sapphire, cat's eye, or gomedha.

The cosmic color to be enhanced is light blue, and the cosmic number is three. The affected element is ether, and the affected sense sound. The affected chakra is the sixth, Ajna, in the middle of the head, just above the eyes.

Stotra of invocation: *Om devanam ca rishinam ca, gurum kanja nasam nibham, budhyi bhutam trilokesam, tam namami brihaspatim.*

Padparadscha

Padparadscha is the most valuable of the fancy (non-blue) sapphires. Padmaraga means "lotus flower." Lotus flowers come in many colors, but the original color is a pinkish-orange. Padparadscha is this color. A true padparadscha has to have a harmonious blend of both colors spread in an even way throughout the entire gem. Some stones may look good from the top but when viewed from the side, show a distinct separation of colors. Such a gem is not a padparadscha but just a fancy sapphire. Some authorities believe padparadscha can only be found in Sri Lanka.

Padparadscha has a good effect on couples desiring children. They can also be favorable for those having trouble getting a promotion or transfer to a better location. Padparadschas should be worn near sunrise on a Thursday.

Emerald (Panna)

Hardness 7.5 to 8, Specific gravity 2.69 to 2.8, Refractive index 1.57, Dispersion 0.014.

An emerald is the green variety of beryl, a silicate of aluminum and beryllium. Emeralds have a low dispersion and a glassy look. Their crystal system is hexagonal.

Pale blue aquamarine, pale green beryl, golden helidor, and pink morganite are also beryls made of the same chemical composition, but each has a different color. If an emerald is too light green, it is not considered a true emeralds, but is called a green beryl. An emerald is a rich translucent green—like green grass glistening in the dew. A flawless emerald is transparent, brilliant, radiant, and has bright spraying rays. Emeralds have almost no fire. They retain their color in artificial light, whereas most green gems do not. Flawless gems are rare. A high quality emerald can cost $20,000 per carat, and is more valuable than a high quality ruby.

Emeralds are mainly mined in Colombia and Brazil, and are also found in Africa, Zambia, Afghanistan, Pakistan, Iran, Russia, Egypt, India (near Ajmer and Udaipur), and Rhodesia. Colombian emeralds are considered the best, and those mined in Muzo are considered the best of those mined in Colombia. About ninety percent of the world's natural emeralds come from Colombia. These emeralds are generally more translucent and possess better color than emeralds from other places. The emeralds from Ajmer are a paler green but still attractive. Emeralds from Udaipur tend to be darker, but they are brittle.

A rectangular step-cut (emerald cut) is generally used for emeralds, because it focuses on the depth of the emerald crystal and brings out the gem's beautiful color. Emeralds are one of the hardest gems to cut. They tend to be brittle, and if handled improperly, will chip or break. They are extremely hard—harder than steel.

Quite a variety of synthetic emeralds have been developed over time. Synthetic emeralds have been produced since 1934. They often command a high price.

The main site for emerald processing and sales is the Indian city of Jaipur. Emeralds from all over the world are sent to Jaipur for processing.

The best colored emeralds are the color of green grass, the green in a peacock feather, the color of a parrot's neck, velvet green, the green on the back of a firefly, and the color of fresh moss. Wearing a flawless emerald of any these shades will greatly benefit the wearer. Light green emeralds have less value.

Most emeralds have tiny cracks or inclusions, reducing their value. Emeralds tend to have more inclusions than most gems. It is best to avoid gems with cracks close to the surface as the durability of the gem can be affected.

Almost all emeralds are placed in oil immediately upon coming from the mines. This helps rid them of inclusions at the surface. Emeralds are also sometimes oiled to conceal cracks or dyed to improve their color. Both of these are fraudulent practices if the seller does not disclose this treatment to the buyer. A good way to examine an emerald is to hold it with tweezers under water. By then looking at it through the glass, it is possible to see if the gem has been dyed or oiled. Emeralds that are dyed, oiled or treated do not have a good effect astrologically, and should not be used for astrological purposes.

Astrological Effects of Emerald

Emeralds are ruled by Mercury. Those who have Mercury as lord of an auspicious house in their birth chart may find emeralds beneficial. If Mercury is in an inauspicious house or is aspected by a malefic planet, it may also be advisable to wear emeralds, but its use in this case should be prescribed by a qualified astrologer. Emeralds can be useful for those under the influence of Gemini or Virgo. Flaws in an emerald can interfere with the transmission of Mercury's cosmic force, so flawed emeralds should not be used. Green is the cosmic color emeralds enhance, and the cosmic number is five.

The best emeralds are smooth, brilliant, transparent, radiant, free of spots, have a rich even color, appear to glow, and have no bad internal or external flaws. They should also be well cut. An emerald should reflect a good light that shines like lightning.

An emerald that does not show glow, appears transparent in the center, or has a lighter tone, is not a first-class stone. An emerald is also considered inferior if it is too dark. An emerald's weaknesses: cracks, rough surface, thick water marks, depressions, no luster, brittleness, more than one color tint, a blackish tinge and a dirty appearance. If the gem is bright like mica, do not purchase it. Do not wear a mixed-colored emerald.

A good emerald without defects will bring wealth, good health, property, and increase a person's intelligence. Emeralds help increase memory, which has the effect of also improving the wearer's education and psychic abilities. Emeralds protect against snakebite, envious people, evil spirits, and curses. They give good children, and pregnant women who wear emeralds are ensured a safe and painless delivery. Emeralds give energy and balance, calm the mind, give mental peace, and help meditation. Emeralds help their wearers practice chastity. They also help the wearers do well on exams, to not lose money in business, to be honest, and to have a good reputation. Wearers can formulate good ideas and will possess the strength to enact them.

Emeralds can be useful for businessmen, printers, publishers, scientists, and writers. They can be good for those working in the chemical business, in public relations, medical equipment, diplomats, mediators, and factory owners. They help with communication and verbal skills, and are therefore good for writers, actors, and public speakers. Businessmen who wear emeralds can learn to communicate better.

Emeralds transmit green, which is by nature a cold color. The color green influences the liver, intestines, kidneys, and the body's flesh. Emeralds also affect the nose. They may help with heart conditions, concentration, insomnia, dysentery, diarrhea, stuttering, asthma, and ulcers. Emeralds can help with diseases caused by imbalances of vital bodily airs. Emeralds are good for purifying the blood, and are useful in treating nervous conditions. Therefore, they may help cure epilepsy, diseases caused by poisons, insanity, stammering, memory loss, hepatitis, stomach problems, depression, bronchitis, flatulence, and dyspepsia. They help strengthen the positive life force, and work with the lungs, tongue, and brain.

Those who wear defective emeralds may find distress, loss of wealth, injury, unhappiness, and will not find happiness in relation to their parents.

Emeralds should be set in gold on a Wednesday. They can also be set on Fridays or Saturdays. The gemstone should not weigh less than one carat, but three carats is recommended. The best sizes are three, five, seven, or ten carats. The proper rituals should be performed, and the following mantra chanted 108 times: *Om bum budhaya namah om*. An installed emerald ring should be worn on the little finger of the right hand within one or two hours after sunrise on a Wednesday of the bright half of the lunar month. The ring should be made when Mercury is in Virgo.

Substitutes: green tourmaline, green jade, aquamarine, green zircon, peridot, chrome tourmaline, chrome diopside, and green agate.

As Mercury is not compatible with the Moon, emerald should not be used with pearl or moonstone. Some authorities say that emeralds should not be worn with yellow sapphires, red coral, or their substitutes.

Depending upon a person's occupation, different color emeralds should be worn. A priest, teacher, scientist, or intellectual should wear light green emeralds. A ruler, soldier, or administrator should wear bluish green. A businessman, farmer, or banker should wear yellowish green. A laborer, artisan, or servant should wear dark green.

Emerald affects the element earth and the sense of smell. It relates to the seventh chakra, Sahasrana (above the head).

Stotra of invocation: *Om priyangu kalika syaman, rupena pratimam budham, somyam somya guno petam, tam budham pranamami aham.*

Pearl
Hardness 2.7–4.5, Specific gravity 2–2.86, Refractive index 1.55–1.65.

Pearls are found in pearl oysters, a species of bivalve mollusk. A pearl glows instead of sparkles. Pearls may be white, black, red, blue, brown, yellowish, and pink.

The location where pearls are grown will cause variations in their characteristics. The rosy white and cream-sheened pearls are considered the best and are thus the most expensive. Pearls of this type are found mainly in the Persian Gulf. Also valuable are the black pearls tinted with iridescent green. Pearl weight is measured by grams rather than carats.

Pearls are mainly found in the Persian Gulf, Sri Lanka (Gulf of Manear), Australia, Vietnam, Japan, Indonesia, Thailand, Malaysia, China, the Pacific Isles, Venezuela, the Red Sea, Panama, and South India. At the present time, the best pearls come from the Persian Gulf, Myanmar (Burma), Australia, and Indonesia. The biggest producer is Australia, then Indonesia and the Philippines. The largest pearls are produced in the South Pacific in white, black, and silver colors.

Natural pearls can be ten times more expensive than cultured ones. A natural pearl is produced when an object—a piece of shell, coral, or sand—becomes lodged in the oyster's shell. To protect from the abrasion, the oyster coats the object with a secretion of calcium carbonate called nacre. Over a number of years, these secretions build up and form a pearl.

Most pearls today are cultivated. The Japanese began pearl cultivation about one hundred years ago, using mostly Akoya oysters, common in Japan. To cultivate a pearl, the pearl farmers place a tiny bead of pearl shell into the oyster's flesh. This stimulates the oyster to secrete nacre and thus begin to form a pearl. The oysters are then returned to the sea for several years while the pearls develop. Cultured Akoya pearls are expensive, while South Sea pearls are the most expensive. Pearls from the South Seas are a good size, ranging from 9–17 mm, while the Akoya pearls usually measure 2–9 mm. Akoya pearls are often bleached, then colored, to give them good variety. South Pacific pearls are found in different colors—cream, silver, gold, shades of blue and pink. Black pearls are found in Tahiti.

Pearls are valued according to their size, shape, color, and shade. There are both saltwater and freshwater pearls. Freshwater pearls are the least expensive, and are often sold for less than costume jewelry. Perfectly round is the most valuable shape in a pearl, then a symmetrical drop, pear shape, and button.

A good pearl is translucent and lustrous. The quality of the pearl's luster helps to tell its value. The surface of the pearl should give an illusion of depth, as if you were looking into a clear pool of water reflecting a cloud.

A natural pearl can often be distinguished from an imitation by its texture. A natural pearl should be smooth; an imitation will feel rough when rubbed on the teeth and possesses a gritty, sandpaper-like texture. It is more difficult to tell the difference between a natural and a cultured pearl. To be sure, one must use X-radiography. Most cultured pearls are bleached, which makes them less useful for astrological purposes. Some black pearls have also been dyed.

Cultured pearls that have a nacreous layer of less than half a millimeter (one-fiftieth of an inch) are considered inferior. Lacquer is often put on pearls to prevent wear and to keep them from cracking. Imitation pearls are often made of glass or plastic, then covered with a coating of synthetic pearl.

The luster on some pearls is only on the outside. On others, the pearl's surface appears dull, but there is an internal luster.

Mother-of-pearl is made by putting shaped items into a mussel shell. Often tiny images of Buddha are used. The oysters then secrete layers of calcium carbonate over the figure, coating them with mother-of-pearl.

Pearls in a necklace should be matched for color, translucency, and luster. They should be strung with knots between the pearls, to stop them from rubbing against one another. Also, if the strand breaks, the pearls will not scatter.

Pearls are damaged by perfume, hair spray, cosmetics, and skin acids. High humidity or excessive dryness can also damage them. Pearls are soft, so if they are placed in a box with other gems, care has to taken that they don't become scratched.

Astrological Effects of Pearls

Pearls are ruled by the Moon. They should be worn by those in whose birth chart the Moon is lord of an auspicious house, and when the lord of an auspicious house is afflicted and is not well placed in the birth chart. Pearls are used to strengthen a weak Moon, and can be worn if the Moon is well-placed in the birth chart.

Pearls are presided over by different Vedic deities: dark pearls by Vishnu, moonlike pearls by Indra, black pearls by Yamaraja, red pearls by Vayu, yellow pearls by Varuna, and pearls that are brilliant like fire or which have the luster of lotuses by Agni.

Pearls strengthen the mind, increase memory, and help control anger. They have a calming and peaceful effect on the mind, and encourage feelings of compassion and love. They also help spiritual meditation.

Ownership of a good pearl brings wealth, sons, popularity, fortune, fame, and freedom from disease and grief. Hindu brides often wear pearl nose rings at their weddings in order to ensure happy marriages and to guard against widowhood.

Those who wear a perfect pearl will be blessed by Goddess Lakshmi to become rich. They will have long lives, good intelligence, attain wealth, happiness, success, general good luck, become famous, and receive important positions in life. They will have patience, determination, purity, a dislike for anger, and a desire to do well. Pearls with a yellow luster give wealth. Red pearls increase intelligence. White pearls give fame. Blue pearls give good fortune. Pearls can help one become self-confident, and can make the work environment more peaceful.

Pearls can help students concentrate better and with more mental peace. They can help young married couples remain harmonious. If one has trouble finding a marriage partner, pearls can be worn to help alleviate this situation. Pearls are good for diplomats and those engaged in charity. They also help one develop creativity.

Pearls and their substitutes transmit the color orange. Orange rays have a cold effect, and can be used to treat the diseases relating to blood and bodily secretions that are caused by extreme heat in the body. Pearls reduce body heat and thus balance bodily fluids.

Pearls can calm the nerves, free one from anxiety, lessen tension, and help with mental problems caused by too much heat in the brain and heart. Pearls are good for women in general. Pearls may also help improve such conditions as tuberculosis, heart disease, ulcers, fever, epilepsy, diabetes, insomnia, eye problems, and uterine problems. Women can wear pearls for menstrual problems.

Wearing defective pearls, however, causes misfortune. Watch for cracks, moles (if it is black, it is very inauspicious), lack of luster, a thin line across the outside of the pearl, spots, internal dirt, or a wood-like material in them.

If a pearl is broken, one will lose his livelihood. If a pearl is in the shape of a bird rather than round, the wearer will lose his or her wealth. If a pearl is shaped like coral, one will become poor. If a pearl does not have luster, one's life will be shortened by wearing it. If a pearl has a spot that looks like a fish's eye, one's children may be lost. Wearing a spotted pearl can cause leprosy.

The most effective pearls astrologically are those that are round and lustrous. A pearl that is long rather than round takes away one's intelligence and makes him foolish. A pearl that has a protrusion on three corners is bad luck. If a pearl is flat, the wearer will get a bad name.

A natural pearl has much more astrological power than a cultured pearl, but since natural pearls are so difficult to find—and are so expensive—some people use cultured pearls as a remedy. One natural pearl can have more effect than a strand of cultured pearls, however. The only way to determine whether one is purchasing a natural pearl or a cultured pearl is to X-ray it to examine its nucleus. Do not drill the pearl; a drilled pearl is of no use astrologically.

A pearl should weigh at least two grams; four, six, nine, or eleven grams are acceptable weights. If one must use a cultured pearl, it should weigh at least three to five grams.

Pearls should be set in silver and worn for the first time on a Monday (best) or Thursday in the evening. They should definitely not be purchased on Saturdays. Pearls should be worshipped with incense and flowers, and the following mantra should be chanted 108 times: *Om som somaya namaha om. Om som chandraya namaha* can also be chanted. The pearl ring should be worn on a Monday morning during the bright half of the lunar month (during the waxing moon, best during a full moon), ideally during one of the constellations ruled by the Moon, such as Rohini, Hasta, Shravan, or Pushya. The ring should ideally be put on during Cancer, Pisces, or Taurus, or while in a friendly sign. The Moon should not be aspected or conjunct with a malefic planet when the pearl is installed.

A pearl should be worn on the ring finger of either hand. The ritual to install the ring should be performed on a Monday evening after moonrise. People often feel a strong effect within a week of the installation.

Moonstone or white sapphire can substitute for pearl. If a moonstone is used, find a stone that weighs at least eight to ten carats.

As the Moon is not compatible with Rahu or Ketu, neither hessonite nor cat's eye or their substitutes should be worn with pearl or its substitutes. Some authorities say that pearls should also not be worn with diamonds, blue sapphires, or emeralds. The Navaratna setting is an exception to this rule.

The cosmic color enhanced by pearl is orange, the cosmic number is two. Pearls affect water, taste, the tongue, blood, and the second chakra, Svadtistana (private area).

Stotra of invocation: "*Om dadhi sankha tusarabham, chira arnava samudbhavam, namami sasinam soman, shambhor mukuta blusanam.*"

To increase a pearl's good effects, soak it in a solution of gold and mercury. To test a pearl's quality, soak it in a solution of warm oil and salt. This will not damage a natural pearl. If a natural pearl is rubbed with a dry cotton cloth containing rice, a genuine pearl will maintain its luster and color.

It is best to drill only oyster pearls through the center.

Pearls can be cleaned by placing them in lightly boiling milk or water, in a covered clay pot. Then they should be rubbed gently with a pure linen cloth.

Depending on a person's occupation, different color pearls should be worn. A priest, teacher, scientist, or intellectual should wear a white pearl. A ruler, soldier, or administrator should wear an orangish white pearl. A businessman, farmer, or banker should wear a greenish white pearl. A laborer, artisan, or servant should wear a black or bluish pearl.

Coral
Hardness 3.25–3.75, Specific gravity 2.65.

Coral is not a mineral but the skeleton-like deposit of coral polyps. Coral polyps build their limestone skeletons by taking calcium out of the seawater. They then deposit calcium carbonate (limestone) around the lower half of the colony. As new polyps grow, the limestone formation becomes larger and larger. Coral comes in different colors—red, white, pink, orange, and yellow. Red is the color most often used for astrological purposes. Red coral contains iron oxide. Of the red corals, blood-red and pink-red are the best. Coral is often stained, and the color fades after a while.

Valuable red coral is found mostly in the Mediterranean, in the waters near Algeria and Tunisia. Coral is also found off the coasts of France, Sicily, Spain, Australia, Mauritius, in the Red Sea, the Persian Gulf, in the seas near Japan, and off Africa's northwest coast.

Coral is found in clear, shallow water at about 5m (15 ft) to 50m (160 ft). The deeper the water, the lighter the coral will be, and vice versa. Imitation coral is made of conch-shell and compacted powdered marble. Plastic, wood, and wax are also used in the making of imitation coral.

Astrological Effects of Coral

Red coral is ruled by Mars. Coral can be worn by those for whom Mars is lord of an auspicious house in the birth chart. If Mars is the lord of an inauspicious house, it may be harmful to wear red coral. A red coral stone or necklace can be worn to strengthen Mars. The darker the coral, the more powerful the effect.

The auspicious qualities of coral: a good red color, a beautiful appearance, freedom from cracks and holes, a perfectly round or oval shape, a smooth surface, a nice sheen, and a regular shape.

Coral's possible flaws: cracks, bores in the body, more than one color in the same piece, black or white spots, depressions, a twisted or bent body.

A flawless, well-polished, brightly dark red-colored piece of coral will have the best result. Such a piece will increase wealth and remove danger and obstacles.

Those who wear red coral will be brave and defeat their enemies. Red coral helps defeat mental depression, and it protects women from widowhood. Red coral protects the wearer from evil spirits and curses, and stops nightmares. It aids meditation and brings happiness. Red coral can help one avoid violence and war.

Coral turns inactive persons into active ones, helps build finances, increases determination, courage, physical strength, vitality, and leadership qualities, and helps one to finish the tasks he has begun. It can help one get a daughter married or to find a new job. It can help marital life. It can also help increase sexual desire, especially in men. It protects against witchcraft, accidents, and lightning.

Red coral can be useful for policemen and soldiers.

Red coral is said to change color if the wearer is about to suffer bad health.

Red coral transmits the cosmic color yellow, which is related to blood, bone marrow, lymph nodes, and the head. Red coral can thus help improve diseases caused by an afflicted Mars or any relating to the above parts of the body. Red coral also affects the genitals, and works with the immune system, can cure smallpox, fever, headache, jaundice, blood diseases, anemia, weakness, typhoid, allergies, cough, bronchitis, pneumonia, wounds, measles, piles, cough, chickenpox, and problems with bile. Red coral used after three months of pregnancy may also be able to prevent miscarriages.

The weight of the coral used should be at least six (some say three) carats or more, or eight, nine, eleven, or twelve carats for a ring. Coral should be set in gold mixed with copper, or, alternatively, silver. The ring should be worn first on a Tuesday, one hour after sunrise, when the moon is waxing (bright half of the lunar month). It can also be worn first on a Monday or Thursday. It should ideally be set when it is in a sign ruled by Mars, a sign friendly to Mars, during a constellation ruled by Mars or ruled by a friend of Mars, or when Mars is exalted. A coral ring should be worn on the ring finger, index finger, or thumb of the right hand. The ring should be made when Mars is in Capricorn (its exalted sign), Scorpio, or Aries (best), on in the constellations of Mirgashira, Anuradha, Dhanistha, or Chitra.

The mantras for red coral: *Om bhom bhomaya namaha om; Om ang angarakaya namaha; Mangalaya namaha; Om kujaya namah; Om mam*. Stotra of invocation: "*Om dharani garbha sambhutam, viddat kanti sama prabham, kumara sakti hastam tam, mangalam pranamami aham.*"

Pink coral, carnelian, bloodstone, and red jasper can be substituted for red coral.

Because Mars in not compatible with Mercury or Saturn, red coral or its substitutes should not be worn with the gems ruled by Mercury and Saturn, emerald and blue sapphire or their substitues. According to some authoritites, red coral should also not be worn with diamonds, cat's eyes, or gomedha and their substitutes. The exception is in the Navaratna setting.

Depending on a person's occupation, different colors of coral should be worn. A priest, teacher, scientist, or intellectual should wear pink-red. A ruler, soldier, or administrator should wear blood red. A businessman, farmer, or banker should wear orange-red. A laborer, artisan, or servant should wear brown-red.

The cosmic number for Mars is nine, the affected element fire, and the affected sense sight. Mars rules the first chakra, Muladhara (base of spine).

Zircon
Hardness 7–7.5, Specific gravity 4.5–4.7, Refractive index 1.91–1.99.

Zircon is a silicate of zirconium and crystals. Zircons come in many different colors, including colorless, yellow, red, brown, green, blue, orange, and other colors. The colorless stones often have an excellent brilliance, good fire or high dispersion, and resemble diamonds. Zircons are often confused with cubic zirconia, the manmade synthetic diamond substitute. Zircon does not have cleavage, but can be brittle, and a slight hit can knock off a corner or crack the gemstone. A zircon can be distinguished from a diamond by the way it refracts light into divergent rays, making the back facets when viewed from above, appear doubled.

The best zircons are found in Sri Lanka, but zircons are also found in Cambodia, south Vietnam near the Cambodian border, New South Wales in Australia, Myanmar (Burma), Canada, Norway, Russia, and France. Zircon is found in Kashmir, Coimbatore, Bihar, Shimla, and Kulu—all in India.

An auspicious zircon will be: transparent, homogenous, radiant, of a good color, lustrous, and soft to the touch. A good color for a zircon is honey or the color of cow urine.

An inauspicious zircon will not be radiant, will be flat-bodied, have a light, blackish hue when seen from a distance, be full of layers, rough, and look like a yellow piece of glass.

A zircon should weigh six, eleven, or thirteen carats and be set in iron or silver. A zircon ring should be worn on the middle finger of the left hand on a Saturday two hours after sunset.

Hessonite

Hardness 7, specific gravity 3.6, refractive index 1.75, dispersion 0.028.

Hessonite is a transparent gemstone. It is actually a type of garnet, and is known as a gomedha in Hindi.

Hessonites come in two colors, golden and cinnamon. A perfectly colored hessonite is a bright golden-orange that resembles a combination of honey, orange and blood and it has an internal fire. Some hessonite has tints of red and brown. The darker garnets should usually not be worn.

Hessonites are found in Africa, Sri Lanka, and Myanmar (Burma).

Astrological Effects of Hessonite Garnet (Gomedha)

Rahu rules hessonite. Rahu is an *aprakash graha,* a lusterless planet, and it gives the results of the lord of the house which it tenants. If Rahu is on the ascendant, wearing hessonite may be recommended. Hessonite may also be good for those born under Aries.

Wearing a good hessonite brings wealth, success, position, prestige, happiness, prosperity, good children, praise, fame, and health. It protects against rivalries and enemies, and thus is good to wear when going into battle. It helps to give good health and appetite, rids the mind of bad thoughts, and gives mental peace. It helps to increase one's social status, and brings one respect from others. It helps protect against evil spirits and the possibility of being poisoned. Brilliant scientists are associated with hessonite, and the gem also helps those who must deal with employees and servants.

Hessonite and its substitutes transmit the cosmic color, ultra-violet. Ultra-violet is the coldest color ray, and should be used for diseases caused by overheating, such as high fevers, insomnia, extreme acid, indigestion, and over-sexuality. It also works with insanity.

A flawed hessonite should not be worn. It is difficult to find a flawless hessonite. A hessonite is flawed if it has a white or bluish color and lacks luster. Wearing a Gomedha with a red color is bad for health. If the gem has a mixture of mica, it ruins wealth..

The gemstone should weigh at least two carats (three is better), and should be set in gold, silver, or a combination of gold, silver, and iron. It should be worn on the middle finger or smallest finger of either hand. Some authorities say it should be worn on the finger ruled by Rahu. The ring should be put on for the first time on a Saturday, during the waxing moon. Rahu should be in a good sign and in the constellations of Swati, Ardra, or Satabisha.

The mantra for hessonite: *Om ram rahave namaha om*. Stotra of invocation: *"Om ardhakaya maha virya, candra dvitya vimardaman, simhika garbha sambhutam, tam rahum pranamami aham."*

Substitute stones are gold-orange zircon, spessertite, golden grossularite garnet, or other gold-orange gems.

Hessonite's cosmic color is ultra-violet, its cosmic number four.

A hessonite gem is often placed in a deceased person's mouth before cremation. This is believed to help the soul remain free of Rahu's obstruction on the journey to future birth.

As Rahu is incompatible with the Sun and Moon, hessonite and its substitutes should not be worn with rubies or pearls and their substitutes. Some experts say that hessonite and its substitutes should also not be worn with yellow sapphire or red coral and their substitutes. The Navaratna setting is the exception to this rule.

Depending on a person's occupation, different colors of hessonite should be worn. A priest, teacher, scientist, or intellectual should wear a honey orange gem. A ruler, soldier, or administrator should wear a reddish orange gem. A businessman, farmer, or banker should wear a golden orange gem. A laborer, artisan, or servant should wear a brownish orange gem.

Jade
Hardness 6–7, Specific gravity 3–3.5, Refractive index 1.6–1.67.

Jade is usually translucent to opaque. Its colors range from apple green to emerald green, and almost-white to greenish white. Jade can be highly polished. Jade is hard and does not scratch easily. Nor is it easily cut. Therefore, well-cut and polished jade is more valuable than uncut stones.

Jade is used as a substitute for emerald to strengthen Mercury. Only green jade is used for this purpose. Good quality jade can be effective in removing the negative effects of badly placed planets.

There are two types of jade, and they are actually two different minerals—jadeite and nephrite. Jadeite is a silicate of sodium and aluminum; nephrite is a silicate of calcium and magnesium. Both are hard and durable, more difficult to carve than steel. Jade will not usually break if hit with a hammer. Jadeite is slightly harder than nephrite, but it is easier to fracture it.

Most of the world's jadeite comes from Upper Myanmar. This jadeite is what we have come to know as "imperial jade," or "Chinese jade." Jadeite is also found in South America, Brazil, Malagasy Republic, South China, Mexico, and Tibet.

British Columbia in Canada is the largest producer in the world of nephrite jade. Nephrite jade is also found in Turkistan, New Zealand, and Siberia.

The color and translucency of jade are the main things that affect its value. Jade can be several different colors. White jade is usually nephrite. The emerald green jade ("Imperial jade") is always jadeite and is the rarest and most valuable form of the stone. Jadeite also comes in orange-red, mauve, blue-green, and lavender. Both types of jade can appear in a variety of colors.

Sometimes jewelers dye jade green, but the dyes are usually not permanent and the stone fades over time. There are many substitutes for jade, one of which is chalcedony.

Jade should be set in gold on a Wednesday. It can also be set on a Friday or Saturday. The piece of jade should weigh at least five carats. The proper rituals should be performed to install the stone in its setting, and the ring should be worn on the little finger of the right hand for men and of the left hand for women, within one or two hours after sunrise on a Wednesday of the bright half of a lunar month. The ring should be made when Mercury is in its own sign of Virgo, or in a friendly sign, a constellation tenanted by Mercury, or a constellation friendly to Mercury.

The mantra to be chanted is: *Om bum budhaya namaha om.*

Jade is worn to help improve kidney disease, skin problems, epilepsy, and allergies. It is said to give one long life and to protect one from accidents.

Cat's Eye
Hardness 8.5, Specific gravity 3.75, Refractive index 1.75.

Cat's eye belongs to the Chrysoberyl family. Chrysoberyl is an aluminate of beryllium. Gems that are a cloudy yellow to brownish green color, which shine with varying colors and luster, are known as cat's eye. Cat's eye resembles the eye of a cat caught in headlights at night. It can appear in two colors—translucent honey brown or apple green. It is cut into a rounded cabochon and has moderate dispersion.

A cat's eye's value is judged by its luster and the richness of its color, the sharpness of the eye and its clarity and shape. A cat's eye with a yellow radiance and white band is considered a high quality gem. The gem is considered superior if the inside band is brilliant and straight. Cat's eye is worth about one-third the cost of a blue sapphire.

Some stones show an effect called "milk-and-honey." If a flashlight is shined at the stone's side, half the stone appears milky white while the other half remains a honey color. The honey-yellow gemstones are the most valuable, the green ones next best. A cat's eye with a band is called alexandarite; without the band it is known as chrysolite.

Cat's eyes are found in Myanmar (Burma), Brazil, China, Sri Lanka, and Thiruvananthapuram (Trivandrum) in India. Those found in the Mogok mines in Myanmar (Burma) and in Sri Lanka are considered the best.

A kind of cat's eye also appears in the quartz family, but it is inferior to the one that appears in the chrysoberyl family. The quartz cat's eye is soft and a lower quality. The quartz cat's eye is a less expensive substitute for the chrysoberyl cat's eye. Quartz cat's eyes are found in India and Sri Lanka.

Tiger's eyes are similar to cat's eyes. They are a yellowish black color (golden yellow to bluish) with a band of green. They actually resemble a tiger's eye. This is another less expensive substitute for the chrysoberyl cat's eye.

Imitation cat's eye can be made by cutting synthetic or natural star sapphires in a way that reveals only one ray of the star. Tourmaline and apatite may appear to be chrysoberyl cat's eyes, but they are softer stones. Quartz and glass can also seem like cat's eyes, but they can be distinguished by their lower specific gravity and lightness.

Astrological Effect of Cat's Eye

One is recommended to wear a cat's eye in reference to Ketu. A badly placed Ketu can give one a bad reputation, rivalries, and bring scandal. Cat's eye can also be used if the Sun is badly placed in the birth chart, but a competent astrologer should make the recommendation for its use. Cat's eye has a good result if Ketu is in the sixth, eighth, or twelfth houses from Venus in the chart. Cat's eye acts quickly and should be worn only after a trial. The cosmic number for cat's eye is seven.

Wearing a good cat's eye makes one wealthy, healthy, strongly determined, knowledgeable, and gives good children, happiness in relation to children, and protection from enemies. It will help one gain insight, psychic powers, and can help one have better perception. It gives gains from speculations, the stock market, and gambling. It is said to help one practice witchcraft, if one is so inclined. It protects one from hidden enemies, and keeps one from jail, intoxication, and drowning.

Cat's eye transmits the cosmic color, infra-red, the hottest cosmic ray. It can therefore help with terminal diseases such as paralysis and cancer. It is good for digestive complications, skin problems, and allergies. It can also help with heart problems.

Politicians can use cat's eye to good benefit, and it can help those in business from losing money.

Some flaws of a cat's eye are if it is dull, has a web, is spotted, or it has depressions. Wearing a stone with webs can send a person to jail. It is especially important not to use a gem that has dark or black imperfections, as these will bring misfortune. A cracked gem can cause injury. If it is spotted, it can cause problems with enemies. A dull or opaque stone causes bad health. If it has black spots, it can cause death. If it is lusterless, it can cause bad fortune to one's children. A depression can cause digestion problems.

A cat's eye should be set in steel or gold, or even platinum, on the small finger of the left hand, at midnight on Thursday (some say Saturday), when the Moon is waxing. Some authorities say that the ring should be worn on the middle finger of the right hand. The stone should weigh more than three carats, but five carats or more is better.

When the ring is made, Ketu should be in a positive sign, such as when Ketu is in Sagittarius, Pisces, or Aries, or in the constellations of Mula, Ashvini, or Magha. The mantra to be chanted for cat's eye: *Om kem ketave namaha*.

Substitute stones are tiger's eye, quartz family cat's eye, tourmaline, and beryl.

Ketu is not compatible with the Sun and Moon, so cat's eye or its substitutes should not be worn with rubies or pearls or their substitutes. Some authorities say that cat's eye or its substitutes should also not be worn with yellow sapphires or red coral. The Navaratna setting is an exception.

Depending on a person's occupation, different shades of cat's eye should be worn. A priest, teacher, scientist, or intellectual should wear a honey yellow stone. A ruler, soldier, or administrator should wear a honey brown stone. A businessman, farmer, or banker should wear a honey green stone. A laborer, artisan, or servant should wear a dark green stone.

Stotra of invocation: "*Om palamsa puspa samkasam, taraka grham astakam, raudram raudrat makam ghoram, tam ketum pranamami aham.*"

Garnet
Hardness 7.5, Specific gravity 3.7–3.8, Refractive index 1.75.

Garnets are good substitutes for rubies. A nice garnet has a good color, and is lively and durable. Superior garnets are often faceted, and the lower quality ones are made into beads. Garnets come in a wide variety of colors, but never in blue.

Pyrope garnet is the most popular of the garnets. It is composed of magnesium and aluminum and has a deep blackish-red, brownish-red, or ruby red color. Such garnets are also called Bohemian garnets, Cape rubies, or Arizona rubies. They are not usually flawed.

Garnets are mined in South Africa, Russia, Australia, Brazil, Myanmar (Burma), and the USA. It is usually best to wear garnet around the neck.

A friendship can be cemented by the gift of a pyrope garnet. It is said that this stone will change color if the wearer is due to suffer in some way. Wearing garnets can help one have a successful career and gain wealth, and can help the wearer's descendants. It can also help women improve their bad health and relieve nightmares. Wearing garnets can make one feel more relaxed.

Turquoise
Hardness 5–6, Specific gravity 2.6–2.8, Refractive index 1.61–1.65.

Turquoise is usually blue green to apple green; sky blue stones are not as common as most people think.

Turquoise is used as a birthstone. It maintains its color in artificial light. The color of turquoise fades over time. It should not be placed in water and should be handled carefully—it is a soft stone that is easy to scratch or break. Turquoise can become discolored by absorbing oils or pigments.

Turquoise is found in Mexico, Australia, Egypt, Russia, Tibet, China, Afghanistan, and the USA. The main source is the USA's northwestern states. Sometimes turquoise is painted with a blue dye, then coated in clear plastic. Pale and chalky turquoise is often treated with oil, clear plastic, or glycerin.

If the stone fades just after it is first put on, it should not be used. It is believed that turquoise will change color to warn the wearer of coming disaster.

One who wears turquoise will find happiness, joy, and honesty. Turquoise can be worn by aristocratic and spiritually-minded people to good benefit. It is said to protect one from curses, violence, accidental death, and enemies. If it is placed against the eyes, it can help eye problems. It can also help with headaches, physical pain, liver problems, and throat infections.

Quartz
Hardness 7, Specific gravity 2.65, Refractive index 1.54–1.55.

Quartz comprises a wide assortment of semi-precious gems, and it makes up the largest mineral group. Quartz is silica (oxide of silicon) and appears in two forms, crystalline, which grows in a single crystal, and chalcedony, which is formed by millions of micro-crystals. Quartz is low in dispersion, and has brilliance, fire, and a glassy luster. Clarity is an important factor when judging quality. Quartz is free from cleavage and is durable. When broken, is has a curved fracture. Quartz is mined mainly in Brazil and Uruguay. It is inexpensive.

Transparent quartz stones: rock crystal, golden topaz (citrine), amethyst, and smoky quartz. Colorless crystalline quartz is known as rock crystal. This is the kind of crystal that is used in crystal balls. Amethyst is the most popular crystalline quartz to be used in jewelry. Tibetan Buddhists consider amethyst sacred to Buddha, and they often wear amethyst beads.

Some chalcedony quartzes: onyx, agate, and jasper.

Chatoyant crystalline stones: the greenish-yellow cat's eye and the golden brown tiger's eye. Chatoyant crystals are stones that reflect a single streak of light when cut in a cabochon.

Quartz is said to help the wearer develop spiritual qualities, and it is therefore of benefit to spiritualists, astrologers, palmists, and philosophers. It is also said to help improve eye, stomach, blood problems, and throat infections.

Rock Crystal

In Hindi, rock crystal is known as *sphatik*. This is the common transparent crystal widely recognized. Rock crystal is an inexpensive substitute for diamonds, but is not very effective. If being used as a diamond substitute, be sure to purchase a stone of at least eleven carats. Rock crystal is best set in gold.

Wearing rock crystal protects against curses, and helps one to have undisturbed sleep. Crystal necklaces are said to aid concentration. If poison is placed in a cup made of rock crystal, the substance will become smoky.

Rock crystal brings good fortune, increases sexual prowess, and protects one from dangerous animals. It is auspicious to wear rock crystal while offering oblations for departed ancestors.

Rock crystal is found in Brazil, the United States, Russia, Japan, Hungary, France, and Madagascar. In India, it can be found in Kashmir, the Vindhyachal Mountains, Spiti, Kulu and Satpura in Madhya Pradesh.

A fractured or discolored crystal should not be used, as it will cause trouble for the wearer.

Topaz

Hardness 8, Specific gravity 3.5–3.6, Reflective index 1.6–1.64.

Topaz has low dispersion and a cleavage perfect in one direction. Topaz is recommended for those whose solar sign is Gemini. It can also be worn by those under the signs of Libra and Scorpio.

Topazes can be orange-yellow, amber-gold, blue, purple, the color of sherry, brown, or pink. The most valuable topaz is known as Imperial topaz, and it is reddish gold. The pink and peach (brownish yellow) topazes are more costly than other colors. Blue topaz is the most common and the least expensive. Blue topaz comes mainly from China. It is colorless or white when it is mined, but irradiation changes the stone to an electric blue. If this is done improperly, the gem can become radioactive, and it is not recommended for astrological use when irradiated.

Other topazes are found in Brazil, Russia, Ukraine, and Pakistan.

Topaz is a hard gem, but it cleaves easily, so a hard blow can crack it. A sudden change in temperature can also cause topaz to crack.

Topaz can have a good influence over the mind and soul. It helps one become more aware, happier, creative, improve one's concentration, increases one's intelligence, and helps one have better clarity of mind. It helps improve wealth, relieves depression, and helps one avoid misfortune. Topaz can help those with dangerous jobs, and can help make life more pleasant. It also helps a couple remain loyal to one another.

Topaz works with the nervous system, relieves exhaustion, mental problems, and diseases of the solar plexus. It can help cure heart complications, migraines, liver problems, diarrhea, rheumatism, ulcers, insomnia, arthritis, jaundice, impotency, and gout.

Citrine

Natural citrine is hard to find, and most of the citrines on the market are actually heat-treated natural amethyst. Natural citrine, however, is a good substitute for yellow sapphire and topaz. Citrines resemble yellow sapphire, and are often sold as topaz, although topaz usually has a richer color.

Citrine comes from Brazil, Uruguay, Madagascar, and France. The best gems come from Brazil. One who wears citrine will have undisturbed sleep.

Opal
Hardness 5.5–6.5, Specific gravity 2–2.25, Refractive index 1.44–1.47.

Opal is hydrated amorphous silica. Opals are used as birthstones. They are said to be good for those born in October.

Opals with variable color changes and that are bright, have a good value. Black opal is rare, and is usually the most valuable. Most good quality opals are found in Australia, although they are generally processed in Asia. Opals are also found in Indonesia.

Opals refract light and then reflect it in a play of colors. Opals can be found in a wide selection of colors and patterns. Water is the main ingredient of opals, so do not allow them to dry out. Opals are easily scratched, especially when set in a ring. They can also be easily shattered either by hitting them or a rapid change in temperature.

Opals help with spiritual and religious life, finances, family life, and they improve one's beauty. They help develop the ability to foretell the future, and many astrologers use them for this purpose. They can also help with legal cases.

With use, opals become dull. After some time, they should be replaced.

Moonstone
Hardness 6, Specific gravity 2.57, Refractive index 1.51–1.52.

Moonstone is an opaque, colorless gem that serves as a substitute for pearl. Moonstones usually have a silvery-white milky sheen called adularescence. There is a band of light, within the body of a moonstone, that is an interplay of light that moves when it is turned.

Some moonstones have a bluish opalescent sheen caused by the reflection of light. Most moonstones with this opalescent sheen are mined in Sri Lanka, and they are both rarer and more expensive than other types of moonstone because their main Sri Lankan source dried up in 1988. The bluer the stone, the more costly it is. The most expensive moonstones cost about US$700 per carat. Whitish stones have little value, and the palest stones are very cheap. Such moonstones are often made into beads.

Moonstones are also found in India, Switzerland, and Myanmar (Burma). Indian moonstones are usually low quality.

Moonstone gives good concentration, mental peace and upliftment, and can help with marriage problems, depression, stomach problems, heart problems, epilepsy, and gynecological problems.

Moonstone is more effective when worn during the bright half of the lunar month; it is weakened during the dark half. Moonstone should be set in silver and worn on the ring (although some say, little) finger.

Peridot
Hardness 6.5–7, Specific gravity 3.22–3.44, Refractive index 1.64–1.69

Peridot is a semi-precious gem that can substitute for emerald. Peridots make up a group of minerals, but most are not used as gemstones. The stones used in jewelry are bright green in color. The greener the color, the more valuable the stone. Any tinge of brown in the stone reduces its value. The darker green stones are called olivines, the lighter green (ranging from yellowish green to bottle green) are called chrysolites. Peridot has an imperfect cleavage in two directions.

Some pale green stones are found in Queensland in Australia, Myanmar (Burma), Pakistan, Brazil, Kenya, China, and North America. Peridot is found in large quantities in small sizes of less than two carats in China. The main source of gem-quality peridot is found in Mogok, in Upper Myanmar (Burma).

Peridots are often mistaken for emeralds, but they are usually clearer, with less inclusions, and much less expensive. Because of peridot's relative softness, care has to be taken to keep it from becoming scratched. The price of peridot per carat does not go up with an increase in stone size.

One who wears peridot will gain wealth, happiness, good health, and have good children. Peridots are believed to cure epilepsy.

Amethyst
Amethyst is a beautiful violet color and is the most valuable type of quartz. It is a good substitute for blue sapphire. The darker the color, the more effective it is.

Amethysts are mined in Brazil and Uruguay, but are also found in the USA, Sri Lanka, Myanmar (Burma), India, and Mexico. The Brazilian amethysts are considered the best, but the ones from Sri Lanka and India are also good quality. Imitation amethysts are often made from glass or synthetic sapphires. Synthetic amethyst is usually made in Russia.

Amethyst can be used to increase financial gain, for general physical well-being, position, and social status. It is said that amethyst will become brighter if it is placed next to a poisonous substance. It is also believed that the stone will change color if the wearer becomes ill.

It can be used with good benefit by social workers, scientists, mathematicians, scholars, and by those engaged in travel, public relations, entertainment, and fashion.

Amethyst is said to be good for those under Pisces or Aquarius, but can also be worn by those under Capricorn.

Bloodstone

Bloodstone is an opaque, dark green stone with red spots. Excellent bloodstones shine brightly. Bloodstone is usually used as a birthstone. A person born under Aries or Scorpio can use this stone with good effect.

It is said that if a person wears bloodstone, he or she will be strong in business and defeat their enemies. They help one increase one's followers, and they protect a wearer from drowning. They can be used to increase courage and mental concentration.

Agate

Agate comes in different colors—yellow, red, milk white, brown, and the less found blue and green colored stones. The best agate is found in Brazil and Uruguay, but the stone is also found in India and the USA.

Sometimes agate is used as a substitute for red coral, but it is not a very effective one. Agates are good for those born under Virgo.

Those who wear agate get long life, family happiness, and prosperity. Their careers improve, and if they are farmers, they are benefited. Agates are also used to improve one's health and financial stability. Agate, it is said, is good to use for countering curses and protecting against jealous rivalries. Physically, it is said to protect against bodily pains, headaches, and excess stomach acid.

Lapis Lazuli

Hardness 5–5.5, Specific gravity 2.7–2.9, Reflective index 1.5.

Lapis lazulis are good for those born under the solar sign of Taurus. They can also be of help in reference to Saturn. Lapis lazuli is a substitute gem for blue sapphire.

They are found mainly in Afghanistan and Chile, although Russia and the United States also mine this stone.

If a child wears a necklace of lapis lazuli beads on a gold chain, it is said that the child will maintain good health and be protected from the bad influences of an evil eye. Lapis lazuli is believed to help women who take part in music, art, dancing, and acting. It is said to help prevent laziness, to increase one's social status, determination, and general happiness. Lapis lazuli also helps overcome depression, diabetes and eye, stomach, and liver problems .

Tourmaline
Hardness 7–7.5, Specific gravity 3.1–3.25, Refractive index 1.61–1. 67.

Tourmaline is found in a variety of colors. The variety is due to the chemical composition. Most tourmalines are composed of silicate and borate of aluminum or magnesia and iron. Tourmaline does not have a cleavage and is a durable gemstone.

Depending on the color, tourmalines are known by different names. Red and pink tourmalines are called rubellite; blue, Brazilian sapphires; colorless, achorite; yellow to yellow green, Ceylonese peridot; green, Brazilian emerald; and violet to red purple, siberite.

Brazil is the main source of tourmaline, but yellow and brown stones are found in Sri Lanka, reds and pinks in California, reds in Myanmar (Burma), reds and greens in Brazil and Russia, and reds, blues, and greens in the USA.

The colors of the stones can be changed by heating or irradiation, but the change is not always permanent. Tourmaline is often cut into a rectangular shape that follows its naturally long and narrow crystal formation. Green tourmaline is often mistaken for emerald, and the blue variety is mistaken for blue sapphire.

Wearing tourmaline increases the wearer's intelligence, and improves concentration. Tourmaline can help someone financially and can be used as a general good-luck stone. Politicians and leaders can wear tourmaline to good effect. It should be set in silver.

Different colors of tourmaline are used to substitute for diamonds, rubies, emeralds, blue sapphires, and yellow sapphires.

Aquamarine
Hardness 6.75, Specific gravity 2.7, Refractive index 1.57–1.58.

Aquamarine is said to be good for those born under Pisces or who have Jupiter well-placed on the ascendant of their birth chart. They are also good for those born under Leo.

Aquamarine is a variety of beryl. A good Aquamarine is transparent, lustrous, and radiant. It has many of the properties of emerald, and can substitute for that gem. Aquamarine is considered a semi-precious stone, and it is therefore much less expensive than an emerald. Aquamarine is often a bright sky blue. The blue color can be produced by heating greenish, greenish yellow, or brownish beryls. It is not good to use a heat-treated gem for astrological purposes. A good aquamarine should not have any inclusions.

Aquamarines are found in Siberia, the Ural Mountains in Russia, Madagascar, and Brazil.

Mothers derive good benefits from aquamarines, and the stones can help solve marital problems. They are also good for spiritual life and for those interested in humanitarian activities. They are beneficial for those in entertainment, teaching, banking, medicine, travel, sailing, or public relations business. They can also help improve personal problems, and they protect the wearers from being exploited. They help improve one's investment abilities.

Spinel
Specific gravity 3.6–4, Refractive index 1.72–1.8.

Red spinel can substitute for ruby and blue spinel for blue sapphire. Spinels can be purple, pink, pink tinged with orange, green, and more rarely, blue. Red spinel is the most valuable. It is rare to find a spinel that weighs more than five carats. Spinel are beautiful, durable gemstones without cleavages and with a moderate dispersion.

Spinel is most commonly a brilliant red, and is often found where rubies are found. Thus people often mistake red spinel for ruby. Some of the well-known "rubies" in the British Crown jewelry collection are actually spinel. Spinel is mined mainly in Myanmar (Burma), although they are also found in Pakistan, Sri Lanka, and Afghanistan.

There are many synthetic spinels on the market, and people are often fooled.

Spinel is said to help the wearer financially, and can protect the wearer from unexpected losses.

Purchasing Gemstones Overseas
It is important to purchase gemstones from a reputable shop. The difficulty lies in being able to distinguish a reputable shop from a disrepu-

table one. Before making any purchase, go to several shops and expect straightforward dealings.

The biggest mistake a person can make when purchasing gemstones overseas is trying to negotiate too good a deal. Something valuable will not be sold for nothing. It is unlikely that a normal buyer will gain an advantage over a professional gem dealer. If you think you have struck too good a bargain, question the quality of the stone you are purchasing. In Southeast Asia there is no shortage of con men.

If someone seems too friendly and accommodating, especially if you have met him on the street, be especially careful. Even if this person takes you to a reputable shop, his commission will be fixed into the price you pay. Such persons often receive a healthy commission, and you, the buyer, will find yourself paying up to fifty percent or more than you would have paid normally. Remember the old saying, "Too much devotion is the sign of a thief." Be just as careful with tour operators, who also often receive commissions for introducing you to particular shops.

A general rule: the closer you are to where the stones are mined, the better chance you have of being cheated. There is more of a likelihood that synthetic stones are for sale along with the real ones. Unless you know the difference, such places are better avoided.

A common scam: "A special government tax has been waived for the next few days. Buy now while the price is right!"

Another scam: You are told that you will be able to resell the gems you are purchasing at home for a huge profit. Or, you are told that you are receiving a wholesale price. Be extremely careful of those who make such statements. If such huge profits were available, these merchants would be making them themselves. Written guarantees mean nothing.

Prices of Gems

A gem's price is determined by the four "Cs": carat (weight), cut, clarity, and color. Another major factor is the buyer's preferences. If a gem is fashionable, its value will increase. Another factor affecting price is whether the gem is common or rare. Whether a gemstone is natural, synthetic, or imitation will affect the price, as will supply and demand. Often speculation can drive the price of gemstones up or down. If a new diamond mine is discovered and the supply uncontrolled, the price of diamonds will drop.

Only flawless, well-colored (or colorless) gems should be used for astrological purposes. Only ten percent of natural gems fall into this category. After flaws are ruled out, the color should be judged. Flawless gems are difficult to find. Still, they are worth seeking out, because their effect is most positive. It is definitely better to pay more for a flawless gem than a flawed one. If a gem has too many flaws, it should not be purchased at all.

Carat—Weight and Size

Carats are the unit of measurement used for selling gems. A carat is one-fifth of a gram. 5 carats =1.0 gram =0.035 ounce. 141.75 carat = 28.35 grams =1 ounce.

Usually, as the weight of a gem increases, so does its value. The value does not usually increase proportionate to the increase in size, because larger stones are rarer and thus more valuable. The price of diamonds, rubies, and emeralds increases greatly with an increase in their weight, because large varieties of these gemstones are rare. For example, a one-carat diamond may cost about $1,000; a two-carat diamond will usually be more than double that price, around $3,000. Aquamarine, topaz, and rock crystal do not increase as much in value as their carat size increases, because large crystals of these gemstones are more common.

When you are shown a gem, you should be able to see its weight. If a gem is cut too deeply, much of the gem cannot be seen. The gem may also be too dark. If the cut of the gem is too shallow, it will lack brilliance and have a flat, washed-out look. If a gem is cut properly, it will look good from any angle.

Color

A gemstone's color is a big factor in its price. Colored stones are usually more valuable than clear ones, except for diamonds. Some gems are fixed in their color. Ruby means red, and emerald means green. Sapphires can be any color but red, but blue sapphires are considered the most valuable, along with the pink-orange "lotus flower" variety (due to their rarity). The rarity of a particular color of gemstone is an important factor in determining its price.

A good colored gem should not be so pale that it is hard to see the color, or so dark that it appears black. A gem's color should be uniform, not blotchy or stronger in one spot than another.

Trust your judgment when looking at gem color. Usually the brighter, more vivid and rich the color, the more valuable the gem. Ask to see a range of colors, and notice the differences. Preference is quite personal. Look at the gems in a variety of lights. Some gems look great in daylight but do not look good under artificial light, and vice versa.

"Fire," the fiery flash in a gem, often increases its value. Fire is caused by refraction, which is the bending of light inward as it enters a denser substance. This is normally seen in the refraction in water, which makes a stick seem to bend under water.

Clarity

Clarity refers to the clearness and clean look of a gem. It is measured by lack of inclusions, cracks, or flaws on the surface or within the gem. The clearer the gem, the better. Inclusions are mineral grains that can be seen, fluids within the stone's body, or bad crystal features, such as twinning. Often, gemstones with cloudy inclusions and air bubbles can be clarified by using heat treatment, but gems treated in this way are not good for astrological use.

How many flaws are acceptable in a gem changes from gem to gem. A good emerald will almost always have some inclusions, and a flawless emerald is often suspect—it may be synthetic. Aquamarine should not have flaws, or very few.

Sometimes inclusions can make a gem more attractive, such as with star stones—star sapphires, cat's eyes, feldspars, and rutilated quartz.

Only glass or a highly superior gem is free of inclusions visible to the eye.

To judge a transparent gem's clarity, hold the gem in thumb and forefinger up to the sun and allow the sunlight to pass through the gem. If the gem is opaque or semi-translucent, it is flawed. These gems should not be used for astrological purposes; they will have a negative effect. Pearls, coral, jade, and agate are the only translucent gems considered to have a positive astrolgical effect. Transparent gems give one a better look at the quality of the gem.

Cut and Polishing

Gems are cut and polished in a variety of ways. The preferred cut for a diamond is the brilliant cut, while the preferred cut for precious opal is a domed solid. Some gems are even carved. A good cut increases the value of a gem; a poor cut reduces its value.

Transparent gems are faceted (a facet is a flat, polished face). This process involves cutting with an abrasive (usually diamond) saw, grinding the gem, then polishing it. How a stone is cut affects its brilliance.

Cut can be judged by shape, type, proportion, and symmetry. Diamonds are usually cut by the brilliant cut because this cut makes the most of their high dispersion. The cut has almost sixty facets, which increases the fire or refraction in a diamond. In a diamond, the light is refracted so strongly that it is trapped inside and reflected before it emerges again. The value of diamonds increased greatly in the 1920s when the brilliant cut was developed. Like a diamond, white zircon and colored cassiterite also have strong fire, and therefore benefit from the brilliant cut.

Hardness

Hardness is the measurement of the strength of a gem's chemical bond. Each mineral is given a number to indicate its degree of hardness. Hardness tells us how resistant a gem is to being scratched.

Gems are measured according to Mohs scale from 1 (softest) to 10 (hardest). Minerals with higher numbers can scratch minerals with lower ones. A diamond is the hardest mineral, and receives a 10 on Mohs scale. The difference in hardness between one number on the scale and another is not proportionate. A diamond receives a 10 and corundum a 9, but diamonds are four times as hard as corundum.

Gems softer than 7 on the scale have a tendency to scratch when set in rings. Most quartz includes some dust, which has a hardness of 7. Therefore gems with a hardness less than 7 tend to become scratched by the quartz in dust.

Mohs scale: 1–talc; 2.5–fingernail; 3–copper coin; 4–fluorite; 5–apatite; 5.5–glass; 6–orthochlase feldspar; 6.5–steel: 7–quartz; 8–topaz; 9–corundum; 10–diamond.

Stability

Stability is judged by how well a gem will stand up to chemicals or deteriorating substances. Opals contain water, and may lose stability in dry air; they may crack due to loss of original volume.

Pearls are damaged by alcohol, perfume, and acids. Some amethysts and kunzites can fade in sunlight. Porous gems such as turquoise can become discolored by skin oils.

Toughness

A gem's toughness is based on how well it resists cracking, chipping, or breaking. Crystals often have a plane of weakness, or a cleavage. Diamonds, which are the hardest mineral, are not actually so tough due to their octahedral cleavage planes. Diamonds may break if dropped or struck.

Topaz has a hardness of 8 but is also not so tough. Topaz has one perfect cleavage, which makes it hard to facet. Some gems have an internal stress, which lowers their toughness. Opal can chip easily if hit sharply.

Nephrite Jade has a hardness of between 6 and 6.5, but it is the toughest gemstone because of its strong, interlocking fiber crystal.

Pearls have a hardness of 3, but it is tough; they do not easily break when dropped.

Luster

Luster is the light reflected from the gem's surface. Some stones flash like the sun, while others have a subtler, softer luster. To have a high luster, the gem must have a smooth surface and be highly reflective. Polishing gems help improve their luster.

Diamonds have the brightest luster. They have an adamantine or hard luster. Most other gemstones possess a glassy or vitreous luster. Quartz is a good example of such a shine. The luster of turquoise is softer.

Brilliance

Brilliance is the reflection of light from within a gem. A brilliant gem is described as being lively, or having life. A gem's brilliance depends on its refractive index and upon the way it is cut. A gem's sparkle is counted as its brilliance.

Refractive Index

The Refractive Index (RI) measures the velocity of light traveling through the gemstone, and how that gem refracts the light that enters it. Refraction is created when the speed of light changes as it moves from air to some other form of matter. A faceted gem will refract back from within itself light that enters it. When light enters a gem, it changes course and is slowed down (refracted).

An instrument called a refractometer measures Refractive Index. It measures the angle that light bends in a gemstone.

The refractivity of a gem is higher in the more dense stones. The most refractive gems, diamond and sapphire, are denser than most gems. All gems except ones that have high symmetry (such as cubical stones) have two or three refractive indexes.

Difference In Light

The light in which one views a gem can make it appear differently. The blue of a sapphire will look bluer under a fluorescent light, because fluorescent light contains many waves in the blue range. A ruby viewed under a fluorescent light will appear weak and have a muddy red color.

A blue sapphire looks best when viewed in strong sunlight in the summer or in the tropics, or under a strong fluorescent light. Winter sunlight will make it appear dull. If it is cloudy the gem may appear a grayish blue.

Specific Gravity

Density is measured by Specific Gravity. Specific Gravity is the weight of a gem compared to an equal volume of water, which is equal to the value in grams per cubic centimeter.

The density of a gem can be measured by weighing it in air and in water. Gems can also be sunk in liquids of various densities. If there are two gems of the same size, the one with higher density will appear heavier when held.

Cleavage

A cleavage is a weakness in a crystal that tends to break along a certain plane. When there are cleavages in gemstones, it can be difficult to cut a face across them. Some gems don't have cleavages. For example, quartz gems break in curved fractures.

Fire

Fire is the play of color in a gem. Dispersion causes fire in a gem. The colors that make up white light bend to different degrees during refraction. As they pass through a gem, they separate into the colors of the rainbow. Fire is usually seen only in clear gems, because the natural color of other gems will cover this phenomenon.

The degree of dispersion varies with each gem. In two different gemstones of the same size and cut, the one with the greater dispersion will show more colors. Thus a diamond has a higher quality fire than a quartz gem.

Synthetic or Treated Gems

A synthetic gem is a manufactured equivalent of a natural one. Such gems are manufactured in laboratory-controlled conditions, and are useless for astrological purposes.

There are different kinds of synthetic gems. An imitation gem resembles a natural gem, but has a totally different composition.

A treated or enhanced gem has been changed chemically or physically.

Gems are often heated or irradiated to enhance or change their color, or to improve their clarity. Some gems are enhanced chemically by dyeing, bleaching, waxing, adding plastic, or oiling.

Some forms of enhancement are considered respectable in the gem business. For example, heating blue sapphires bring out their blue color. Such enhancements permanently alter the gem. Jewelers are required to inform customers about enhancements, if the customer inquires.

Dying is common in the gem business. To test whether or not a gem has been dyed, rub the stone with a cotton ball dipped in fingernail polish remover (acetone). Acetone will dissolve the dye and it will rub off onto the cotton ball.

Most rubies and sapphires are heat treated to improve their color because treating increases the sale value. Amethyst, spinel, topaz, peridot, garnet, citrine, and tourmaline are also frequently treated. Since jewelers are usually good at what they do, it is difficult to tell whether gems have been treated.

Once a gem has been altered, it greatly reduces its astrological value. Great care should be taken, therefore, to purchase untreated, high quality gems.

Gem Substitutes

There are two types of man-made substitutes, synthetics and simulants. A synthetic gem is made of exactly the same substance as the natural gem, but it is grown in a laboratory. It can sometimes be difficult to tell a natural gem from a synthetic one. Natural stones often have inclusions, which help with identification. Synthetics sometimes have lines or bubbles by which they can be identified.

Occasionally, a substitute substance or gem may be passed off as the real thing. For example, a cheaper gem may be substituted for a more expensive one—citrine quartz can be substituted for the more precious topaz. Such substitutions are fraudulent.

Simulants are not composed of exactly the same substance as real gems, but when one examines them, they appear to closely resemble the natural stone. Cubic zirconia (zirconinum oxide) highly resembles a diamond and may be sold as such. Imitation gems are often made of glass, plastic, or a combination of two (doublets) or three (triplets) substances. The parts may be imitation or real.

Birthstones According to the Sidereal System

Sign of Zodiac	Birthstone Gemstone	Substitute	Ruling Planet
Aries	Red Coral	Jasper, Bloodstone	Mars
Taurus	Diamond	White Topaz	Venus
Gemini	Emerald	Green Jade, Peridot	Mercury
Cancer	Pearl	Moonstone	Moon
Leo	Ruby	Bloodstone	Sun
Virgo	Emerald	Green Jade, Peridot	Mercury
Libra	Diamond	White Topaz	Venus
Scorpio	Red Coral	Jaspter, Bloodstone	Mars
Sagittarius	Yellow Sapphire	Yellow Topaz, Citrine	Jupiter
Capricorn	Blue Sapphire	Lapis Lazuli, Amethyst	Saturn
Aquarius	Blue Sapphire	Lapis Lazuli, Amethyst	Saturn
Pisces	Yellow Sapphire	Yellow Topaz, Citrine	Jupiter
	Hessonite		Rahu
	Cat's Eye		Ketu

Birthstones according to National Association of Jewelers

According to what was decided at a meeting of the National Association of Jewelers held in Kansas City, USA in 1912, the following birthstone chart was devised. According to Vedic astrology, there is no correlation with this list and the signs of the zodiac. This is because the Sun changes signs around the third week of every month; therefore gemstones cannot be assigned to particular months but should be assigned to zodiacal signs. According to the Tropical (Western) system of astrology, the Sun's location at birth determines the birth sign. Measuring gemstones against only the sun's placement is not a reliable way to judge their use. But here is the chart:

Month of Birth	Birth Stone	Significance
January	Garnet	Constancy
February	Amethyst	Success
March	Blood Stone or Aquamarine	Courage
April	Diamond	Innocence
May	Emerald	Fidelity
June	Pearl or Moonstone	Sincerity
July	Ruby	Nobility

August	Sardonyx or Peridot	Virtue
September	Blue Sapphire	Prosperity
October	Opal or Pink Tourmaline	Happy Dreams
November	Topaz or Citrine	True Love
December	Turquoise or Zircon	Wisdom

Constellations and Gems

Each constellation is ruled by a particular planet and is related to a particular gemstone:

Twenty-seven Constellations	Planets	Gemstones
Ashwini	Ketu	Cat's Eye
Bharani	Venus	Diamond
Krittika	Sun	Ruby
Rohini	Moon	Pearl
Mrigashira	Mars	Coral
Ardra	Rahu	Hessonite
Punarvasu	Jupiter	Yellow Sapphire
Pushya	Saturn	Blue Sapphire
Ashlesha	Mercury	Emerald
Magha	Ketu	Cat's Eye
Purva Phalguni	Venus	Diamond
Uttar Phalguni	Sun	Ruby
Hasta	Moon	Pearl
Chitra	Mars	Coral
Swati	Rahu	Hessonite
Vishakha	Jupiter	Yellow Sapphire
Anuradha	Saturn	Blue Sapphire
Jyeshtha	Mercury	Emerald
Mula	Ketu	Cat's Eye
Purva Shadha	Venus	Diamond
Uttar Shadha	Sun	Ruby
Shravana	Moon	Pearl
Dhanistha	Mars	Coral
Purva Badra	Jupiter	Yellow Sapphire
Uttar Bhadra	Saturn	Blue Sapphire
Revati	Mercury	Emerald

Navaratna Ring or Pendant

The Navaratna ring or pendant contains all nine planetary gems. Substitute gems should not be used in such settings, and substituting for the more expensive stones should not be necessary because each gemstone used is actually quite small. All the gems should be real and flawless. The following gems are to be set in a Navaratna arrangement: diamond, emerald, ruby, pearl, coral, cat's eye, sapphire, topaz, and hessonite.

A Navaratna ring is believed to bring happiness, prosperity, honor, fame, mental peace, long life, and wealth. A Navaratna ring will enhance the good effects of any planets in their own signs or in signs of their exaltation.

This ring should be prescribed by an astrologer. The astrologer should also set the auspicious day and time at which to wear the ring. A qualified person should perform the *puja* (worship).

The ring can be set either in gold or silver, and the nine gems should be set in a prescribed order—which an Indian goldsmith should know.

The mantra to be chanted for this ring: "*Om Surya namaha, Chandraye namaha, Budhaye namaha, Brihaspataye namaha, Mangala namaha, Shukraye namaha, Shaniaye namaha, Rahuaye namaha, Ketuaye namaha, Nava grahaye namaha.*" This mantra should be chanted one thousand times a day for fifty days.

Prescribing a Gem

Using gemstones as astrological remedies is a complicated science, and it is best to consult a qualified astrologer before making any decisions in this regard. Wearing an incorrect gem can be severely detrimental to one's health and happiness.

There are those who think that if a *krura-graha,* cruel planet, is badly placed in the chart, one should not use its gemstone to improve its effects. This is because the gemstone may also strengthen the planet's bad effects. It would be better, these experts say, to use another gem—one that would strengthen the positive planets in the chart and therefore improve one's situation overall. Other experts say that wearing gemstones filters out the negative rays of the afflicting planets and allows only their positive aspects to work on the wearer. Whatever one's point of view, it is certainly not a good idea to wear a gem to strengthen an afflicted planet without having that gem prescribed by a qualified astrologer.

In prescribing gems, the birth chart must be drawn to see how the various planets are positioned in the *rasis* (zodiacal signs) and *bhavas* (houses).

An astrologer would then look at the position of the planets in the signs and houses, whether they are in friendly signs, are exalted, are well-aspected, or are in *mulatrikona*. All these things give positive effects and strengthen a chart. Besides checking the birth house chart, a *navamsa* chart is often also drawn and examined in Sidereal astrology.

Astrologers may also prescribe gemstones based on *prashna* charts, which are charts drawn up to reply to particular questions. Gemstones may be prescribed to help with specific problems addressed by the native's question.

Things astrologers may check to prescribe a gem
1. The *lagna* (rising) sign, and whether it is positively situated.
2. The *mahadasha* or major planetary period. Sometimes gems will be prescribed to help during a particular *mahadasha*, and then removed after that planetary period has passed.
3. The Moon's position in the chart.
4. The position of the twenty-seven constellations the Moon tenants. Different gems may be worn during different constellations.
5. Then the overall chart is assessed: what planets are exalted, sign ownership, aspects, and other positions.

VASTU SASTRA

Where we live can influence our happiness, wealth, health, and prosperity. The Vastu Shastra is the Vedic science of building. When one studies the Vastu Shastra, he learns to create buildings that favorably influence those things that bring us happiness

The Vastu Shastra considers the astrological placement of the Sun, Earth, and other planets during the actual construction. It also considers where the building site is located, the site's shape, the proposed building's shape, the direction the building will face, the location of gates, entry doors, room doors, windows, and the building's general design. North and east are considered important directions—east because it is the direction from which the sun rises.

Assessing the Land

When purchasing a property, it is a good idea to stand on the land and feel its vibration for a few moments. Trust your feelings. If you feel positive about it, consider buying the land. If not, it is probably not good for you. It is best to buy land where happy and successful people have lived. A house sold by a person in distress or who is impoverished, should be purchased only with caution. A dilapidated or haunted house should not be purchased at all.

The land should be cultivatable and should smell good. It is best not to build on nonarable land. Land that contains many rocks, anthills, many worms, bones, broken pottery, sludge, and thorny trees should not be purchased. If the center of the land is humped like the shell of a turtle, it should not be purchased.

The color of the soil should also be considered. White soil is good for *brahmans* (priests, teachers, scientists, or intellectuals), red for *ksatriyas* (rulers, soldiers, or administrators), yellow for *vaisyas* (businessmen, farmers or bankers), and black for *sudras* (laborers, artisans, craftsmen, or servants).

When you assess the soil, do not just make a surface check, but also dig about 4m (12 ft) down. If the soil is black up to 1m (3 ft) down and white or red below that, the land can be purchased. According to Vastu Shastra, black and clayey soil is not good for building. If the soil is crumbly rock, money can easily be gotten. Yellow soil is good for businessmen.

Another test of land quality is to dig a knee-deep hole (2/3m or 2'x2'x2') and then refill it. If after filling the hole you have some soil left over, the land is good. If there is no soil left after filling the hole, the land is average. If the returned soil does not even fill the hole, this is not a good sign. Such land should not be purchased. This shows the soil's natural moisture and aeration.

Again dig the same sized hole. This time, fill it with water. If it takes more than an hour for the water to be absorbed, this is a good sign. If there are many cracks in the hole after the water has been absorbed, the construction may cost more than you expect. This is a percolation test done even in the U.S. to test for clay deposits. The cracks indicate clay soil, which is not best for water drainage and can cause foundation problems, etc. Also, wastes are not carried away properly, which can bring disease.

Do not purchase land that has been used as a crematorium, cemetery, or a *samadhi* (tomb for a holy person). The land should not be purchased if in the recent past someone has committed suicide on it, or if there have been several deaths over the period of a couple of months.

It is usually best not to purchase land next to a bridge. If the bridge is on the north or east sides, it definitely should not be purchased. If it is on the south or west sides, that is a safer purchase.

It is also usually best not to purchase land that shares a well with another property. The land can be purchased, however, if the water supply is a common well on the north, east, or northeast side.

A plot of land situated on a hill is also not a good purchase in most cases. It is better to purchase level ground. If the land to be purchased is on the side of a hill, however, and the land slopes down toward the north or east, that is all right. If the land slopes to the west, do not purchase it.

After choosing and purchasing land, plants should be grown on the land. Also, if possible, keep a cow and her calf on the land for a while to make it more auspicious.

The Land

The direction that the front of a property faces is important. The best shapes for plots of land are square or rectangular, facing squarely on the four cardinal directions. A land tilt of 20 degrees, off square by 20 degrees, is acceptable. If the plot is rectangular, it is better that the longer sides run north to south rather than west to east.

If the plot of land does not squarely face the four cardinal directions, and if the road does not run in one of the four cardinal directions, the house should be built facing the four directions The house should be square or rectangular, and the faces of the building should each be toward a cardinal direction, and not built facing the road.

It is not good to purchase a piece of land squeezed between two larger pieces of land as such land will bring its owner poverty.

The northeast side of the land should be the lowest side. If the northeast side is at a higher elevation than other sides of the property, you can dig soil from that one side and use it to build up the other parts. The land should either slope down toward the north or east, but not toward the west or south. Land sloping north brings riches, sloping east brings good fortune, sloping south brings ruin, and sloping west brings financial loss.

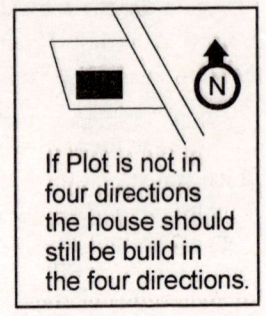

If Plot is not in four directions the house should still be build in the four directions.

It is auspicious if tall buildings or hills do not obstruct the north, northeast, and east sides of the land. Do not purchase land with such obstructions to those sides because the sun's rays will be blocked.

Having those same obstructions blocking the west or south sides, however, bring health and wealth—light coming from the southwest is not beneficial. The sun's rays traveling westward are considered harmful. Thus such obstructions block out harmful rays.

Larger Plot	Not a Good Plot	Larger Plot

For the same reason, a water source located on the southwest side of a building will cause the owner misery. Similarly, there should be a minimum number of doors and windows set into the southwest side of a building; the majority of windows should be set in the northeast side.

The boundary walls around a property should be higher in the west and south and lower in the north and east.

It is auspicious if the plot has a river or a stream flowing through it on the northeast, or if there is a lake on the same side. It is not auspicious if there is an electrical power supply or large electric pole on the northeast side of the plot. A telephone pole is not negative in the northeast, however.

There should not be any valley, a depression in the land, or large pit around the land.

Construction

Construction should not stop once it begins. Workers should not be unnecessarily pushed to speed up their work; work for the day should stop at sunset. No construction should be done at night. A qualified engineer should always oversee the construction.

Building materials should be stored in the southwest corner of the property during construction. The storage area or structure can also be built in the southeast corner, at least 1m (3 ft) from the property boundary. The guard should stay in a house in the southeast corner. Thieves will be a danger if the guard stays in the northwest corner, and the guard should not stay in the southwest corner.

Order of construction: the well, the storage house, and then the boundary wall.

Roads in Relation to Land

A square piece of land surrounded by roads on four sides is considered very good. It should be purchased even if at a high cost. A person who owns this land will become wealthy, healthy, and happy.

If a road runs alongside the property and ends at the northeast corner, that is also very good. If a road ends on any other parts of the property, however, that plot is usually not good.

A road on the north side of the property is good, but a road on the south side is not so good. If there is only one road, it is best if it is located on the east side. It is not so good if it is located on the west side.

If there are roads on only the east and north side, that is good. If there are roads on the west and north, it is average. Roads on the north, west, and east—that is, only on these three sides—is not so good. Roads on the north, south, and west is also not so good. It is inauspicious if there are three roads only on the east, south, and west.

Land should also not be next to a T or Y intersection.

Road to East is very good.

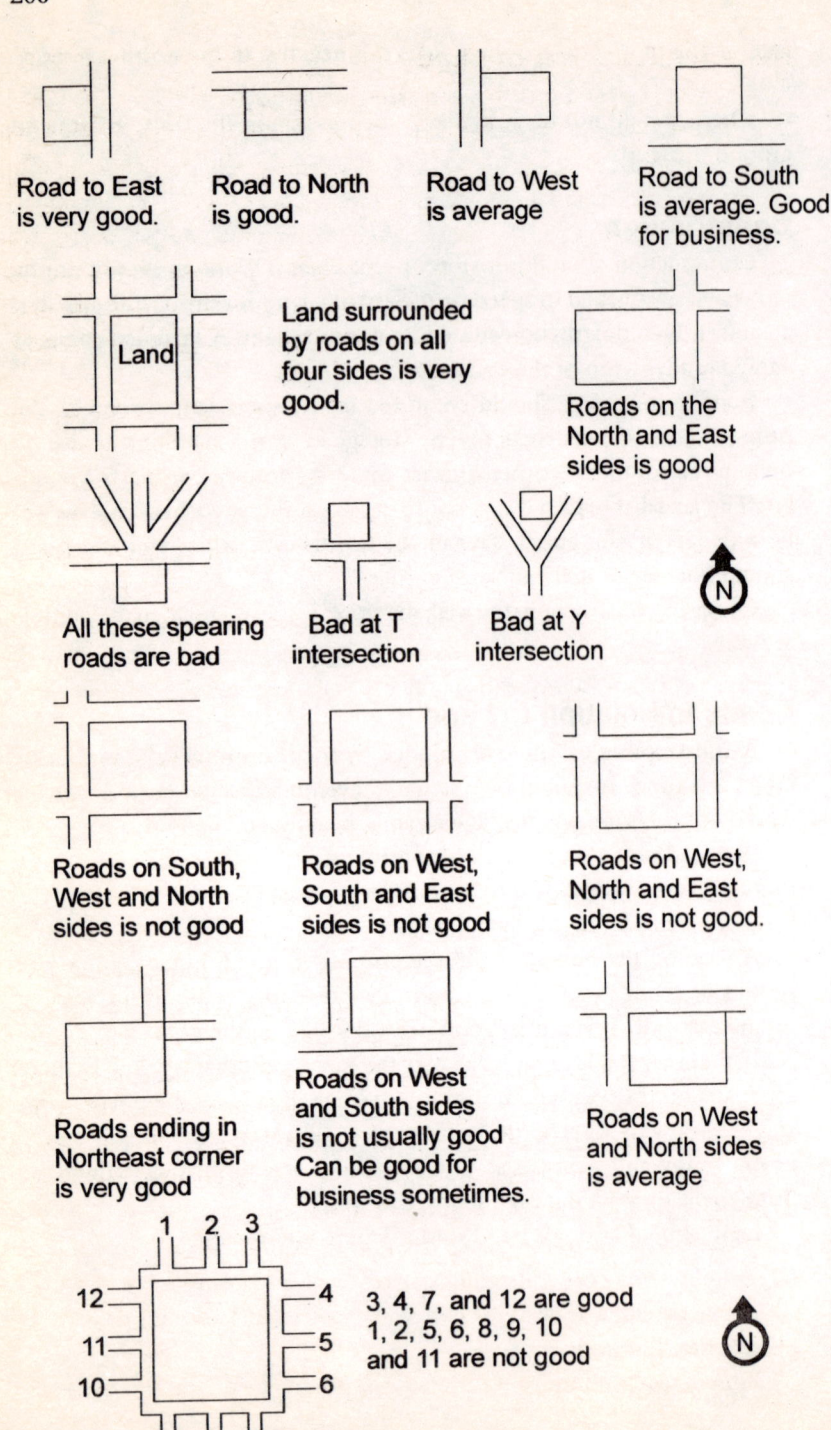

Road to North is good.

Road to West is average

Road to South is average. Good for business.

Land surrounded by roads on all four sides is very good.

Roads on the North and East sides is good

All these spearing roads are bad

Bad at T intersection

Bad at Y intersection

Roads on South, West and North sides is not good

Roads on West, South and East sides is not good

Roads on West, North and East sides is not good.

Roads ending in Northeast corner is very good

Roads on West and South sides is not usually good Can be good for business sometimes.

Roads on West and North sides is average

3, 4, 7, and 12 are good
1, 2, 5, 6, 8, 9, 10 and 11 are not good

Negative Location of Land

There are other aspects of land assessment that should be considered. The plot should not be within twice the distance of the height of the house to a public place—a hospital, factory, temple, church, marriage hall, courthouse, cemetery, or cremation grounds. There should not be a laundry place, shoe shop, meat shop, or workshop with loud machinery opposite the property.

The house should be at least 25m (80 ft) from the entrance of a temple. The property's gate should not face a temple or church, and the shadow of a temple or church should not fall on the house.

If the public place is twice the distance of the height of the house away from the house, it will have no effect.

Building Material

Only new bricks, wood, and materials should be used when building a new house. Materials from an old building should not usually be used to build a new one in case those old materials repeat negative incidents that occurred in the old house. There is unhappiness in using old things. If there are old materials available, better to sell them and use the money to buy new materials.

Wood from thorny trees should not be used, as it will have a negative effect. Materials that have been stored for a long time should also not be used. Iron grills should only be used when needed.

Shape of the Land

The best properties are either square or rectangular. If the plot is not a perfect rectangle, it is best if at least the southwest and southeast sides of the land are at 90° angles from one another. The southwest side of the quadrilateral should definitely not be extended past the southeast side, even if that means giving away a portion of the plot. Land that extends past the northeast side of the quadrilateral, however, brings wealth, happiness, and good name. Land extending on the northeast side is very good. Extensions on any other side are inauspicious. Extensions of the northwest side will cause you to lose money and peace.

If the land is cut in the corner this is not good. If possible the land to fill in the missing corner should be purchased. If the land is cut short on the northeast side it is very bad and is not aspicious; do not purchase it. It is like a headless body.

Round, oval, and triangular plots should be avoided. The house should not be built in the shape of a diamond, with the corner facing north. L-shaped plots are also inauspicious and should not be purchased.

It is good if the plot is narrower at the entrance and wider at its rear, but the opposite is not good.

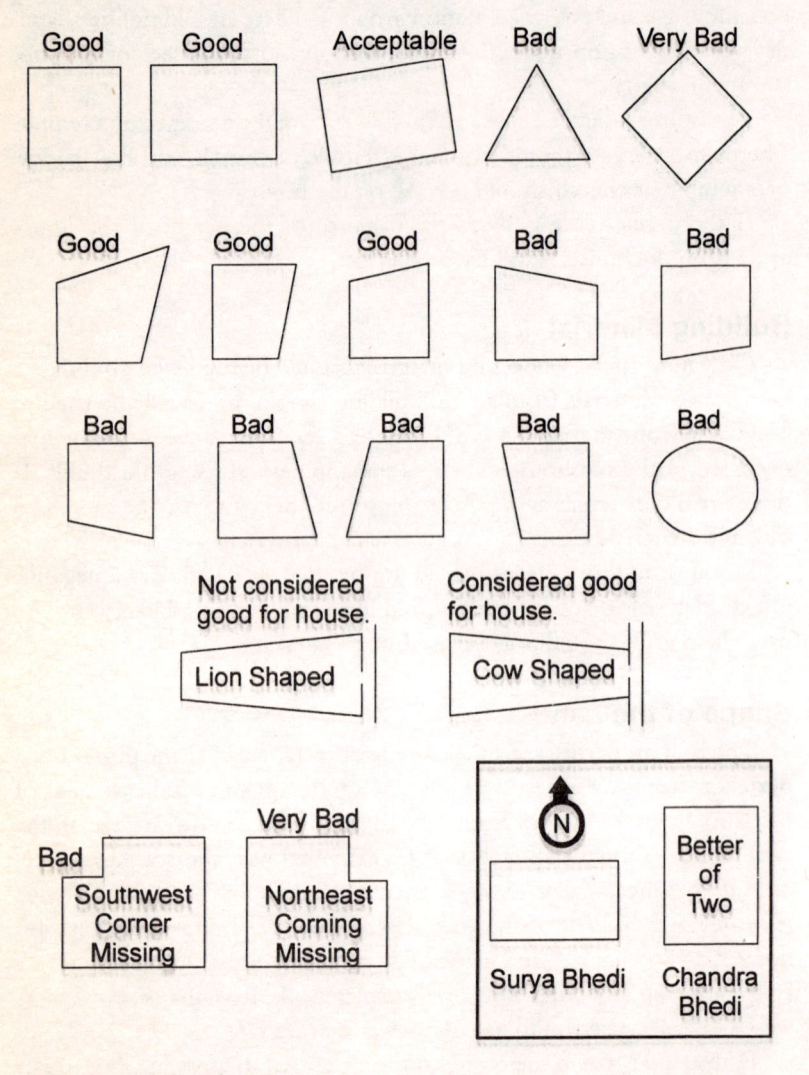

| Good | Good | Acceptable | Bad | Very Bad |

| Good | Good | Good | Bad | Bad |

| Bad | Bad | Bad | Bad | Bad |

Not considered good for house.
Lion Shaped

Considered good for house.
Cow Shaped

Bad — Southwest Corner Missing
Very Bad — Northeast Corning Missing

Surya Bhedi | Chandra Bhedi (Better of Two)

Well or Water Source

It is advised that the first construction project for the new house is to dig the well. If water is used from this well for the construction, it is auspicious for the family who will live in the house. It is best that the well or water source is on the north or northeast side of the land, or if water comes from the municipality, it should enter from the northeast side. If you draw a line from the southeast corner to the northeast corner, the well should be to the right or left of the line, not on it.

The well can also be in the north or east sides of the property. The well should not be in the northwest or southeast corners, as this is inauspicious. It is especially inauspicious if the well is dug in the southwest corner. It is also inauspicious to have a well in the middle of a house.

Wells should be round. Ideally, the well water should be exposed to sunlight for five hours a day. It is not recommended to share wells between two properties.

The well should be dug after *puja* (worship) has been performed on the land at an astrologically auspicious time. This will insure that the water will be pure.

The well should be dug under an auspicious star, such as Rohini, Hasta, Uttara Bhadrapada, Uttara, etc. It should be dug on an auspicious day—a Monday, Wednesday, Thursday, or Friday. The well should be dug during a downward-facing constellation or star, such as, Krittika, Purva Phalguni, Mula, Bharani, Ashlesha, Purva Bhadrapada, or Purvashadha.

Water departing from the kitchen and bathroom should flow to the northeast and leave the house from this side.

Compound Wall and Gate

The compound wall should be built before the house is constructed. Construction should begin during an auspicious constellation, and on a favorable day—a Monday, Wednesday, Thursday, or Friday. It should also be begun during an auspicious day of the lunar month—Pratipada, Panchami, Shashthi, Dashami, Ekadashi, or Purnima.

The compound wall should not be higher than the house, and construction of it should begin on the southwest side.

The southwest part of the wall should be higher than the rest of the wall. The walls on the north and east sides should be 53cm (21 inches) shorter than on the west and south sides. If this is not possible, then the north and east sides should be a minimum of 8cm (3 inches) shorter.

Do not set the gate on the south side. It is best that there are two gates to the compound, so evil things entering one gate will exit from the other.

Outside of Main Building

It is best if the house is built on the southwest section of the land. Any open space should be to the north and east. Open space on the west side of the land is not good for the family's male members. It is also good to keep a tulasi plant in the northeast corner.

The electric generators should be situated on the southeast section of the plot, not the northeast, which is inauspicious. Loud machinery should not be placed near the house.

If there is to be a swimming pool, waterfalls, or fountains, they should be set to the north, east, or northeast. Gardens, plants, or the lawns should also be set to the north, east, or northeast. Plants should be less than 1m (3 ft) in height. Swings should be to the north or east, and should swing from east to west.

North

Best Place for House in Southwest

Outdoor seats should be placed in the south or west of the open area, and people should face north or east while sitting.

It is considered inauspicious to block the entrance to a house, such as with a tree or telephone pole. If one of these things is more than twice the distance of the house's height away, it will not have any effect.

Trash or dirty water should not be kept near a house's entrance (or the entrance to a place of business), and neither should it be kept near the property's entrance. An unclean stream or pool of unclean water should not be located in front of the house.

Annexes or outhouses should not be on the north or east sides of the house, and they definitely should not touch the eastern or northern boundary walls.

A garage, building, or servants' quarters built separately from the house should be located to the southeast or northwest of the main house but should not touch any of the boundary walls. Ideally such quarters should not touch the southeast corner, but should be slightly west (without touching the east wall). They should also not touch the northwest corner but should be slightly south (without touching the north wall). They should be established about 1m (3 ft) from the wall.

Parking

Cars should be parked facing east or north. A car should never be parked facing south. If a car is parked facing west or northwest, the owner will spend a long time traveling.

The parking lot should be in the northwest corner of the property. It should not be located to the southwest or northeast. Parking can also be located in the basement, on the north or east side.

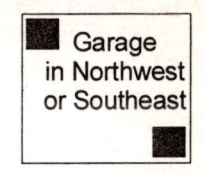

> Garage in Northwest or Southeast

A parking garage should not be connected to the compound wall or the main building.

The parking garage should be painted a light color, not a dark color.

Roof

The roof of the house should slope towards the northeast and rainwater should flow to the north, east, or northeast direction.

Balconies and Verandahs

Balconies, verandahs, and terraces should ideally be built on the north, northeast, or east sides of the house, not on the south or west sides. If a balcony is on the southwest side of a house, it should be covered and closed.

The floor or roof over a balcony or terrace should be lower than the floor or roof of the main building. It is best if the verandah's roof is slanted toward the northeast. Tin is a good roofing material for such structures. The verandah's corners should not be rounded, and balconies should not have arches.

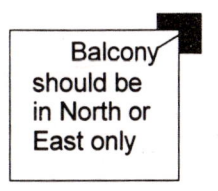

> Balcony should be in North or East only

Flowerpots on the verandah should be small. No creepers should be planted on a verandah. The seats on the verandah should be set on the south or west sides.

Shoes can be removed and placed on the verandah. They should not be placed to the northeast.

Inside the Building

Furniture, such as sofas, should be placed in the southeast, south, or west sides of a room. The house's owner should sit facing north or east, and his guests should sit facing west or south.

It is best that the northeast corner of each room in the house be left empty. If furniture must be set in the northeast corner, it should be set 15cm (six inches) from the wall.

Do not align doors within the house. One door should not lead directly into another.

It is best when a student studies that he face north, northeast, or east. Therefore a table in a study room should be placed in the south or west sides of the room. Books should be stored in the southwest side of the room.

Do not keep money in a place facing south.

When one prays, he should face either north or east.

Beds should face either west or south to insure that when a person rises in the morning, he is facing either north or east. While asleep, one should place his head to the south, east, or west, not north. If one's place of worship is in the bedroom (in the northeast), one should sleep with his head facing east to avoid pointing his feet toward the altar.

Mirrors should be placed on the north or east walls, not on the south or west walls. Do not keep broken mirrors in the house. Clocks should be placed on the west, north, or east walls. Clothes should be washed in the southeast corner of the house.

Medicine should be kept in the northeast corner of the house, and a person should face northeast while taking it. It is best to nurse those who are ill in the southwest corner of the house, although the northwest corner is also good.

Rainwater and wastewater should leave the house from the northeast side. It should flow west to east or south to north.

There should be an even number of columns and beams in the house, not odd.

Doors should generally be made from a single piece of wood and should open on the left side.

A television can be placed in the southeast side of a room. An overhead water tank should be located in the southwest side of a building.

Stairways should be on the south, southwest, or west sides of a building.

Certain pictures should not be hung in a house such as nudes, animals fighting, captured elephants, hunting scenes, trees without fruits or flowers, snakes, owls, bats, vultures and pigeons.

Entrance Gate and Main Door

The main door of the house should be larger than the other doors entering the house. The main door should have two shutters and open to the inside of the building. Teak is a good material for the entrance door.

It is best that a house has two entrances. The exit door should be smaller than the entrance, and it should have only one shutter. If there are two external doors for the house, they should not be set in a straight line.

When one enters the house, there should not be a wall in front of the entrance. There should be a door that opens to the next room. A shadow should not fall on the main door. The main door of the house should not be below ground. Neither should the main door be in the center of the house, nor in the extreme corners. If the door is set in the north wall, move it east of center; if it's in the east wall, move it north of center. If it is set in the south wall, it should be moved east of center; if it is in the west wall, move it south of center. Some authorities say that if the house's entrance is in the west wall. It should be centered.

Some Vastu authorities say that to figure out where to place a main door, divide the house into nine parts. The door should be in the fourth section of the house from the left hand side. From the right side of the house, the entrance is in the sixth division from the right.

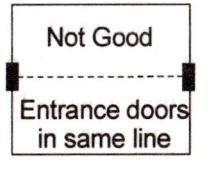

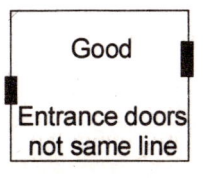

The main door should not be situated across from the main door of another house. The entrance doors of two houses should not be exactly opposing one another. Neither should two houses share a common entrance.

If the entrance of the house is to the south, there should not be a balcony or verandah in front of the door.

It is good to set gates to both the property and the entrance to the house on the north or east sides. It is also all right to have the main door on the west wall. It is not advised to have the main entrance on the south side.

It is considered auspicious if the entrance to the property and the main door of the house are on the same side. It is not considered good if the main door to the house is on the opposite side to the entrance of the property.

There should not be an underground tank, septic tank, or canal under the main entrance. There should not be any abandoned, wrecked buildings in front of the main entrance.

It is good to decorate a house's entrance with

pictures or statues of Laksmi, Ganesh or Kuvera and auspicious signs such as OM or the Swastika. Inauspious pictures should not be on the door. Doors should have thresholds. Shoes should not be kept in front of the door, but to the side.

The door should not be slanted, sliding, or circular.

Overhead Water Tank

The overhead water tank should be in the southwest (best) or west corners of the building. An overhead water tank should not be located in the northeast or southeast corners, or in the middle of the roof. It is also best that it is not located in the northwest unless the tank is small and is located approximately 1m (2 or 3 ft) from the building's corner. The tank should be elevated at least 1m (2 or 3 ft) above the roof, on a platform.

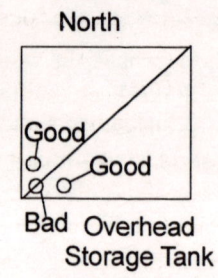

If possible, the tank should not be made of plastic. If it must be plastic, however, it should either be black or dark blue plastic, because such colors aid the absorption of sunlight. A dark water tank while absorbing sun for heat doesn't encourage microbial growth as quickly as a light-colored tank would do.

If possible, there should be different tanks for the kitchen and bathrooms.

The House

It is best if the building's walls are higher on the west and south sides and lower on the north and east sides. Also, the south and west walls should be thicker than the north and east walls, if possible. The building's floor and roof should be higher on the south and west sides, lower on the north and east sides. Neither the ground nor the building should be higher in the northeast than in the southwest.

ROOMS IN THE HOUSE

Worship (Temple) Room

Worship should be done in the northeast, north, or east sides of the house. It is best that the temple room is in the northeast corner of the house. The worship room should not be to the south. The place of worship should be on the ground floor and not upstairs.

The altar should be located on the northeast side of the temple room. The deities or pictures of the deities should either face east or west, and should not face north or south. It is best that the Deities face west and the worshipers face east.

The altar should not be set into the wall but should be at least 2.5 cm (an inch) from it. The door to the temple room should have two shutters.

Toilets should never be above or below the place of worship. White, light yellow, or light blue are good colors for a temple room. It is good if the worship room is shaped like a pyramid, sloping inward as it goes upward toward the roof in the four directions.

Kitchen

The kitchen should ideally be in the southeast corner of the house, its windows on the east and south sides. There can also be a window on the west side. If the kitchen cannot be in the southeast corner, it is all right to place it in the northwest corner. But in general, the kitchen should not be in the north, and should certainly not be in the northeast corner. Locating the kitchen to the southwest will cause problems.

The kitchen should not be next to or across from a toilet, nor should it be directly in front of the main door.

Cooking should be done in the southeast corner or on the east side of the kitchen. It is best to cook while facing east, but facing north is also all right. It is advisable not to put the stove on the northern wall. The cooking platform should not touch the wall but should be placed at least 8 cm (3 inches) from the wall. The stove should not be in front of the kitchen's door.

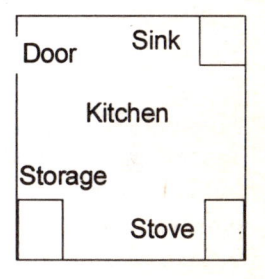

Electrical items such as microwaves, grinders, and mixers should be placed in the southeast corner of the kitchen. The sink should be in the northeast corner. The southwest wall should be used for storage.

The refrigerator should be in the northwest, southeast, south, or west. It should not be placed on the northeast side. If it is on the southwest side of the kitchen, be sure to set it away from the wall.

If there is a dining table in the kitchen, it should be placed on the north or west side. The door to the toilet should not face the dining table.

Kitchens should be painted yellow, rose, red, orange, or chocolate brown. If possible, do not paint the walls white or black.

Living (Sitting) Room

The living room should be on the north side of the house. Furniture should be square or rectangular, not round or oval. It is good if the ceiling slopes down toward the northeast direction. The air-conditioner should be in the west, not the southeast. Furniture should mainly be in the west and south section of the room.

The walls should be painted white, yellow, green, or blue, never red or black. Depressing paintings should not be placed on the walls.

> Furniture in Living room in South or West

Bedrooms

The main bedroom should be on the southwest or northwest side of the house. If there is an upper story in the house, the master bedroom should be on this floor, in the southwest corner. Adult married children can also use this room. Younger children, however, should not use it because that will cause trouble in the household. Bedrooms on the northeast side of the house will also cause trouble.

The children's bedrooms should be in the northwest or west. The younger children's bedroom can also be on the east side of the house, Newly married couples should not use a bedroom on the east side.

Guest bedrooms are best located in the northwest corner, but can also be located in the northeast corner.

Bedroom walls should be painted a light rose, dark blue, dark green, gray, etc. Some authorities say that the walls should not be painted white or a light yellow. The door should be set in the east, west or north, and should ideally be one shutter.

One should sleep in his own house with his head facing east or south. If one is staying in someone else's house, or while traveling, he should sleep with his head facing west. One should never sleep with his head facing north. Upon rising from bed, the right foot should be placed on the floor first.

If one is to study in the bedroom, the east side should be used. The wardrobe should be located on the northwest or southwest side of the bedroom. TV, heaters, and air conditioners should be located in the southeast corner.

The southwest corner of the room should not be vacant. An attached bathroom could be built on the west or north sides of the room. It is best not to keep the safe in a bedroom, but if this is the only place for the safe, it should be located on the south wall, opening north.

Safe Room

Money, valuables, or a safe should be stored in a room on the north side of the house. This is the side of Kubera, the god of wealth. The door to this room should be facing north or east. The walls should be painted yellow, because yellow leads to an increase of wealth.

If a safe is large, it can be placed in the south, southwest, or west sides of the house, but it should always be set a few inches from the wall. It should not be in the southwest or southeast corner, and should definitely not be in a northeast corner. The safe should face north and open toward the north or east. It is inauspicious to have a safe opening to the south—this will cause a loss of money. The safe should not be located under any beams.

Safes should be installed on a Monday, Wednesday, Thursday, or Friday, when the Sun is in the constellations of Dhanishtha, Rohini, Uttara, Swati, Shravan or Punarvasu.

Dining Room

The dining room should be located on the west side of the house, or on the east or north side of the building. If the kitchen is on the ground floor, the dining room should not be on an upper floor but should also be located on the ground floor.

The door leading into the dining room should be on the east, north, or west side of the room. It should not have arches. The house's main entrance door should not face the dining room's door.

It is best to face east or west while eating. The head of the family should face east during meals. Other members of the family can face east, north, or west, but it is not advisable to face south.

The dining table should not be round or oval but either square or rectangular. It should not fold from the wall or be attached to the wall.

A sink can be located in the northeast corner of the dining room, or on the north or east sides of the room. No toilets should be attached to the dining room.

Bathrooms

Bathrooms can be on the west or northwest sides of the building, but not on the eastern or northeastern sides. The toilet room should also not be located on the southeast, the southwest, or in the center of the building. The morning sun falling on the body after bathing is good, so windows should be set in the north or east sides of the room.

Ideally, toilets should face south, not east or west (in the direction of the sun). The toilet should be located on the west or northwest side of the room and should be built 30–60cm (1 or 2 feet) above the ground.

An attached bathroom should be on the west or northwest side of a room, never on the northeast side.

Sinks should be placed on the northeast, north, or east sides of the room. Bathtubs should be located on the northeast, west, or east sides.

Bathroom walls should be painted white, sky blue, or another light shade. Do not use black or dark red.

Water should leave the bathroom from the east or northeast side. Water should not leave from the southwest or southeast directions. The overhead septic tank should be on the northwest side of the house.

Study Room

The library or study should be located on the west side of the building, but should not be located in the corners of the house. When using a library or study, it is best to sit facing east or north.

The bookshelves should not be in the northwest or southwest corner. Books should be in the east, north, or west sides of the room.

The door should be two-shuttered and should be located in the northeast, north, or west. Windows can be set on the east, north, or west walls. The walls should be painted white, sky blue, cream, or light green.

If one will not sleep in the room, a pyramidal shape (walls sloping inward as they go upward towards the ceiling) will help study and meditation.

Storage Area

The storage areas should be located in the northwest part of the building, but not in the north or east. The storage room door should not be on the southwest side of the room. Storage cabinets should be located on the west or north sides of the room. Butter, ghee, oil, and cooking gas should be kept in the southeast corner.

Stairways

Best to build stairways on the southwest, or if necessary, on the south or west sides of the house. Do not build stairways on the northeast side, as it will cause loss of wealth. The staircase should go up from east to west or north to south. The same stairway that goes to the upper floor should not also go down to the basement.

Stairways should be built with an odd number of stairs—9, 11, or 15 steps, for example. The number of stairs should not end with a zero if you must build an even number—there should not be 10 or 20 steps—because it is best to begin climbing steps with the right foot and also to end the climb on the right foot. This is not possible when there is an even number of stairs. The right foot is equated with gain, the left with loss.

Circular stairways are not good. The doorway at the top of the stairway should be at least 20cm (8 inches) lower than the doorway at the bottom of the stairs. Broken stairs should be repaired immediately to avoid accidents.

The stairway should be painted a light color. The worship room, safe, or toilet should not be located under a staircase.

Basement

Basements should ideally not be built under the entire house. If that is impossible, use only the northeast section. Heavy equipment can be kept on the south and west sides.

It is best that the basement should only be in the northeast side of a house. It can also be located on the east side of the house. It should not, however, be located only on the south, southeast, or west side.

The floor of the basement should slope downward towards the northeast. The walls should be at least 3m (9 ft) high. The basement should be painted white but should not be blue. The heater, water heater, or electrical panels should be in the southeast corner of the basement.

Since sunrays do not enter basements, this highly reduces the basement's positive effect on the persons living in them. Therefore, a basement should not be used for living as far as possible. Basements are also not good places to conduct business. The basement's effects will be improved if one-fourth of the basement is above ground.

Mezzanine

A mezzanine or loft should be built on the south, west, or southwest sides of a room.

Position of Rooms

Directions	Ruling Planet	Room
North	Mercury	Living (Sitting) room, safe
Northeast	Jupiter	Worship room, living room
East	Sun	Living room, bathing room (no toilet)
Southeast	Venus	Kitchen
South	Mars	Kitchen, storeroom
Southwest	Rahu	Master bedroom, heavy storage
West	Saturn	Children's bedroom, store room, study
Northwest	Moon	Guest room, bathroom, grain storage room

Northeast Dining Room Storage Guest Bedroom	North Living Room Safe	Northeast Pooja or Worship Room
West Children's Bedroom Study	Open Area	East Study Room Bathroom (but no toilet)
Southwest Master Bedroom Library Stairway	South Bedroom Storage	Southeast Kitchen

Upper Floor

It is best that there are more doors and windows on the north and east sides of the building. There should be fewer windows and doors on the upper floors than on the lower ones. It is also said that the number of doors and windows on the upper floor should not equal the amount of doors and windows on the ground floor. The ceiling height of the rooms on the upper floor should be less than the ceiling height of the rooms on the ground floor.

If only part of the upper floor is used, this part should be built in the southwest area. The balcony should be on the north, east, or northeast side. The balcony should not be in the southwest corner.

Bedrooms and studies should be located on the upper floor. A storage area for heavy items should be located on the lower floor, and not the upper.

Trees and Plants

It is always good to grow a tulasi plant on one's property. Tulasi should be located on the north, northeast, or east sides of the house, or in front of the house.

Trees should not be planted directly in front of the house's main entrance. There should be an even number of trees on one's property, not an odd number.

Trees should be planted on the south or west sides of the house. Ideally, they should be planted on both these sides rather than on only one side. It is not good to plant a tall tree on the north, northeast, or east sides of a building. Smaller trees may be planted on the east or north sides, but no trees should be planted in the northeast corner. Tall trees should not be too close to a building as they block the sunlight. A tree's shadow should not fall on the house.

Large trees should not be located too near the house as their roots can damage the foundation and compound wall. Also, the roots of large trees absorb sunlight quickly, meaning these positive rays will not be received by the building. Do not allow tree branches to touch the house.

Stone sculptures and rock gardens should be located on the southwest side of the house because they are heavy.

Thorny plants should not be planted near the house. Cactus should not be planted at all. Thorny plants other than roses have a negative energy. Ideally all thorny plants should be pulled up and destroyed.

A list of good trees to plant: coconut, neem, betal, sandalwood, lemon, pineapple, bilva, almond, jackfruit, pomegranate, mango, amla, and katha. Banyan and pipal (aswatha) are sacred trees; they should usually only be planted near a temple or at a sacred place.

Creepers or other plants should not be grown by using the building or compound wall as support. Creepers should only be grown in a garden, and they should have their own independent supports.

Plants should be planted during auspicious constellations. Saplings should first be planted in clay pots and only later placed in the ground. This enables them to grow better.

If a tree must be removed because it is inauspicious or for other reasons, it should be removed in the months of Magh or Bhadrapada. The day before cutting the tree, worship it and express regret that it must be removed from its rooting. Promise to plant a new tree in its place. Do so within three months. When cutting the tree, it should fall east or north, not south or west.

Worship of Land

Certain rituals can be performed before construction on the plot begins. The land should be installed at an auspicious time, during an auspicious constellation. Mondays and Thursdays are auspicious days for such rituals. Ideally, a qualified astrologer should set the time of installation. Worship should be done in the northeast corner of the land.

Before installing the land, it should be cleared. Dirt, stones, holes in the ground, and trash should be removed. Thorny bushes should also be uprooted and removed.

The installation should not be done if a woman in the household is more than seven months pregnant. The groundbreaking ceremony for the house should only be done during the Uttarayan period, when the sun is in the northern hemisphere, and when the days are longer than the nights, from June 21 through December 20.

House Warming

Before entering a new house, a house-warming ceremony should be performed. A good time to enter a new house is in the period of Uttarayan, from June 21 through December 20, in the months of Vaishaka, Shravan, and Margashirsh, in the constellation of Uttara, Magha, Ashwini, Swati, Pushya, and Revati, on an auspicious day. It is good to confirm this time with a qualified astrologer.

Ganesh-puja, Navagraha-puja (worship of the nine planets), and worship of the Vastupratima (building deity) should be performed. The residents of the building should then circumambulate the building. Then *puja* should be done to the threshold.

Purchasing the Adjacent Plot

If one wishes to purchase the land adjacent to one's own property, it should be purchased on a Monday, Thursday, or Friday, during an auspicious constellation such as Vaishaka, Purva, Ashlesha, Mrig, Revati, Mul, or Anuradha.

The land one already owns can be extended to the north, east, or northeast. The northwest corner should not be extended. If a plot is available in the southwest, west, or south sides, it should not be purchased, as it will cause misfortune and loss.

If the northeast plot is available, purchase it. It is best if the adjacent lot on the northeast side is at a lower elevation than the land already owned. If such land is purchased, the dividing wall should be taken down. As far as possible, you should not construct buildings on this land.

General Information

One should not sit or sleep under a beam. One should not hang paintings depicting violence, war, crime, or distress on the walls. Sweep all cobwebs from the house—they are inauspicious. Cobwebs are signs of the mode of ignorance. Creaking doors are also inauspicious and should be oiled immediately. Such sounds cut the ether and allow subtle living entities to enter through the "hole," as does whistling.

The shadow of a temple should not fall on the house. There should not be a mountain on the east side of the house, close enough that its shadow falls on the house.

The sun's rays from 6 to 9 a.m. are the most beneficial because at this time, they are coming from the east. When the sun's rays are coming from the west between 3 and 6 p.m., the sun's rays are not considered beneficial.

Sometimes after a house is constructed, it can be remodeled to make the vibrations more favorable to the residents. Often by making positive changes according to the Vastu Shastra to an already-built house, the fortunes of the residents change radically for the better.

It is also best that persons own their homes and do not live in rental properties. If part of the house is to be rented out to others, it should be the north or northeast side. Only the owner should use the south side.

It is not good to leave a house vacant for more than four months. The ground floor of the house should be kept occupied; but it is acceptable if the upper floor is vacant.

Suggested Reading

A good book to read on Vastu Shastra is the illustrated *The Little Book on Vaastu,* by Gyan C. Jain, published by BPB Publications. The illustrations make it easy to understand the subject.

Vaastu Shilpa Shaastra, by Derebail Muralidhar Rao, published by S.B.S. Publishers, is a detailed book on the subject of Vaastu, with good, detailed illustrations. It is a bit difficult to read, but it is informative.

Vastushastra, An Edifice Science, by AR Tarkhedkar, published by Cosmo Publishing House, is a three-book set containing good, detailed information.

The Pocket Book of Vaastu, by Rakesh Chawla, published by Full Circle, is an easy to understand book but is not so detailed.

FESTIVALS

Religious festivals in India are a time for celebration and purification. People will often fast to become purified. The temples are decorated and sumptuous foodstuffs are offered to the deities.

Holidays and festivals normally follow the Indian lunar (Vikramaditya) calendar, and therefore each year they fall on a different day of the normal western calendar. The calendar is based on lunar months, which begin with the full moon. The lunar calendar adds a thirteenth month every thirty months to make sure the months stay the same as the seasons. This system is 57 or 58 years ahead of the Christian calendar.

Months

The Indian lunar months and the western equivalents (Indian Calendar)

Magha	January-February
Phalguna	February-March
Chaitra	March-April
Vaishaka	April-May
Jyaistha	May-June
Asadha	June-July
Sravana	July-August
Bhadra	August-September
Asvina	September-October
Kartika	October-November
Aghan	November-December
Pausa	December-January

Magha (Jan-Feb)

Makara Sankranti (Pongal) It falls on January 14, which is when the Sun is in the zodiac of Makara (Capricorn). This is the day the Sun enters the sign of Makara. Makara Sankranti is considered an auspicious day, and people focus on giving charity to the poor and the less fortunate. **Pongal**

is a harvest festival celebrated in Tamil Nadu. The festival is celebrated by processions, decorated cows, chalk designs on the doorways of people's houses. Pongal, sweet porridge made of rice is distributed, even to the cows.

Vasant Panchami and Saraswati Puja Vasant Panchami is a spring festival. On this day worship is done to Saraswati, the wife of Brahma. She is the goddess of knowledge. People wear yellow on this day, and children fly kites (*patangs*).

Phalguna (Feb-March)
Siva-ratri This is the appearance day of Lord Siva. Special festivals are held in Varanasi, Kalahasti, Chidambaram, Srisailam, and other places where there are important Siva temples.

Tibetan New Year This is celebrated among the Tibetan communities, especially in Dharamsala.

Chaitanya Mahaprabhu's Appearance Day This important Gaudiya Vaishnava festival falls at the same time as Holi in Feb/March. On this day there is a large festival at the birthplace of Sri Chaitanya in Sri Dhama Mayapur, which is located about 150km north of Calcutta in West Bengal. About a quarter of a million people come to Mayapur on Sri Chaitanya Mahaprabhu's appearance day.

Holi Holi is celebrated on the full moon day in February/March. People celebrate Holi by throwing powdered dye and colored water on each other. This is joyfully celebrated in Braja (the area around Vrindavan), especially in Varsana and Nandagram.

One story about Holi is that Prahlada Maharaja refused to worship his father and wanted to worship his father's enemy, Lord Vishnu. His father's sister, Holika, who was immune to being burned, sat with the boy in a big fire, in an attempt to kill the boy. Prahlada's devotion was so great that Holika was burnt to death and Prahlada was unharmed. Huge bonfires are lit on the eve of Holi, and grains from the new harvest are thrown into the fire.

WARNING! You should be careful if you are in India during Holi (Feb/March). During Holi the locals throw a pink dye on everyone they can, and many times it will not come out of your clothes. The more you resist, the more they will try to cover you with dye. If you walk on the street, expect to get covered with dye and to take it with a smile.

Khajuraho Dance Festival Famous dancer and musicians come from all over India for this interesting festival.

Chaitra (March-April)
Ramanavami This is the appearance day of Lord Rama. On this day devotees read the *Ramayana*, which glorifies Lord Rama. The temples are decorated with flower, lights and other auspicious items. Devotees fast on this day and constantly chant the names of Lord Rama.

Hanuman Jayanti This popular festival celebrates the birth of Hanuman. The deity of Hanuman in temples is given a new coat of paint mixed with ghee (clarified butter). The glories of Hanuman are read from the Ramayana. Fasting is done and the temples are decorated.

Mahavir Jayanti This festival honors the birth of Mahavira, the founder of Jainism.

Vaishaka (April-May)
Narasimha's Jayanti This festival celebrates the appearance of Lord Narasimha and the killing of the demon Hiranyakasipu. People fast on this day, usually until dusk, because this is when Lord Narasimha appeared. Devotees meditate on Lord Narasimha, read stories about Him, and pray to receive the good qualities of devotion which were exhibited by Prahlad Maharaja.

Puram Festival This is an interesting festival in Thrissur in Kerala, where there is an elephant parade and elephant competition.

Jyaistha (May-June)
Buddha Purnima This is the celebration of the birth, enlightenment, death, and salvation of Lord Buddha, which takes place on the full moon of the fourth lunar month. There is a special festival at Bodhgaya in Bihar, Sarnath in UP, Sikkim, and places associated with Lord Buddha.

Asadha (June-July)
Ratha-yatra Festival During this festival, the deities of Jagannath, Bal-

arama, and Subhadra are carried out of the temple and are then placed upon three large chariots, which are pulled with ropes by thousands of devotees.

This famous festival begins on the second day of the bright fortnight of Asadha. The deities are pulled on their carts the entire length of Grand Road, from the Jagannath Temple to the Gundicha Temple (about 3km). The deities stay at Gundicha for nine days, then return to the main temple on the tenth day. This is called **Bahuda-yatra**, or the return cart festival. The festivals—cart and return cart—are the only opportunities in the year for non-Hindus to see the Jagannath Deity.

The chariot of Lord Jagannath, known as Nandighosh, is 13.7m (45 ft) high. It has eighteen wheels and is covered with brightly colored yellow and red fabric. A wheel rests on top of the car. Lord Balarama's chariot is 13.2m (44 ft) high and has sixteen wheels. It is called **Taladwaja**, and the fabric on the roof is red and green. It is crowned with a *tala* fruit. Lady Subhadra's cart is 12.9m (43 ft) high and has fourteen wheels. It is named **Padmadhwaj** or Darpadalan and is covered with red and black fabric. There are side deities on each of the carts. With the exception of the *kalasa* (the pinnacles on top of the chariots), the fourteen side deities, and the wooden charioteers and horses, which are all reused, the carts are newly constructed each year according to strict and ancient specifications.

The **Pahandi**, or Deity procession from the temple to the carts, is the most colorful part of the festival. First, Sudarsana Cakra is brought from the temple and placed on Subhadra's chariot. Then Balarama, Subhadra, and finally Jagannath are each placed on their respective carts. The deities are extremely heavy, and it takes many strong men to move them step by step. The king of Orissa then sweeps the street in front of the carts with a golden-handled broom.

There is no steering system for the carts. If a cart does not reach the Gundicha Temple by sundown, the journey continues the next day. Not reaching the destination is common; the streets are so crowded with pilgrims that the journey always takes longer than expected.

When the festival is over, the carts are dismantled and broken into pieces, then sold as sacred relics.

Raksha Bandhan This festival takes place in July/August. It is said that during a battle between the demigods and demons the demigods lost their heavenly kingdom. Then the consort of Indra tied a Rakhi on his wrist and because of this the demigods were able to win back their kingdom.

During this festival a sister ties a Rakhi, which is a handspun cotton (or silk) thread dyed yellow with turmeric, around the wrist of her brother. The brother then gives her presents, and promises to be responsible for her safety. The Rakhi can be given to any one, but is usually given to one's brother. This celebration symbolizes the protection of women. The person on whose wrist the Rakhi is tied is duty bound to protect the person who ties it on.

Sravana (July-Aug)
Jhulan Yatra Mahotsava (Swing Festival) During this festival, the Radha-Krishna Deities in the temples are swung on a swing. This festival lasts for 13 days. In Vrindavan this is one of the biggest festivals of the year. Often the swings are made of gold or silver.

Balarama's Appearance Day On this day Lord Balarama appeared in Gokula near Vrindavan.

Bhadra (Aug-Sept)
Janmasthami This festival celebrates the appearance of Lord Krishna. He appeared in Mathura about 5,000 years ago. Janmasthami falls on the 8th day of the dark half of Bhadra. As part of the celebration devotees fast until 12 midnight, because this is the time Krishna appeared. The temples are decorated and special dresses are usually offered to the Deities. They will also usually have a special public bathing of the Deity of Krishna (called *abhishek*). The Deity is bathed with various items such as milk, yogurt, ghee, honey, flowers and water from a holy river, such as the Yamuna or the Ganges.

This festival is celebrated all over India, especially in Gujarat, Rajasthan, Mathura and Vrindavan. This is usually the most crowded day of the year in Krishna temples. Temples will usually organize plays and dances depicting different pastimes of Lord Krishna. There is a huge *arati* at 12 midnight in Krishna temples throughout India.

Radhastami This is the appearance day of Srimati Radharani, the consort of Sri Krishna. This is a popular festival in Vrindavan.

Ganesh Chaturthi The birth of Ganesh is celebrated on this day. A statue of Ganesh, sometimes 10 metres (33 feet) high, is made of clay, cloth or other substances. It is worshiped for seven to ten days and is then submerged in the sea or in a lake. Sweet-rice pudding, *laddoos* (sweet flour balls), and coconuts are offered to Ganesh during this festival.

Asvina (Sept-Oct)

Sraddha This event is a time when homage is paid to the dead ancestors. These homages are done to make sure there is peace for the departed souls of the ancestors. During the Sraddha period one does not take part in any kind of celebrations and does not make unnecessary purchases.

Durga Puja This is one of the most popular festivals in India. It symbolizes victory of good over evil. Durga is the consort of Lord Siva who controls the material energy and punishes the demons.

Dussera This festival celebrates the victory of Lord Rama over Ravana. Ravana is the demon that kidnapped Rama's wife Sita. This is a 10-day festival, and on the tenth day a large image of Ravana is shot and killed (usually burnt) by Rama.

Durga's victory over the buffalo demon, Mahishsura, is also celebrated at the same time. This festival also goes for 10 days. On each night of the first nine days, a different form of Durga is worshiped. On the tenth day, many cities have big parades. The Dussera processions in Mysore and Jaipur are major events.

The nine forms of Durga are: Shailputri, Brahmacarini, Candraghanta, Kushmanda, Skandamata, Katyayani, Kalaratri, Mahagauri, and Siddhidhatri.

Navaratri This is a nine-day festival. *Nava* means "nine." During this festival the three main goddesses are worshiped. On the first three days, Durga is worshiped, then Lakshmi and then Saraswati. The last day of this festival is called Dussera or Vijaya Dasami.

In Gujarat, women, and sometimes men, dance the *garbha* dance. They dance around in a big circle with swaying steps and rhythmically clap to the music. It is a big social and spiritual event. It usually begins in late September when the moon is almost full.

Kartika (Oct-Nov)

Dipawali (Deepavali) *Dipawali* means "row of lights." It is celebrated 20 days after Dussera. It celebrates the return of Lord Rama to his kingdom Ayodhya, after his victory over Ravana. This is celebrated by burning lamps and candles in temples and homes. On Dipawali, fireworks are set off all over India. People visit friends and relatives and give each other gifts and sweets.

Some people also celebrate Dipawali as the time when Lord Krishna killed Narakasura. Narakasura was the son of the earth and because of boons he had received from Siva and Brahma he was able to conquer not only the earth, but also the heavenly planets. Krishna killed him with the help of his queen Satyabhama who acted as his charioteer. After he died his mother requested Krishna to make the day that her son was killed a day of celebration. Thus Dipawali also celebrates the earth and heaven being delivered from Narakasura.

On this day fireworks are set off all over India. A new commercial year begins for businessmen. Houses are cleaned completely and are often freshly painted. People visit friends and relatives on this day and give each other gifts and sweets.

This festival is also associated with Laksmi because it is believed that wealth (Laksmi) will not enter one's house on this day if it is dark. On this day a special *puja* (worship) is offered to Laksmi in most people's homes.

Govardhana Puja (Annakuta Festival) This festival is celebrated during the month of Kartika (Oct/Nov), on the day after Dipawali. This festival celebrates the offering of a mountain of food items to Govardhan Hill by Nanda Maharaja and the residences of Braja.

On this day Govardhana Hill is worshiped. In most of the temples of Vrindavan and Braja, huge quantities of sumptuous food are prepared for this ceremony and are distributed to the general public. A large hill of *prasada* (sacred food) is made in many temples. Devotees circle the hill and then honor the *prasada* from this hill. Also models of Govardhana Hill are made of cow dung.

Camel Festival The Camel Festival at Pushkar draws a couple hundred thousand people, and a lot of camels too. This festival takes place for three days around the full moon day of Kartika (Oct/Nov). It is considered especially auspicious to bathe in the lake at Pushkar on the full moon day of Kartika.

Nanak Jayanti This is the birthday of Guru Nanak, the founder of the Sikh religion. It is especially celebrated in Amritsar and the Punjab.

Aghan (Nov-Dec)

Gita Jayanti This is the birthday of the *Bhagavad Gita*. There is a special festival in Kurukshetra, the place where Krishna spoke the *Bhagavad Gita* to Arjuna. The *Bhagavad Gita* is considered to be the most important scripture by many Hindus. This day is celebrated on the eleventh day (Ekadashi) of the bright (first) half of the moon in the month of December/January.

Pausa (Dec-Jan)

Onam This festival celebrates the memory of the king of the demons, Bali Maharaja. It is a major festival in Kerala. Bali Maharaja was removed as king of the earth by Vamana, an incarnation of Lord Vishnu, and he was sent to the underworld. The king is so attached to his subjects that he returns once a year to see them. In Trichur there is a large festival with colorfully decorated elephants. At Kottayam, Aranmula, and Champakulam, there are snake boat races, with large crews of oarsmen rowing to the rhythm of drums and cymbals.

Glossary

abhisek - formal bathing of the deity in a temple.
acharya - a guru, spiritual teacher, or guide who teaches by example.
Adinath - first of the twenty-four Jain *tirthankaras*.
Agni - fire, the fire-god.
ahimsa - nonviolence.
akhandpath - continuous reading of the Adi Granth, the Sikh holy book.
Alwars - Tamil Nadu saints who were devotees of Lord Vishnu.
amrita - immortality, nectar.
ananda - transcendental bliss.
ananta - unlimited
Ananta - the snake bed of Lord Vishnu.
Annapurna - Durga manifested in her form of supplier of food.
Apsara - heavenly dancing girls.
arati (arotika) - the standard worship ceremony of offering lamps and other items to the Lord in his Deity form, accompanied by bell-ringing and chanting.
Archa-vigraha - the form of God manifested through material elements, as in a statue of Krishna or Vishnu. Actually present in this form, the Lord accepts worship from his devotees.
Aristasura - a demon who took the form of a bull to kill Krishna.
Arjuna - one of the five Pandavas from the *Mahabharata*. Krishna spoke the *Bhagavad-gita* to him on the battlefield of Kurukshetra.
Aryan - a follower of Vedic culture. A spiritually advanced person.
asana - yogic posture.
Ashoka - the king who spread Buddhism in India in the 3rd century BC.
ashrama - living quarters at a temple or holy place. It is usually a basic place. It also refers to the four spiritual orders of life according to the Vedic social system. This includes *brahmacarya* (student life), *grihastha* (married life), *vanaprastha* (retired life), and *sannyasa* (renounced order). Refuge, spiritual community.

asura - demon or one envious of God.
asvamedha yajna - a very elaborate sacrifice, usually performed by kings.
atma (atman) - the soul.
avatara - literally, "one who descends". A partially or fully empowered incarnation of God who comes to the world for a particular mission.
Ayurvedic medicine - natural herbal medical science originating in the *Vedas*.
Balarama - older brother of Krishna. Also known as Dauji, Balabhadra, or Baladeva.
Bali Maharaja - a demon king who gave the dwarf *Brahmin*, Vamanadeva, an incarnation of Lord Vishnu, three paces of land and who then lost his entire kingdom.
banyan tree - a sacred tree of the fig family which consists of many trees connected to one main trunk.
Bhadrakali - Durga in her terrifying feature.
Bhagavad-gita - literally, "Song of God." This is the sacred scripture in which Lord Krishna, the Supreme Personality of Godhead, instructs Arjuna about spiritual life and the importance of serving Krishna (God). The main spiritual scripture of India.
Bhagiratha - the king who performed austerities to bring the Ganges to earth to save his ancestors.
Bhairava - the terrify aspect of Lord Siva, who chopped off the fifth head of Brahma.
bhajana (bhajan) - song; hearing and chanting about God.
bhajana-kutir - a place where a saintly person performs personal mediation.
bhakta - devotee.
bhakti - devotional service to God in a personalized form.
Brahma - the first created being in the universe and the secondary creator of the material worlds. Directed by Vishnu, he creates all life forms in the universe. He also rules the mode of passion.
Bharata - half-brother of Rama who ruled Ayodhya when Rama was in exile.
Bhima - one of the Pandavas, known for his strength and strong appetite.

Bhudevi - consort of Lord Vishnu.
bhumi - the earth or goddess of the earth.
bodhi tree (bo tree) - peepal tree, considered sacred; the tree under which the Buddha meditated and became enlightened.
Brahmin (brahman) - a member of the highest order in Vedic society according to the occupational divisions of society.
brahmacari - celibate student, first of the four asramas.
Brajabasis (Brijabasis) - the residents of Vrindavan.
Buddha - the founder of Buddhism who lived during the 5th century BC.
Caitanya Caritamrita - biography of Sri Caitanya Mahaprabhu written in the late 16th century by Krishnadasa Kaviraja.
Caitanya Mahaprabhu - an incarnation of Krishna who appeared in Navadvipa, West Bengal, in the late 15th century, and who inaugurated the congregational chanting of the holy names of the God.
caranamrita - water used to bathe the feet of the Deity of the Lord. This water is offered to pilgrims at temples.
Caturmasya - the four months of the rainy season, when special austerities are performed.
Chandra - the moon-god, or moon.
Chakra - disc weapon of Lord Vishnu. Chakras are installed on top of Vishnu temples to indicate who is being worshipped within. Focus of power in the body.
cintamani - touchstone, which grants all desires.
danda - staff or stick.
dandavat - bowing down, falling flat on the ground like a stick.
darshan - viewing the deity or saintly person.
dharamshala - pilgrim accommodation.
dasa - male servant of God.
Dasaratha - the king of Ayodhya and father of Lord Rama.
dasi - female servant of God.
demigod - living beings who are especially empowered by the Supreme Lord to act as controllers in universal affairs.
deva - demigod.
devadasi - temple dancer.
devi - goddess.
dham - an important holy place.
dharamshala - a basic pilgrim guesthouse.
dharma - the moralistic occupational duty of man. In Buddhism it means the law of nature and truth.
dhoop - incense.
Digambara - sky-clad. A strict Jain sect whose monks wear no clothes.
dikpalas - guardian deities of the four directions.
diksa guru - the initiating spiritual master (guru).
Divya Desam temples - 108 important Vishnu temples sung about by the twelve Alwar devotees of Tamil Nadu.
Draupadi - wife of the five Pandavas brothers, from the *Mahabharata*.
Durga - Lord Siva's wife in a fierce form, riding a tiger.
Dvapara-yuga - the third age of a *maha-yuga*, lasting 864,000 years.
Dwarka (Dvaraka) - the site of Lord Krishna's city in his pastimes as an opulent prince. Dwarka is a city in India on the coast of Gujarat.
ekadashi - the eleventh day of the waxing and waning moon. Abstinence from grains and beans is prescribed on this day.
gada - club, mace.
Ganesh - the son of Lord Siva and Parvati, who has an elephant head. He is the god of prosperity (wealth) and wisdom. He rides on a rat.
Ganga - the name used in India for the Ganges. It is consider holy.
Ganga Devi - the female goddess of the Ganga.
Garuda - The half-man, half-eagle carrier of Lord Vishnu. He is found facing the entrance of many Vishnu temples.
Gaudiya Vaishnava - the school of Vaishnavism following in the line of Sri Chaitanya Mahaprabhu.
Gayatri - a sacred mantra chanted by Brahmins for purification three times a day.
ghat - steps leading down to a holy river, a holy lake, or a *kund*.
Gita Govinda - a poem by Jayadeva Goswami about the intimate pastimes of Krishna with the *gopis*.
gopis - Krishna's cowherd girl friends in Vrindavan. His most confidential servitors.
gosvami (goswami) - a swami, one fully in

control of his senses.
guru - spiritual master, spiritual instructor.
gurudwara - Sikh temple.
Hanuman - the monkey follower and servant of Rama in the *Ramayana*.
haj - pilgrimage to Mecca by a Muslim.
haji - a Muslim who has made the pilgrimage to Mecca.
Hara - a name of Lord Siva.
Hari - a name of Lord Vishnu.
Hinayana - literally, "lesser vehicle". One of the two major Buddhist sects.
Indra - the chief of the administrative demigods and the presiding deity of rain.
ishwara - controller, a name of God.
japa - mantra chanted softly to oneself, usually the names of God.
Jagannatha - Lord of the universe. The main place of his worship is at Puri in Orissa.
Janaka - father of Sita, the wife of Rama.
ji - honorific title added to almost any name as a term of endearment.
jyotir-linga - one of the important twelve, self-manifest Siva-lingas.
Kailasa (Kailash) - the home of Lord Siva in the Himalayas.
Kali - the black form of Lord Siva's wife.
Kali-yuga - The "age of quarrel and hypocrisy." It began 5,000 years ago and lasts for a total of 432,000 years.
Kaliya Serpent - the snake Krishna punished for poisoning the Yamuna River.
Kama - Cupid, god of love.
Kanyakumari - a virgin maiden; another name for Lord Siva's wife.
karma - material activities. The concept that whatever you do creates a future reaction.
kartals - hand-held cymbals.
Kartikkeya - the son of Lord Siva and the god of war. Also known as Subrahmanya or Skanda.
Kathakali - Keralan religious dance.
kirtan - chanting the holy names of the Lord in public.
kovil - name for a temple in South India.
Krishna - According to Vaishnavas, Krishna is the Supreme Personality of Godhead. Also known as Govinda or Gopala.
ksatriya - the administrative and military class in Vedic culture, the second social order.
kumbha - pitcher.

kund - lake or pond; a *kund* often has steps leading to the water.
Kuvera - god of wealth.
Laksman - the younger brother of Rama.
Lakshmi (Laxmi) - Vishnu's consort; the goddess of wealth and good fortune.
Linga - phallic symbol used in the worship of Lord Siva.
lama - Tibetan Buddhist monk.
lila - a transcendental "pastime" or activity performed by God.
Mahabharata - story of Lord Krishna and the battle between the Pandavas and the Kauravas.
Mahadeva - Lord Siva.
maha-prasada - food taken from the Deity's plate after an offering.
mahant - head of a monastery or temple.
maharaja, maharao, maharana - king, ruler.
mahatma - great soul; saintly person.
Mahavir - the twenty-fourth and last *tirthankara* (teacher) of the Jains.
Mahisha - buffalo demon who was killed by Durga.
mandir - temple.
mani stone - sacred stone with the Tibetan Buddhist mantra *"Om mani padme hum"* ("Hail to the jewel in the lotus") imprinted upon it.
mantra - a transcendental sound or Vedic hymn, a prayer or chant.
Maratha - ruling group from Maharashtra during the 16th to the 18th centuries.
masjid - mosque
math (mutt) - monastery.
maya - that which is not, unreality, deception, forgetfulness. Material illusion.
mela - fair, festival.
Mohammed - the founder of Islam; "the praised."
moksa - liberation.
mudra - hand gesture used to symbolize different things in Hinduism and Buddhism.
muni - a sage.
murti - the form of the deity on the altar in temples.
namaste - Hindu greeting, obeisance. Said with hands joined together.
Nanda Maharaja - the leader of the cowherd man of Vrindavan who raised Lord Krishna.
Nandi - the bull carrier of Siva, found in

many Siva temples.
Narasimha (Narsingha) - half-man, half-lion incarnation of Lord Vishnu who killed Hiranyakasipu and saved Prahlada Maharaja.
Narayana - the four-armed form of Lord Krishna who presides over the Vaikuntha planets; Lord Vishnu.
Nataraja - Siva as the cosmic dancer.
navagraha - nine planets.
nirvana - freedom from material existence.
padayatra - foot journey; to go on pilgrimage by foot.
padma - lotus.
panda - a *Brahmin* guide.
Pandavas - the five sons of King Pandu: Yudhisthira, Bhima, Arjuna, Nakula, and Sahadeva. The heroes of the *Mahabharata*.
pandit - learned scholar or priest.
parampara - disciplic succession of gurus and disciples.
Parasurama - the sixth incarnation of Lord Vishnu who killed twenty-one generations of *ksatriyas* (warriors).
Parikrama - circumambulating a sacred place, temple, mountain, or shrine. Should only be done clockwise.
Parsi - follower of Zoroastrianism.
Parvati - another name for Siva's wife; literaaly, "daughter of the mountain."
prabhu - master.
pranayama - breath control used in meditation by yogis.
prasadam - sanctified food; food offered with devotion to Lord Krishna or Lord Vishnu; "the Lord's mercy."
prayag - the auspicious confluence of two holy rivers.
prema - love of Godhead.
puja - offering of worship.
pujaris - Brahmin priests who perform the actual worship on the altars.
Puranas - the eighteen historical supplements to the *Vedas* written in Sanskrit.
purnima - full moon.
Radha (Radharani, Radhika, Radhe) - the favorite consort of Krishna in Vrindavan. Often she is the female Deity standing next to Krishna on the altar.
Rama - Lord Ramacandra, an incarnation of Lord Vishnu who appeared in Ayodhya as the perfect king.
Ramayana - the story of Rama and Sita and the killing of Ravana.
ratha - temple cart or chariot, used during religious festivals to carry the Deities.
rasa - the transcendental "taste" of a particular spiritual relationship with the Supreme Lord.
rasa-lila - pastimes of Krishna dancing with the *gopis*.
Ravana - the ten-headed demon king of Lanka; was killed by Rama for kidnapping Sita.
Rinpoche (Rimpoche) - highly respected Tibetan Buddhist lama who is considered to be a reincarnation of a previous teacher.
rishi - a sage; a saintly person.
rudraksha - beads worn by devotees of Siva.
Rukmini - one of the main wives of Lord Krishna.
sadhu - a saint or wandering holy man.
salaam - literally, "peace;" Muslim greeting.
samadhi - trance; complete absorption in God consciousness. A great saint's tomb or memorial.
sampradaya - the four authorized disciplic successions coming from the Supreme Personality of Godhead: Brahma, Kumara, Sri, and Rudra.
sangam - meeting point of two rivers.
Sankaracarya (Sankara) - the great philosopher who established the doctrine of *advaita* (non-dualism).
sankirtan - congregational chanting of the holy names of God.
sannyasa - the renounced order of life.
sannyasi - a person in the renounced order of life.
Sanskrit - the oldest language in the world. The *Vedas*, India's holy scriptures, are written in Sanskrit.
Saraswati - wife of Brahma; the goddess of learning.
Sati - the wife of Siva, who burned herself alive when her father insulted her husband, Lord Siva.
sati - a widow who burns herself in her husband's funeral fire.
Satya-yuga - the first age of a *maha-yuga*. It lasts for 1,728,000 years.
seva - voluntary service to a temple, God, or the general public.
shalagrama-shila - a sacred stone that is nondifferent from Lord Krishna or Lord

Vishnu and his incarnations. Often taken from the Gandaki River in Nepal.
Shaivaite - follower of Lord Siva.
shakti - female creative energy.
shankha - conch, symbol of Lord Vishnu.
shastra - revealed scriptures; Vedic literature.
Shesha - the sacred serpent upon which Lord Vishnu lies.
shiksa-guru - the instructing spiritual master (guru).
shishya - a disciple or student.
Sita - the wife of Rama, who was abducted by Ravana.
Siva - the demigod who supervises the material mode of ignorance *(tamo-guna)* and who annihilates the material cosmos.
Sivaratri - appearance day of Lord Siva in Feb-March.
sloka - verse from the Vedic scriptures.
sraddha - offering of sacrifice to save one's ancestors from a hellish existence after death.
Sri (sree, shree, shri) - honorific prefix used before speaking the Deities' name.
Srimad Bhagavatam - the *purana* or history written by Vyasadeva to give a deep understanding of the position of Lord Krishna. It deals exclusively with the subject of pure devotional service to the Supreme Lord.
Subhadra - sister of Krishna. She is the yellow deity found with Lord Jagannatha.
Subrahmanya - Karttikeya, the son of Lord Siva and the god of war. Also known as Skanda.
Sudarsana-cakra - the disc weapon of Lord Vishnu.
sudra - a member of the laborer class.
surabhi - a cow from the spiritual world that can give unlimited milk.
Surya - the sun-god.
svami (swami) - one fully in control of his senses; a person in the renounced order of life.
Svetambara - "white-clad" sect of the Jain religion.
tabla - a two-drum set.
tapasya - austerities.
Theravada - "small-vehicle," one of the main Buddhist sects.
tilak - sacred clay which is put on a person's body and forehead to show whom he worships. Vishnu tilak is also known as *gopicandana*.

tirtha - a crossing place. A sacred place made holy by the fact that God celebrated a pastime there. Such places are usually inhabited by saints.
tirthankara - "ford maker"; one of the twenty-four main Jain teachers.
Treta-yuga - the second age of a *maha-yuga*, lasting 864,000 years.
Trimurti - the Hindu trinity of Brahma, Vishnu, and Siva.
Upanisads - 108 philosophical treatises appearing within the *Vedas*.
Vaikunthas - the eternal planets of the spiritual world.
Vaishnava - a devotee of Lord Krishna or Lord Vishnu.
vahana - the carrier of a deity, such as Lord Siva's Nandi.
Valmika - author of the *Ramayana*.
Vamana - Lord Vishnu in his fifth incarnation as a dwarf Brahman.
vaishya - member of the mercantile and agricultural class.
vanaprastha - a man who has retired from married life to cultivate renunciation.
varna - literally means "color"; the social classes of *Brahmins, kshatriyas, vaishyas,* and *sudras*.
Varaha - the boar incarnation of Lord Vishnu.
varnasrama-dharma - the Vedic social system which organizes society into four occupational and four spiritual divisions.
Vedas - the religious scriptures.
Vedanta-sutra - the philosophical conclusion of the *Vedas*.
Vishnu - The Supreme Godhead.
Vrindavan - Krishna's personal abode; a village in North India where Krishna performed his most intimate pastimes during his appearance on this planet.
Vyasadeva - the literary incarnation of the Lord.
yajna - sacrifice; a fire yajna is sanctified over fire and is taken very seriously.
Yamaraja - god of death who passes judgment on nondevotees at the time of death.
yantra - a geometric design often used in meditation.
yatra - pilgrimage.
yatri - pilgrim.
yoga - to connect with god.

yogi - a *sadhu* or saintly person who performs yoga.
yoni - the symbol of the female sexual organ on the base of a Siva-linga.
yuga - an age.

Architecture

Anda - the spherical part of a stupa; literally "egg."
antarala - pillared hall.
cenotaph - a memorial.
chaitya - Buddhist temple, Buddhist hall of worship.
chorten - Tibetan Buddhist monument equivalent to a stupa that often contains relics or prayers.
cupola - small dome.
deul - in Orissan temples it corresponds to the vimana or towered sanctum. It is a cubical, inner apartment in which the main deity is located, and has a tower over it.
darwaza - door, gateway.
dhvajastambha - flagstaff.
dwarapala - the doorkeeper sculptures by the doorways of Hindu and Buddhist temples.
garbha-griha - inner sanctuary or altar room that contains the main deity of the temple. Literally, "womb-chamber."
gompa - Tibetan or Ladakhi monastery.
gopuram (gopura) - highly carved soaring towers over the temple gates.
gurudwara - Sikh religious complex; usually includes a temple and guest house.
kalsasha - pot-like top of a temple tower.
makara - crocodile-like animal found on temple doorways.
mandapam (mandapa) - halls of the temple, often with many pillars.
mihrab - niche in the wall which indicates the direction of Mecca from that site, and thus the direction to be faced during prayers. It is in the west wall in India.
minaret - high thin towers, often found next to mosques.
nandavana – flower garden.
nrita-mandapa - dance hall.
prakara - the high walls surrounding the temple grounds.
pitha - the pedestal or altar of the deity. The pitha is in the sanctum sanctorum (inner sanctum).
sanctum sanctorum - inner sanctuary or altar room containing the main temple deity.
shikhara - curved temple tower or spire. The roof of the sanctum sanctorum.
stambha - free-standing pillar.
stupa - hemispheric Buddhist monument of worship.
vahana mandapa - where the mount of the deity *(vahana)* such as Lord Vishnu's carrier Garuda or Siva's bull Nandi is located.
verandah - an enlarged porch-like outside hallway.
vihara - Buddhist monastery.
vimana - the tower over the deity sanctum.

Names of Krishna

Acyuta - one who always protects His devotees; one who never fails.
Arisudana - one who kills His enemies.
Banke Bihari - *Banke* means "bent in three places," and *bihari* means "supreme enjoyer."
Bhagavan - possessor of all opulence.
Braja-bihari - one who frolics in the land of Braja
Brajendranandana - son of the king of Braja.
Damodara - *Dama* means "ropes" and *udara* means "abdomen". One who was bound by a rope around the abdomen.
Dina Bandhu - friend of the poor.
Giriraja - Krishna in the form of Govardhan Hill.
Gokulacandra - The moon of Gokula.
Gopala - the herder and protector of cows.
Gopinatha - Lord of the *gopis*.
Gopijana Vallabha - the transcendental lover of the *gopis*.
Govardhana-natha - Lord of Govardhan Hill.
Govinda - He who pleases the spiritual senses and the cows.
Hrisikesa - He who is the master of the senses.
Janardana - One who destroys obstacles on the path of devotional service.
Kesava - One who has beautiful black hair; He who killed the Kesi demon.
Kesisudana - He who killed the Kesi demon.
Kunja-bihari - One who frolics in the forest groves of Vrindavan.

Krishna - the all-attractive one.
Madana-Mohan - Krishna, who is the enchanter of Cupid.
Mohana - He who enchants everyone.
Madhusudana - He who killed the demon Madhu.
Madhava - He who is the husband of the Goddess of fortune; He who appears in the dynasty of Madhu.
Mukunda - the giver of liberation.
Murari - killer of the Mura demon.
Paramesvara - supreme controller.
Purusottama - He who is superior to everyone; He who is the best man.
Radha-natha - Lord of Srimati Radharani.
Radha-Raman - He who sports with the Radha.
Radhika-Raman - He who sports with Radhika.
Rasa-bihari - The supreme enjoyer of the *rasas*.
Rasaraja - Lord of the *rasas*
Shyamasundara - Krishna, who is the beautiful color of a fresh blackish rain cloud.
Vaasudeva - Krishna, the son of Vasudeva.
Visvamurti - He who is all-pervading and spread across the entire universe.
Visvarupa - The universal form of the Supreme Lord.
Vrindavana-candra - moon of Vrindavan
Yajnesvara - the Lord of all sacrifices.
Yogesvara - Lord of all the *yogis*.

Astrology Glossary

Ayanamsha–difference between Tropical and Sidereal zodiacs. About 23º.
Bhava–house.
Bhava chakra–house chart.
Budha – Mercury.
Chandra – the Moon.
Dasha – period.
Dhanus – Sagittarius.
Drishti – planetary aspect.
Ghati – twenty-four minutes of time.
Graha–planet.
Guru–Jupiter.
Hora–of a sign, planetary hours.
Jaimini–author of a system of Vedic astrology.
Jathaka–horoscope.
Kanya–Virgo.
Karaka–indicator.
Kataka–Cancer.
Kendra–angular house; fourth, seventh, and tenth houses.
Ketu–Dragon's tail or the Moon's southern node.
Kuja–Mars.
Kumbha–Aquarius.
Lagna–rising sign or ascendant.
Makara–Capricorn.
Mangala–name for Mars.
Maraka–Death or death-inflicting planet. It usually causes a negative effect.
Meena–Pisces.
Mesha–Aries.
Mithuna–Gemini.
Mitra–friend.
Moolatrikona–a favorable position for the planets, almost as good as exaltation.
Navamsa–nine divisions of a sign; harmonic ninth chart.
Nirayana–fixed zodiac.
Parashara–author of the main Vedic system of astrology.
Rahu–Dragon's Head or the Moon's northern node.
Rajayoga–a good combination of planets for power, success, money, and political success.
Rashi–sign of the zodiac.
Rashi chakra–sign chart.
Ravi–Sun.
Sambhanda–relationship between planets.
Shani–Saturn.
Sayana–movable zodiac.
Simha–Leo.
Shukra–Venus.
Thula–Libra.
Trikona–Trine house.
Vrischika–Scorpio.
Vrishabha–Taurus.
Yoga–special combination of planets.

Please visit our web Site at:
www.spiritualguides.net

The site includes:

The entire Spiritual India book done by Spiritual Guides, which includes a detailed account of the holy places, temples, forts, beaches, palaces, treks, wildlife parks and much more.

- Information on Vrindavana, Mayapur and Jagannath Puri
- Astrology Section
- Vastu Sastra
- Fengshui
- Vedic Gemology
- Tarot Card Reading
- Good Shopping Sources in India
- Vegetarian Restaurants in the US and other Countries
- Vegetarian recipes and ingredients

Updates of the India, Vrindavan books will be put on the site regularly. Such as:

New Restaurants and Hotel (also restaurants that have closed).
Updated phone numbers.
Updated taxi prices from airports and train stations.
Present taxi prices between Delhi and Vrindavan.
Updated train and plane schedules and prices in India.

The site will include articles and comments from travelers in India.

Also Included: Important India, Nepal, spiritual, vegetarian, natural health shops, and travel web links.

Index

A

Adjacent Plot 223
Agate 188
Agni 32
Ahimsa 50
Alwars 85
Amethyst 187
Ananta Shesha 5, 29
Anantadeva 29
Andal 71
Andhra Pradesh Temples 80
Angles 129
Antardasha 134
Aquamarine 189
Aquarius 119
Aries 115
Arjuna 42
Asana 51
Ascendant 131
Ashrama 51
Ashtanga Yoga 51
Ashutosha 20
Ashwini 103
Aspect 130
Assessing the Land 202
Astrological Remedial Measures 147
Astrology 101
Astronomy 88
Atharva Veda 40
Atman 52
AUM 39
Avastha 129
Avatara 8
Ayanamsa 104
Ayodhya 17
Ayurvedic medicine 56

B

Balabhadra 18
Baladeva 18
Balarama 18, 24, 229
Balconies 211
Bali Maharaja 232
Banyan Tree 75
Basement 219
Bathrooms 217
Bedrooms 216
Benefic planets 125
Bhadrakali 26
Bhagavad Gita Verses 97
Bhagavad-gita 42
Bhagavata Purana 45
Bhagiratha 61
Bhairava 20
Bhakti 50
Bhaktivedanta Swami Prabhupada 71
Bharata Natyam 58
Bhima 42
Bhudevi 5
Bhutanatha 20
Bindu 86
Birthstone 198
Bloodstone 188
Blue Sapphire 162
Bodhi tree 75
Brahma 22, 65
Brahmacharya 84
Braja Mandala 56
Brihaspati 35
Brilliance of Gems 195
Buddha Purnima 227
Buddhism 90
Budha 18, 31, 35, 91, 227
Building Material 207

C

Cadent houses 129
Caitanya Mahaprabhu 69, 226
Chakra 53
Camel Festival 231
Cancer 116
Capricorn 119
Carat 192
Cat's Eye 180
Caturmasya 52
Chakras 49
Chamunda 26
Chandra 31
Chanting Hare Krishna 95
Chart designs 144
Citrine 186
Clarity of gems 193
Cleavage 196
Color of gems 192
Colors 148
Combust 130
Compound Wall 209
Conjunction 129
Constellations 122-124
Coral 175
Cow 57
Cusp 104
Cut of Gem 193

D

Daksha 57
Dance 58
Debilitation 128, 129
Dhamas, four main 55
Diamond 152
Digambaras 94
Diksa-guru 46
Dining Room 217
Dipawali 230
Diwali 23
Draupadi 43
Dravidian Temple Design 78
Durga 20, 21, 25, 230
Durga Puja 230
Durva Grass 75
Dussera 230
Dvapara yuga 65

E

Ecliptic 103
Ekadanta 27
Ekadasi 64
Emerald 167
Temple Room 214
Enemies in Astrology 126
Entrance Gate 212
Ephemeris 102
Exaltation 128-129

F

Favorable Gemstone 197
Fingers 150
Fire in Gems 196
Foods 66
Friends in Astrology 126
Funeral Rites 66

G

Ganesh 26, 229
Ganesh Chaturthi 229
Ganga 28
Gangadhara 20
Ganges 28, 60
  story of 61
Garbhodaksayi Vishnu 8
Garnet 183
Garuda 5, 27, 29
Gate of House 209
Gautama Buddha 90
Gayatri 22
Gemini 115
Gems for Health 147
Gita Jayanti 232
Gomedha 180
Govardhana Hill 76
Govardhana Puja 231

Grahas 105
Granth Sahib 93
Grihasta 85
Guru Parampara 45

H

Hanuman 17, 27, 227
Hanuman Jayanti 227
Hardness of gems 194
Hare Krishna Mantra 95
Harmonic chart 139
Harmonium 68
Hayagriva 19
Hessonite 178
Himavan 76
Hinayana 90
Hindu 38
Hindu Trinity 39
Hinduism 37
Holi 226
Holy Places 55
House Warming 222
Houses 121

I

Incarnations of Vishnu 8
Indra 29
Indradyumna, King 25
Inside the Building 211
Islam 88

J

Jade 182
Jagannatha 24
Jainism 93
Jamadagni 16
Janma Rashi 132
Janmastami 229
Jhulan Yatra Mahotsava 229
Judgment of a Horoscope 141
Jupiter 35, 109
Jyothisha 62, 101
Jyotirlingas 55

K

Kailash, Mount 75
Kali 21, 26
Kali yuga 65
Kalki 19
Kalpa 65
Kamadeva 32
Karaka 112
Karma 48
Karttikeya 27
Kathakali 59
Kendras 129
Kerala Temple Design 81
Ketu 106, 112
Kitchen 215
Krishna 3, 42, 229
Krishnayattam 60
Kshirodakshayi Vishnu 8
Kumbha-mela 62-63
Kundalini Yoga 49
Kurma 12
Kusha Grass 75
Kuvera 30

L

Lagna 131
Lakshmi 5, 23
Laksman 17
Land quality 203
Leo 116
Libra 117
Linga 54
Living (Sitting) Room 216
Lotus Flower 74
Lunar 124
Luster of gem 195

M

Madhvacarya 69
Maha-Vishnu 8
Mahabharata 42
Mahadashas 134-135, 138

Mahadeva 20
Mahakali 26
Mahavir 93
Mahisasura 230
Main Door of House 212
Major periods 134
Makara Sankranti 225
Malefic planets 125
Mandala 73
Mandara 76
Mangala 34
Manipuri dance style 60
Mantra 50
Manu 73
Marriage 64
Marriage Selection Astrology 142
Mars 34, 108
Mathura 56
Matsya 9
Mercury 35, 109
Meru 75
Mezzanine 219
Mohini Murti 19
Moksha 73
Months 225
Moolatrikona 128
Moon 34, 107
Moonstone 186
Movement of the Planets 139
Mudra 74
Muhammad 88
Music 67
Musical instruments 67
Muslims 89

N

Namaskar 68
Namaste 68
Nandi 28
Narada Muni 28
Narasimha 13, 227
Narasimha's Jayanti 227
Narayana 8

Nataraja Siva 21
Nathaji 23
Nathdwar 24
Navamsa Chart 139
Navaratna ring 200
Navaratri 230
Nirvana 74
North India Temples 82

O

Odissi 60
OM 39
Onam 232
Opal 186
Orissan-style Temples 81
Overhead Water Tank 214
Ownership 128

P

Padma 74
Padparadscha 167
Panaparas 129
Pandavas 43
Pandu 43
Parasurama 16
Parking 210
Parsis 94
Parvati 20, 21
Pearl 170
Peridot 187
Pisces 120
Planetary War 130
Planets 105-107
Plants around house 221
Polishing of Gems 193
Prabhupada, A.C. Bhaktvedanta 71
Pranayama 51
Prasada 66
Prashna 102
Predictions 132
Prescribing a Gem 200
Puranas 41
Puri 24

Q

Quartz 184

R

Radha 5
Radharani 229
Radhastami 229
Radhika 5
Raghunath 17
Rahu 36, 106, 111
Rajasic foods 66
Rama 44, 227, 230
Rama-naumi 227
Ramacandra 17
Ramanujacarya 69
Ramayana 17, 44
Rashi 113
Ratha-yatra 227
Ravi 34
Refractive Index 195
Reincarnation 48
Retrograde 141
Rig Veda 40
Rock Crystal 184
Roof 211
Ruby 158
Rudraksha Beads 74

S

Sabhanayaka Nataraja Temple 22
Sadhu 72
Safe Room in house 217
Sagittarius 118
Sama Veda 40
Samadhi 51
Samsara 49
Samskara 72
Sankaracarya 70
Sankarsana 29
Sannyasa 85
Sapphire 161
Saraswati 22
Saraswati Puja 226
Sati 21
Sattvic foods 66
Saturn 35, 110
Satya Yuga 65
Satyavrata, King 9
Scorpio 118
Setting in a Ring 149
Shaivites 46, 72
Shaktas 46
Shakti 25
Shalagram-shilas 54
Shani 35
Shankha 68
Shape of the Land 207
Shridevi 5
Shukra 35
Siddharta Gautama 90
Sidereal Astrology 103
Signs 113, 121
Sikhism 92
Sikhs 92
Siksa-guru 46
Sita 17
Sitar 68
Sitting Room 216
Siva 19, 58, 226
Siva Jyotirlingas 55
Siva-linga 54
Siva-ratri 226
Skanda 28
Smartas 46
Solar Year 124
Soma 31, 34
Specific Gravity 196
Spinel 190
Sraddha 230
Sri Yantra 86
Srikurman 12
Srimad-Bhagavatam 45
Stairways 218
Storage Area 218
Study Room 218
Sub-periods 134
Subhadra 24

Subrahmanya 28
Succeedent houses 129
Sudarsana Cakra 53
Sun 34, 107
Sun god 34
Surya 30, 34
    defined 30
Svetambaras 94
Swastika 53
Synthetic Gems 196

T

Tablas 68
Tamasic foods 66
Tanpura 68
Tantra 53
Taurus 115
Temple Design 77
Temple Priests 82
Temple Worship 83
Temples 76
Theravada 90
Tirthankaras 93
Tithis 124
Topaz 185
Tourmaline 189
Treated Gems 196
Trees around house 221
Treta yuga 65
Trikonas 129
Trines 129
Trivikrama 16
Tropical 103
Tulasi 75
Turquoise 183

U

Uma 21
Upanishads 41
Upper floor of house 221

V

Vaishnava Sadhu 72
Vaishnavas 46-47
Vamana 13, 16
Vanaprastha 85
Varaha 12
Varuna 32
Vasant Panchami 226
Vayu 33
Veda Vyasa 19
Vedas 40
Vedic astrology 101
Venus 35, 110
Verandahs 211
Vinayaka 27
Virgo 117
Vishnu 5
Vishwakarma 33
Vrindavana 56
Vyasadeva 26

W

Water Source for House 208
Well 208
Worship 40
Worship (Temple) Room 214
Worship of Land 222

Y

Yajur Veda 40
Yamaraja 33
Yantra 86
Yantras 87
Yellow Sapphire 164
Yoga 88
Yogas 133
Yudhisthira 42
Yugas 65

Z

Zircon 177
Zodiac 103

Distributors

India

The Variety Book Depot
A.V.G. Bhawan, M3 Connaught Circus, P.O. Box 505
New Delhi 110001, India
Phone: 011 332-7175, 332-2567, 335-0039; Fax: 011 371-4335, 011 625-2117; Email: variety@nde.vsnl.net.in

UBS Publishers' Distributors Ltd
5 Ansari Road, P.O. Box 7015, New Delhi 110 002
Phone: 011 327-3601, 011 326-6647; Fax: 327-6593
Distributes: *Holy Places and Temples of India* and *Hinduism, Vastu Sastra, Vedic Astrology and Gemology*

Munshiram Manoharlal
54 Rani Jhansi Road, P.O. Box 5715, New Delhi 110 055
Phone: 011 777-1668, 011 777-3650; Fax: 91 11 361-2745
Email: mrml@mantraonline.com, mrmlpub.mrml@axcess.net.in
Distributes *Hinduism, Vastu Sastra, Vedic Astrology and Gemology, Vrindavan and Braja Mandala, Sri Navadvipa and Jagannatha Puri,* and *Holy Places and Temples of India.*

Motilal Banarsidass
41 UA Bungalow Road, Jawahar Nagar, Delhi 110 007
Phone: 011 291-1985, 011 291-8335; Fax: 011 293-0689
Website: www.mlbbooks.com
Distributes: *Hinduism, What It Really Is, Vastu Sastra, Vedic Astrology and Gemology, Holy Places and Temples of India*

Jada Bharata, Spiritual Guides
Krishna Balarama Mandir, Bhaktivedanta Swami Marg Vrindavana, Mathura Dist, UP India; Residence: MVT, 6-C 201
Phone: 0565-446-008; Fax: 91-565-446-008; Email: spiritualguides@hotmail.com; Website: www.spiritualguides.net

USA

Krishna Culture
PO Box 926337, Houston TX
Phone (800) 829-2579, (713) 290-8715; fax (713) 290-8720
Email: krsnacultr@aol.com; Website: www.krishnaculture.com

BTG Service Center
P.O. Box 255, Sandy Ridge, NC 27046
Phone: (800) 800-3284; fax (336) 871-3641; email: archives@earthlink.net; Website: www.krsna.com or www.krishna.com

John Howley
Spiritual Guides
197 Ocean Avenue
Freeport, New York
Phone: 516 223-4015; Email: spiritualguides@hotmail.com
Website: www.spiritualguides.net

For Wholesale orders to the trade:
New Leaf Distributing Company
401 Thornton Road, Lithia Spring, Georgia 30057-1557
Phone: (800) 326-2665; Fax (800) 326-1066
Email: newleaf@newleaf-dist.com; Website: www.newleaf-dist.com
Distributes *Holy Places and Temples of India* and *India: A Practical Guide* (ISBN: 0-9653858-4-1).

England

BBL Distribution
PO Box 324, Borehamwood, Herts, WD6 1NB UK
Phone 44-208-905-1244; Fax 44-208-905-1108;
Email: BBL@com.bbt.se; Website: www.krishna.co.uk

Australia

The Temple Shop
PO Box 30
Cammeray NSW 2062 Australia
Phone: 61-2-9904-9119; Email: sraddhavan@hotmail.com

Europe

Bhaktivedanta Library Services
Petite Somme 2, 6940 Durbuy, Belgium
Phone: 32 86 323280; Fax: 32 86 322029;
Email: bls.orders@pamho.net; Website: www.blservices.com.

Once in the website, click on "product catalogue" at the top of the page. Then on the left side a frame appears with the categories of books. Click on "Lords Holy Dhama" and the books published by Spiritual Guides come up. To find *Hinduism, What It Really Is, Sanatana Dharma, Vastu Sastra, Vedic Astrology and Gemology*, you click on Philosophical Books and you will find this book in that category.

For more information on distributors please check our website. Expect several more to be added in the near future.

Website: www.spiritualguides.net

Books Published by Spiritual Guides

For details and updates check our website at: **www.spiritualguides.net**

India: A Practical Guide by Jada Bharata, John Howley

This book gives a detailed explanation of places in India, including: temples, forts, beaches, holy places, palaces, wildlife parks, the Himalayan mountains, museums and much more. It has easy to understand introductional information, so is very useful for a first time visitor to India or Southeast Asia. It has 196 maps. Contains detailed practical information including: hotels, restaurants, travel information, in all price ranges. Also it has sections on health, history, festivals, what to bring, and religious information. Over 500 towns and cities listed, and thousands of places described.

INDIA, published by Spiritual Guides, is an invaluable asset for a person planning to make a visit to India. It is very detailed and covers most of the major places covered in other travel books written on India, plus many other places. The practical advice on India is very helpful and is written in a street-smart manner. This book explains how to to have a pleasant and inexpensive trip to this exotic country.

This books is an updated version of the Holy Places and Temples of India book below, so I would recommend that you purchase this book instead. It basically has everything as the book below, but also includes double the information.

Price: $20; ISBN Number: 0-9653858-4-1; Pages 1093

Holy Places and Temples of India

Detailed descriptions of holy places and temples in Inda. Lists over 30 holy places, 200 temples and has 63 maps. Extenisve accommodations, good list of vegetarian restaurants, transportation, and much more.

Price $15; ISBN 0-9653858-0-9; Pages 672

Vrindavan and Braja Mandala by Jada Bharata Dasa

Vrindavana is the land of Krishna. For a devotee of Krishna this is the most important place in the world to visit. This is the place where Krishna appeared on this earth and where He had many of His pastimes.

Many places are listed in this book such as: Vrindavana, Mathura, Govardhana Hill, Radha Kunda, Gokula, the twelve forests of Vrindavana. Also listed is Uchagrama, the village of Lalita Sakhi; Prema Sarovara; Sanket, where Radha and Krishna would meet; Javat, the village where Radharani lived after She got married; Raval, where Radharani appeared; Baldeo, where there is an ancient Deity of Balarama; and Kamyavana, which has many important places in it.

There is also much practical information in this book. There is a list of places to stay and eat at while in Vrindavana. There is also travel information for within Braja and travel information telling how to get to Vrindavana. There is also a good section on where to shop in Vrindavana and a health section.

There are also sections on Delhi and Jaipur.
Price: $12; ISBN 0-9653858-1-7 Pages 505

Sri Navadvipa and Jagannatha Puri by Jada Bharata Dasa
Contains a detailed description of Mayapur and the Navadvipa Dhama area. Included in this book are most of the major places that are visited on Navadvipa Dhama Parikrama. All the nine islands are described. It also describes Gaura Mandala or the places that Lord Caitanya and his associates had their pastimes, in Bengal and Bangladesh.

There is also a section about Jagannatha Puri. A short section on Calcutta is included as most people going to Mayapur will pass through Calcutta. Included are what each place is and what its significance is, stories about the places, maps, and descriptions of how to get to the places.

There is also a lot of practical information in this book. There is a list of places to stay and eat at while in Mayapur, Jagannatha Puri and Calcutta. Also travel information is included and valuable practical hints.
Price: $10 ISBN 0-9653858-2-5 Pages: 264

Hinduism, What It Really Is, Sanatana Dharma, Vastu Sastra, Vedic Astrology and Gemology
Price: $9.95 ISBN 0-9653858 Pages: 250

Books to Come
Natural Eating Places in the USA and Canada Lists vegetarian restaurants, natural food stores, vegetarian options in fast food restaurants, and vegetarian ingredients in foods. Also vegetarian websites will be listed. This books can be seen on Spiritual Guides' Website (www.spiritualguides.net). On the website vegetarian restaurants in other countries besides the USA will be listed. The website will be active around June, 2001. The book is expected to be published in January of 2001.

To order these books in the USA please send a check or money order to:

John Howley, C/O Noel Dela Merced
Spiritual Guides
197 Ocean Avenue
Freeport, NY 11520
516 223-4015

Please add $4 for postage and handling for any number of books up to five. Please make the check payable to John Howley. Allow 14 days for delivery. Prices good until December, 2002. Thank you.

Name_____

Address_____

City/State/Zip_____

Phone_____

Email_____

☐ To have updates on new Spiritual Guide books sent to you please check here.

You can also get copies of *India: A Practical Guide* and *Holy Places and Temples of India* from Amazon.com and other internet suppliers. Please check our website at www.spiritualguides.net for more information on internet and other mailorder suppliers.

Reviews of *India: A Practical Guide*

The travel guide *India* would be of much help for those travellers who want to explore the spiritual aspects of India. The book is a compilation of recollections by the authors themselves as they devoted years in travelling across the country. Therefore, facts given by them are first hand information and born out of practical experience. Written in simple and narrative English, it is a good handbook for a traveller who comes here to discover the spiritual wealth of India.
　　The Hindustan Times

India's spiritual richness is vast and incomparable, but often the physical difficulties make them less easy to appreciate. John Howley has given nice practical advice on how to survive the difficulties, to find the spiritual essence that is the real India. I recommend this book.
　　Bhakti Vikasa Swami England

I would like to congratulate Jada Bharata Dasa on the publication of his book, *India*. This outstanding book will fulfill the desires of many sincere visitors to India by guiding them safely and intelligently to the real treasures of India, the holy places. I wish him all success in his continuing project of providing the best spiritual guidebooks available.
　　His Holiness Hridayananda dasa Gosvami

You have done a great service in writing your book, Holy Places and Temples of India. All the practical information on dealing with India is as welcome as the information on the holy sites.
　　W. Fox, Maharishi Institute of Management

I used *India* as my one and only guidebook while on an extended pilgrimage in India. When you have the best, what need is there for the second rate. A chock full, jammed packed, overflowing encyclopedia of reliable information on negotiating your way through spiritual India. For those jaded travelers who are tired of the hype and pressures of the Taj Mahal type tourist beat, this book guides you, lifts you, and directs you perfectly to and through India's spiritual destinations.
　　S. Zansal, USA

Your book is great. I lived in India ten years and I finally got a book that had information that I always wanted. Thank you very much.
　　Braja Bihari
　　Vaishnava Institute for Higher Education, India

Please visit our web Site at:
www.spiritualguides.net

The site includes:

The entire Spiritual India book done by Spiritual Guides, which includes a detailed account of the holy places, temples, forts, beaches, palaces, treks, wildlife parks and much more.

- Information on Vrindavana, Mayapur and Jagannath Puri
- Astrology Section
- Vastu Sastra
- Fengshui
- Vedic Gemology
- Tarot Card Reading
- Good Shopping Sources in India
- Vegetarian Restaurants in the US and other Countries
- Vegetarian recipes and ingredients

Updates of the India, Vrindavan books will be put on the site regularly. Such as:

New Restaurants and Hotel (also restaurants that have closed).
Updated phone numbers.
Updated taxi prices from airports and train stations.
Present taxi prices between Delhi and Vrindavan.
Updated train and plane schedules and prices in India.

The site will include articles and comments from travelers in India.

Also Included: Important India, Nepal, spiritual, vegetarian, natural health shops, and travel web links.